THE RIGHT OF PASSAGE

THE RIGHT OF PASSAGE

ONE JEWISH FAMILY'S STRUGGLE TO ESCAPE THE HOLOCAUST

JULIAN BEECROFT
WITH SHERI BLANEY

Praise for *The Right of Passage*

'Sometimes the dates and numbers of the past obscure the individual human dramas that comprise our history. Fortunately, *The Right of Passage* makes visceral and intimate – and all the more meaningful – the story of the Holocaust and a family's struggle to escape its unspeakable evils.'
Ken Burns, filmmaker, director of *The US and the Holocaust*

'An evocative and urgent reminder of the perils of being a bystander at a time of burgeoning threats to democratic freedoms around the world. ... *The Right of Passage* is a work of meticulous research and rare devotion. What began with a serendipitous discovery of a cache of negatives in a rubbish bin in Massachusetts almost half a century ago became the book you hold now in your hands: one-part gripping detective story, one-part page-turning tragedy about the untold potential lost to antisemitism and the Holocaust. ... a work of great historical importance with deep resonance for our current moment.'
Kelly Horan, author of *Devotion and Defiance*

'What begins with a box of abandoned negatives and notebooks yields a thrilling piece of detective work and the revelation of a family history shaped by flight, tragedy, and exile.'
Joseph Pearson, author of My Grandfather's Knife: Hidden Stories from the Second World War

'A well-researched reconstruction of how a gifted German-Jewish logician had to flee to Belgium but finally ended up in the Nazi camps. The reader can follow, in Grelling's own words, how even during difficult times friendship and love and even intellectual exchange was not destroyed by the brutality of Nazism.'
Frank Caestecker, Professor of History, University of Ghent

'Snapshots of an unbroken but acutely endangered belief in the power of reason ... the painstaking and detailed research reveals an important insight: as the number of contemporary witnesses continues to dwindle, our knowledge and future generations' understanding of the Nazi reign of terror and the Holocaust depends on the rescue, careful research and publication of letters, diaries and other personal documents that document human behaviour in inhumane times, but which are largely not yet kept in archives. One such accidentally preserved collection of letters and photographs forms the basis for this extraordinary and exemplary book.'
Joachim Schloer, Emeritus Professor of History, University of Southampton

'The fate of the Grelling family kept me spellbound. Their brilliance and resilience in desperate times told through letters, photographs and personal reflections is moving and a must-read in a world that is still grappling with one of history's darkest chapters.'

Helene Munson, author of *Boy Soldiers: A Personal Story of Nazi Elite Schooling and Its Legacy of Trauma*

'This book tells the story of one Jewish family's experience during the Nazi era in Germany ... a detailed and engrossing examination of one extended family's travails during that dark time. But it is impossible to read it without recognizing how enormously relevant it is to today ...

Sheila Suess Kennedy, J.D., Professor Emerita Law & Public Policy O'Neill School of Public & Environmental Affairs, Indiana University, Purdue University, Indianapolis

'*The Right of Passage* is a meticulously researched book that is both intellectually fascinating and deeply moving. Although subtitled *One Jewish Family's Struggle to Escape the Holocaust*, it tells a broader story about the fate of German Jewry under the Nazis and their willing accomplices in Vichy France, a fate made worse by the unwillingness of western democracies, sometimes driven by home-grown antisemitism, to accommodate refugees fleeing genocidal tyranny. ... Assembled from a treasure-trove of family correspondence, interviews, private memoirs and photographs, *The Right of Passage* is a must-read for anyone interested in Holocaust studies.'

John Jay, author of *Ninette's War: A Jewish Story of Survival in 1940s France*

'*The Right of Passage* is an intimate Holocaust narrative that conjures full lives from fragments – letters, photographs, interviews and archival materials. ... There is heroism in the devotion of Kurt Grelling and his circle of European intellectuals to their work and to one another, in the resilience of the Grelling family, and in many small acts of kindness at the story's edges. There is also a grand and pitiless combination of human forces that corrupts or pulverizes all it touches. However dramatic, this is a history of individuals and small communities, memorialized as they must be if we are to remember the many millions.'

Noah Chafets, Cyril O. Houle Chair, Basic Program of Liberal Education for Adults, University of Chicago

Cover image: The *C.G. Francklyn* (aka the *Rügen*) in the harbour at Reval (Tallinn), Estonia, August 1929. (© Sheri Blaney, Samter Archive).

First published 2025

The History Press
97 St George's Place, Cheltenham,
Gloucestershire, GL50 3QB
www.thehistorypress.co.uk

© Julian Beecroft & Sheri Blaney, 2025

The right of Julian Beecroft & Sheri Blaney to be identified
as the Authors of this work has been asserted in accordance
with the Copyright, Designs and Patents Act 1988.

All rights reserved. No part of this book may be reprinted
or reproduced or utilised in any form or by any electronic,
mechanical or other means, now known or hereafter invented,
including photocopying and recording, or in any information
storage or retrieval system, without the permission in writing
from the Publishers.

British Library Cataloguing in Publication Data.
A catalogue record for this book is available from the British Library.

ISBN 978 1 80399 705 6

Typesetting and origination by The History Press
Printed and bound in Great Britain by TJ Books, Padstow, Cornwall.

The History Press proudly supports

Trees for Life

www.treesforlife.org.uk

EU Authorised Representative: Easy Access System Europe
Mustamäe tee 50, 10621 Tallinn, Estonia
gpst.request@easproject.com

CONTENTS

GERMANY	**9**
Discovery	11
The Gypsy Life Isn't Beautiful	33
An Irretrievable Separation	49
BELGIUM	**63**
A Man of Letters	65
J'accuse!	81
The Invariant of Transpositions	95
Everything Is a Risk	113
Letters from America	127
Many People Are Disappearing from Brussels	139
FRANCE	**153**
The Camp on the Beach	155
The New School	169
A Book of Essays	183
A Man in My Position	197
How Nerve-shredding this Constant Waiting Is	209
On Love Alone	225
The Choice	237
Stolperstein	249
Afterlife	251
Acknowledgements	263
Text Credits	267
Endnotes	269
Select Bibliography	281
Index of Names	285

'A man discovers what he is actually worth in this world when he faces society merely as a man, without money, name or powerful connections, stripped of all but his native potentialities. He soon finds that nothing has less weight than his human qualities.'

Max Horkheimer, from
'The Latest Attack on Metaphysics', 1937

GERMANY

DISCOVERY

This book began with some notebooks and a cache of old negatives, offered as a gift one summer evening more than forty years ago. The images were taken by a talented but unknown photographer first identified by Sheri Blaney, without whose original research this story would not have come to light. Sheri has worked with and been fascinated by photographs her entire life. But, even so, the negatives she was given, once she had found the time to examine them, were quite unexpected in what they revealed: a forgotten world of freedom, of travel and friendship and family ties, during the brief period after the end of the First World War in which democracy flourished in many parts of Europe. Slowly, she found living descendants of the people in the photographs. From what they told her, a picture emerged of a notable family of German Jews, including scientists and intellectuals whose influence on national life had been significant, before the madness that took hold of Germany in 1933.

Having found a lot of valuable information, Sheri approached me for help in developing her brief early manuscript into a full-length book. In the course of further research in university archives in the USA and western Europe, I found collections of extraordinary letters in various languages – in English and in French but above all in German – that reflected the cosmopolitan background of those who wrote them. As my wife Ulla and I began translating them, it was clear, almost from the start, the scope of the story that was there to be told and needed to be told.

At the centre of most of the letters, either writing or receiving them or else being written about, was Kurt Grelling, with whose fate this book is mainly concerned. A distinguished logician, mathematician and philosopher of science, the German translator of several works by Bertrand Russell, Grelling was a friend or colleague of some of the most important thinkers of the time, members of the Vienna Circle and in particular the closely related Berlin Group, in which he was a leading light. Beginning in 1934, the letters tell a story of how democratic freedoms, which had flourished across large parts of Europe since the end of the First World War, came increasingly under threat. Grelling's frank exchange of views with fellow philosophers, especially Jewish figures such as Otto Neurath and Paul Oppenheim, shows how Nazi ideology had impinged upon their freedom of thought, forcing them to reckon with the rise of antisemitism as a political issue that for Jews was existential. Most of his friends and colleagues were among the hundreds of thousands who were able to emigrate, mainly to the USA, though often by the skin of their teeth. Grelling was not among them. From the summer of 1940, stuck in a French internment camp, frustrated by the US immigration system, which grew increasingly hostile to Jews, Grelling's letters turned more desperate, as the efforts of friends to secure him a visa and passage on a ship finally came to nothing.

Sheri could not have known any of this back in 1980, when her friend had given her the notebooks and the various sheets of negatives. He had found them lying on a pavement outside a house in Arlington, Massachusetts, not far from where she was living at the time. As she wrote in her original manuscript: *I had already worked for many years in the field of publishing, copyright, and photography, which has been my professional specialty ever since. My friend was working on construction at the house and discovered them out front on the sidewalk. He imagined that the new owner had found them, left behind by the previous occupant in an attic or closet, and put them out there so that anyone with enough curiosity might pick them up. Knowing my interests, my friend brought me what turned out to be a treasure trove of fifty-year-old images: 400 medium-format, black-and-white negatives, plus a dozen or so strips of the more modern 35mm negatives which I put to one side, assuming they were of no importance or had no connection to the older-format negatives.*

Along with the medium-format negatives there were several notebooks. Three of them contained handwritten, brief – almost cryptic – numbered descriptions written mostly in German, dating from the years 1929 to 1935, corresponding to about 250 of the numbered negatives. Nowhere was there any contact information that would have enabled me to return the material immediately to its owner, as I would like to have done. So, to preserve the negatives, I transferred them from their original glassine sleeves to archival pages, hoping one day to have the time to fully appreciate them; to find the people – perhaps a family – who had owned them, and to share with them the lives the images portray so intimately.

After four busy decades in which Sheri had sometimes wondered about the negatives, in 2020, when the Covid pandemic confined everyone in their homes, she suddenly had the time and attention she had always promised she would give them.

Several of the negatives and notebooks that were given to Sheri in 1980. (© Sheri Blaney)

I woke up thinking about the negatives, fearful that my children might toss them out after I was gone, and that once again they would end up on a sidewalk for the landfill. Being semi-retired already, with extra time on my hands I started to examine the notebooks and negatives, to scan any images that seemed arresting enough to reproduce, and to research the people and places they depicted, with no real idea of what I would find.

It seemed unlikely that any of the people who appeared in the photographs would be alive today, but very likely they were someone's parents, grandparents, relatives, or friends. Was there a friend or relative out there who could shed light on these mysterious photos or could tell me who had taken them?

The photographs themselves were sometimes of a rare beauty and narrative scope. From their unity of style, it was clear they were the work of someone with a keen eye, technical competence and, in some of the more artful shots, an awareness of trends in the photography of the time. They were carefully composed and accomplished across a wide variety of situations, including everything from lakes and snowy mountain landscapes to thoughtfully posed portraits and amusing snapshots of people in period clothing, engaged in travel or activities of one kind or another, or often just relaxing at home. There was a woman on the telephone and another one listening to the radio. There was someone operating a MADAS machine (a manual, mechanical calculator) and a family standing by a 1930s LaSalle sedan, both state-of-the-art technologies at the time. There was a large number of outdoor shots showing people enjoying their pets or skiing or sitting in a café, a girl of college age smoking a pipe and a group of young men in swimsuits clowning around. But there were also other kinds of studied or documentary images – still-life interiors, parades on the streets of a city, and European scenery and architecture photographed with great skill. The range of subjects and the recurrence of certain people across different sets of photos suggested that these were not the work of a professional but that of a gifted amateur with a natural feel for the use of light and an instinct for composition.

Saying goodbye at the train station in Basel, Switzerland, *c.* 1935. (© Sheri Blaney, Samter Archive)

A busy street scene in Geneva, Switzerland, c.1934. (© Sheri Blaney, Samter Archive)

Nebelmeer (sea of fog), Rigi-Kaltbad, Switzerland, December/January 1932/33. (© Sheri Blaney, Samter Archive)

Hikers at Mer de Glace, Chamonix, France. (© Sheri Blaney, Samter Archive)

A man posing with his two dachshunds. (© Sheri Blaney, Samter Archive)

Skijoring, a winter sport showing a woman on skis being pulled by a horse and rider, Adelboden, Switzerland, 1934. (© Sheri Blaney, Samter Archive)

A woman working at a MADAS machine. (© Sheri Blaney, Samter Archive)

Mutti on the telephone, Berlin, early 1930s. (© Sheri Blaney, Samter Archive)

A group of young men clowning around, Switzerland. (© Sheri Blaney, Samter Archive)

The Swiss Alps with tourists enjoying the view, c.1934. (© Sheri Blaney, Samter Archive)

Women listening to a guitar player, Salève, Saint-Claude, Jura, eastern France, August 1932. The note for this photo is simply *Heimatklange* (sounds of home). (© Sheri Blaney, Samter Archive)

As each negative emerged as a positive image through my photo scanner, I was intrigued to see pictures that for nearly a century had been hidden away. I found it strangely moving to view this forgotten world, and my own instinct told me that others would find it as fascinating as I did. I noted the photographer had taken time to organize the negatives and record dates, events, and some names that might offer insight into the lives of the people in the photographs. But there was not enough information to address the many unanswered questions I was left with. Above all, I wondered who had taken these photographs, how they had come from Europe to New England, and why they had been left behind for the trash back in 1980.

Sheri turned to the notebooks for clues. Each notebook contained pages for handwritten notes with individual columns for dates, locations and descriptions, followed by bound glassine-sleeved pages that held the corresponding numbered negatives. Most of the text was in German with a few English and French words, depending on where the photos had been taken. The photographer was clearly a very methodical person; the written record they had kept would have crystallised any memories that might be triggered by seeing these images sometime in the future. But the records were also incomplete. Many of the negatives lacked the corresponding written notes, leaving little clue as to whose faces were captured, or where and when they were taken. But through a bit of research and by matching up some of the faces to people already identified in the notebooks, Sheri was able to make a few connections, although even at the time of writing, more than three years later, many mysteries remain.

Some of the place names in the notebooks were unfamiliar, where one-time German names had now been changed. But she realised that Stettin meant Szczecin, once in German East Prussia on the Baltic coast but a part of Poland since the end of the Second World War; one photo depicted a bascule bridge in the city, the central section of the *Bahnhofsbrücke* or station bridge that spanned the River Oder, a rare image of a structure that is no longer there. Reval was even more obscure but turned out to be the old German name for Tallinn, the capital of Estonia, a newly independent republic after the Treaty of Versailles. And Helsingfors is the Swedish name, and the old German name, for Helsinki, the capital of Finland, another young democratic nation a few hours by ferry across the Baltic Sea.

These were just the first few images in one of the books. All were taken in August 1929, the earliest recorded date. Whoever had shot them had clearly been making a journey. The image from Reval was of a ship, which we have since identified as the *Rügen*, the name given in the notebooks to describe the image. The *Rügen* had entered service as a mine-laying ship

The bascule bridge, Stettin, East Prussia (now Szczecin, Poland), August 1929. (© Sheri Blaney, Samter Archive)

in the Baltic in late 1914 and served as a hospital ship in the early 1940s. But the records Sheri found contained no information about the ship's activity during the years 1919 to 1939. As she wrote in her manuscript, *I had already noticed that the smokestacks bear the letters 'C' and 'G', and at one point discovered that the* C.G. Francklyn, *a Cunard ship whose profile matches the one in the photograph, was sailing out of Stettin in the late 1920s. It certainly looks like a passenger ship in the photo.*

The next several images, a dozen or so, are light-damaged or underexposed, like most of those that were taken on this first trip. But together they confirm the impression of a journey going north across eastern Finland, through the region known as Karelia. This remote territory had a long border with the Soviet Union, which invaded soon after the outbreak of the Second World War; the often-forgotten conflict was ended with Finland ceding territory in Karelia to its much larger neighbour – territory that remains in Russian hands. But these were images of a peaceful world in which people at leisure could go wherever they pleased and did so with a lust for life that was heightened after years of war and the economic hardship which had followed. The Austrian-Jewish writer Stefan Zweig, one of the most cosmopolitan figures during that brief window of European freedom, said as much in his memoir *The World of Yesterday*. 'There was never so much travelling as in those years', he wrote of the peaceful period between 1918 and 1933: 'was it the impatience of the young to make up for what they had missed when countries were cut off from each other? Or was it, perhaps, a dark foreboding, a sense that we must take our chance to break out of confinement before the barriers began coming down again?"[1]

There is little sense of dark foreboding in these photographs of the trip to Finland or in most of the images that the mystery photographer took over the next few years. Whoever this person was, they were clearly exercising not only a freedom to travel but a sense of adventure in the way they experimented with the camera, as if seeing the world, or at least the places they were shooting, for the very first time, as we now realise was almost certainly the case. There are atmospheric images of Finland's largest lake, Lake Saimaa, including a silhouette, taken facing the sun, of a woman standing at the deck rail of a ship. In fact, there are several pictures of the same woman in this brief travelogue, and Sheri also noticed that the woman appeared in many more images taken in various locations across Europe over the following few years. Referred to in the notebooks as *Mutti*, the German word for Mummy, she is still quite young, no more than early middle age. On this evidence, it seemed likely that the photographer, presumably the woman's child, was no more than a teenager when these images were made.

Mutti in Florence, at the Basilica di San Lorenzo, spring 1935. (© Sheri Blaney, Samter Archive)

View from the belltower of the Transfiguration Monastery, Valamo, Finland (now Valaam, Russia), August 1929. (© Sheri Blaney, Samter Archive)

The journey through Finland seems to have taken them at one point to the Orthodox Transfiguration Monastery on the island of Valamo (today Valaam) on Lake Ladoga, an enormous body of water, north of St Petersburg, that covers an area of almost 7,000 square miles. Both lake and island now lie wholly within the borders of Russia, but at the time, the monastery was the most important in the Finnish Orthodox Church. There is even a sweeping panorama taken from the top of the bell tower of this building, the *Glockenturm* referred to in the notebook entry for this image. Clearly, the photographer was making the most of their freedom.

Subsequent sets of photos, in 1931 and 1933, record trips to southern England, to the cities of Winchester and Bristol among other places, where the photographer seems to have had relatives or friends; and in almost every year from 1930 to 1935 there were visits to different parts of Switzerland around the cities of Zurich, Bern and Geneva and the Jura region of eastern France. The photographer is alive to the drama of natural light in the stark images of snowy landscapes captured in different parts of the Swiss Alps, a technical but also an aesthetic achievement that becomes a feature even in some of the interior shots taken later on.

The arches of the understorey of the Vasari Corridor, Ponte Vecchio, Florence, Italy, 1935. (© Sheri Blaney, Samter Archive)

The final trip, to Italy from March to May 1935, may well have been the longest. These photos are aesthetically more daring, with striking images such as an abstract shot of the understorey of the Vasari Corridor in Florence, a vanishing tunnel of arches whose unknown destination induces a sense of unease. But there were also more named individuals among the notebook entries for this trip, including someone called Tante Grete, suggesting time spent with family and friends in cities such as Florence, Siena and Perugia, but also at a place called Villa Incontri, though what that was, and where, was still a mystery. And then there were more images of Switzerland – of Zurich and Bern and Lake Lugano – whose date was unknown, as there were no more notebooks with information on when and where they were taken or what their subjects were. But their technical competence suggested a date that came later than the summer of 1935.

Then one day, looking more closely at one of the negatives, Sheri discovered an important clue. *In the photo of the woman listening to the radio there appears to be a drawing or a print of The Star of David partially visible on the wall, to the right of the radio, which I only happened to notice with the help of my Schneider 4X Lupe, a jeweler's magnifier that was used in the printing industry to examine photographic film before the advent of digital photography. Had I not had this tool to view it, and had I not been raised by Jewish parents, I might have missed this familiar symbol of Jewish identity. But even having found this out did not tell me who this woman was. I could find no information for the negative. Based on the span of years recorded in the notebooks, but also her clothing and the wireless radio, the photo was likely taken between 1929 and 1936, though I couldn't say what relationship she had to people in the photos I had already scanned, or even who had taken the picture. Was it the same woman who had travelled so extensively, or had the photo-maker now become the subject? Whatever was the case, since much of the handwritten content of the notebooks appeared to be in German, I suspected the woman and her family were of German origin and almost certainly Jewish.*

Encouraged by this discovery, Sheri kept looking. The unknown photographer's habit of shooting home interiors offered further clues to the family's background and identity. In one negative Sheri noticed a print of a Käthe Kollwitz image of a mother and child, *Mutter mit Kind* from 1933, hung on a wall.

Having been a Kollwitz fan since my teens, I immediately recognized her style of drawing. Kollwitz was a Berliner, a fiercely political artist who despised Hitler, war, and the devastation it brought, which she had seen first-hand in the conditions that existed in the capital city at the end of the First World War. When I visited Berlin after the Wall came down, I had sought out Kollwitz's neighborhood and went to the park, Kollwitzplatz, where a sculpture of the artist was installed in her honor. I was now beginning to feel more closely connected to these mysterious negatives which had landed serendipitously in my lap over forty years earlier.

After concentrating for several months on the older, large-format negatives, I began examining the strips of 35mm negatives. From the dates on the documents, and markings on the negatives, I determined that they were photographed in 1941, using Agfa film, with a Leica camera. To my surprise, these apparently unrelated strips held important clues to the photographer's identity as well as that of several other family members. These images were not only of people, but for some reason known only to the photographer, contained several shots of the same young woman as well as various documents, including an employment letter, a tax payment and other bank information for a Marion E. Samter living at 165 Coolidge Street in Brookline, Massachusetts. The employment letter stated Marion's yearly salary of $1,041, paid to her by the Liberty Mutual Insurance Company in Boston. Also shown are copies of a few of the documents this woman would have photographed, presumably as proof

Marion by the radio, and the Star of David on the wall, undated. (© Sheri Blaney, Samter Archive)

of employment for some official purpose, including a letter from the Franklin Savings Bank, again based in Boston.

Could I assume that Marion E. Samter was the photographer who had taken all those earlier images at so many locations across Europe, as well as these mundane bureaucratic shots? Certainly, the woman sitting on a wall in one of the 35mm negs was very likely the same woman listening to the radio with The Star of David in the background. She wasn't facing the camera in the earlier shot, but the hair, the general physique, and the profile seemed to indicate that the same person was the subject of both pictures.

It was a fair supposition, but without clear evidence Sheri couldn't be sure, so she turned to the New England Historic Genealogical Society, searching their online database for a Marion E. Samter. Finding some matching records, she contacted the society's Wyner Family Jewish Heritage Center, from whom she was given some additional information. The documents she had on the film were an exact match with online records as well as others that came up for a Marion E. Samter of Brookline, close to Boston. These new records included a ship's manifest of 'alien passengers', her social security application and a 'HIAS'[2] case file from August 1941.

I felt like I had found the woman I was looking for, but still I had no definitive proof that Marion E. Samter of Brookline had any connection to the older negatives and notebooks going back to 1929. I needed to find a living relative who could identify the person in the 35mm negatives and confirm that she was the same woman as appeared in the earlier European shots. By digging into Ancestry.com, I was able to find the child of a Marion E. Samter, a daughter named Anita who lived in Oregon. I telephoned her, not knowing but hoping that she was indeed the daughter of 'my' Marion, the young woman in the photos.

Marion's professor in front of a blackboard with various mathematical equations, Bern, 1935–38. (© Sheri Blaney, Samter Archive)

Anita was thrilled to hear of the existence of the negatives and notebooks. She exchanged photos and documents by email with Sheri and had soon confirmed that her family and the one in the images that Marion had taken were one and the same, that the woman standing by the radio was indeed her mother Marion, at home in Berlin, and that *Mutti* was her grandmother Else. Anita also said that Marion was an avid fan of the artist Käthe Kollwitz, whose artwork is on display in the family home. She added that members of her family tree included an accomplished writer, a scientist and a logician, each with an international reputation.

Anita also recalled that her mother, Marion, had attended college in Berlin. But, with increasing Nazi persecution of the Jewish community, in 1935 – the same year as the Nuremberg race laws were introduced – she had gone to Switzerland to finish her education, obtaining a PhD in Actuarial Mathematics from the University of Bern in 1938. The chronology of the photographs certainly fits this timeline of growing oppression, with the last of the European trips documented in the notebooks, the one to Italy, being made in the spring of 1935, when things were already difficult for German Jews but travel abroad was not yet impossible. Thereafter, the photos seem to be of places in Switzerland, including a shot of a lecturer at a blackboard graffitied with advanced equations, taken perhaps surreptitiously from a desk several rows back in the classroom. It strongly suggested that she was living there to pursue her doctoral degree. It was certainly a move that made sense.

The impact of the new laws, which downgraded the rights of Germans of Jewish background, forbidding them from marrying non-Jews and turning them from citizens into 'subjects' of the state, had the effect of sending Jewish Germans into internal exile within their own country. Jewish university students had already been barred from studying for ordinary degrees, let alone doctorates, so Marion's decision to develop her talents abroad was one that many in her position would have taken given the means. She needed to become as attractive as she could be for any country that would have her as an immigrant; clearly, there was no going back.

Having few options inside the German-speaking world, of those available, it seems likely that her familiarity with Switzerland, as shown in the annual visits she had made to every region of the country, made it the obvious choice. Given what was happening in Germany during the years she spent in Switzerland, Marion may well have been reluctant to come home. She may already have left when, in the summer of 1935, her mother Else moved into the top-floor flat in a house she had jointly bought with

Marion in ski clothing with her camera, Switzerland, 1935. (© Sheri Blaney, Samter Archive)

her brother, Kurt Grelling, at Wilhelmstrasse 13 in Lichterfelde-Ost, a suburb in the south of Berlin; Kurt, his non-Jewish wife Greta and their two children all lived in the ground-floor flat. Anita doesn't recall her mother ever speaking about the property, though for brief periods Marion must have stayed there. She often mentioned the multiple times she came back to Berlin to gather up her documents and belongings. This must have been in 1938; her studies had ended and her choice to emigrate to America had been made. At that point, the USA had not yet tightened its immigration laws to the extent that would later present such difficulties for other Jewish academics – among them her uncle Kurt – with far greater experience and reputation than a young woman who had only just finished her PhD.

In October that year, she returned to Berlin one last time, to collect her last belongings and also her passport. Official Nazi policy at this point was still to encourage Jews to emigrate, though with most no longer able to work or study, with businesses being confiscated, and with Jews racially vilified as a group by public officials, she must have wondered how long it would be before even this was forbidden, as soon it would be. As later became clear in the correspondence of other members of the family, especially that of Marion's uncle, Kurt Grelling, with his friends and colleagues

– and as famous accounts like the private diaries of Dresden professor Victor Klemperer bear out – German Jews were very aware of the growing threat they faced. The range of places and situations in every continent where they looked for refuge during the later 1930s was a measure of how bad things became, both in Germany and in the many countries that, increasingly, would not take them in.

America was the place where most Jews wanted to go. But for most of the world's people, the land of immigrants had been hard to get into for many years. The Johnson–Reed Act (aka the Immigration Act), passed by the US Congress in 1924, had set maximum annual quotas for immigrants from each country. Informed by the rise of scientific racism in the early twentieth century, whose bogus scientific claims made racial bias a politically respectable creed, the act saw quotas assigned to people from countries in western Europe, and especially northern Europe, that were far larger than the quotas given to other places. Prospective immigrants could only apply for a visa for the country of their birth, not their country of citizenship if the two happened to differ, out of a need to define them by race. There was no official US asylum or refugee policy, just these very particular immigration quotas, with by far the largest – 65,721 per annum, a very specific number – allotted to the white Anglo-Saxon Protestants of the UK. Germany had the second-largest quota, but this figure – at 25,957, less than half the British quota – was applied to a population almost half as large again. US immigration since the turn of the century had come mostly from what the framers of the law regarded as 'less desirable' nations in southern and eastern Europe. With the goal of preserving the existing balance of ethnicities in America, the new law set quotas for those places that were derisory at best. When war broke out, these paltry amounts and the quotas in general effectively barred most of the large numbers of Jews from all over Europe who wanted to escape.

For German Jews, demand soared after the pogrom of 9 November 1938, known as Kristallnacht. That night of murderous terror in cities and towns across Austria and Germany took place the month after Marion had come back to Berlin that one last time. Even before this had happened, in September that year, the list of German Jews waiting for a US quota visa had grown to 220,000, more than a third of the Jewish population. Kristallnacht and its aftermath would soon swell that number. Assuming that she had acted quickly and applied for her US visa on returning to Switzerland, Marion had probably just got ahead of the flood of applicants that would follow over the next two and a half years, among them her mother, her aunt Charlotte and her uncle Kurt.

But even this piece of excellent timing was no guarantee of success. Prospective immigrants needed to get hold of many different documents within a short window – some were valid for a limited period, some dependent on possession of the others. With quotas running out toward the end of the year, obtaining a visa involved a tricky combination of administrative dexterity, timing and luck. Marion was certainly lucky, in part because she had taken the decision – presumably with Else's blessing – to emigrate without her mother. Else would have to find her own way of getting out.

Anita provided Sheri with copies of Marion's passport and the handwritten note she had written in her late eighties, describing her last trip back into Germany from Switzerland. Re-entering the country where she was now regarded as something less than fully human, she was strip-searched. The passport, dated 15 October 1938, may not have been newly issued but instead an existing one crudely altered by a new measure that gave clear evidence of the Nazis' direction of travel. Following the Decree on Passports of Jews that came into force on 5 October, all new or existing passports for Jewish-German nationals had to be stamped on the front with a big red J. So, on her last trip home, one way or another this act of

Marion Samter's German passport from 1938. (Courtesy of Anita Savio)

conspicuous branding was applied to Marion's passport under the new law. In fact, while the Nazis would have needed no encouragement, negotiations with the Swiss federal government, increasingly reluctant to take in Jewish refugees, had persuaded them to adopt the new rule, emblazoning the scarlet letter on the passports of German Jews. This single measure saw an immediate change of attitude towards her when Marion returned to the Alpine nation. As she later wrote, *That stopped me from being admitted back into Switzerland after a brief stay in Berlin for the purpose of packing some more stuff. How did I finally manage to get back into Switzerland? A Swiss friend of mine, the widow of my math professor, purchased an Albanian visa for me so that the Swiss felt safe that they could kick me out to Albania when they wanted to get rid of me.*[3]

The teacher in the photo that Marion took of the maths class may well have been the same professor whose widow would later help her to get the visa she mentions in her note. But whoever it was, she soon had the documents she needed, including the prized US visa that so many Jewish refugees were hoping to obtain. Securing a berth on the steamer SS *Noordam*, she left the Dutch port of Rotterdam on 18 February 1939, bound for New York City. The 'List or Manifest for Alien Passengers to the United States Immigrant Inspector at Port of Arrival' records her as passenger twenty-four out of twenty-four. The document as a whole is something of a group portrait of the range of people fleeing the coming storm, with one defining thing in common.

All are listed as reading German, though under the heading of 'Nationality', one family of five is given as Polish, the remaining nineteen being German. Under the next heading of 'Race or people', all are listed as 'Hebrew', a racial designation that persisted in US immigration policy until 1943. The ages range from 2 to 85 years old; there are several families, and there are five children under 16. Most of the men are merchants, but there are also two physicians and one professor. Marion is listed as 'Dr. Phil.'; the other women are without profession.

The majority of the twenty-four were born in various cities in Germany, with the remaining passengers from Poland, Czechoslovakia and even, in one case, Australia. Next to the serial number of their individual immigration visas is the place where each was issued. In Marion's case this was Zurich, on 3 February 1939; the same city is also given as her last residence or address. Her mother Else is listed as living at Wilhelmstrasse 13, Berlin, in the flat above that of her brother Kurt, his wife Greta and their children, where by that point only Greta remained. Marion's final destination is given as New York. The form confirms that she has paid her own passage and possesses more than the minimum sum of $50 required to enter the country. As in every case where the word 'MORE' has been written in this column, a handwritten figure has been scrawled over the top, which in her own case appears to be '250'.

Every passenger has stated their intention not to return to their country of origin, to remain in the United States and to become a US citizen. Each one gives the address of the person they will live with upon entering the country, which in the case of Marion is someone she lists as an acquaintance: Frida Schoenfeld of 615 Fort Washington Avenue in Washington Heights, NYC. It is possible that Ms Schoenfeld acted as the financial sponsor that every immigrant needed to secure a visa. She may have been an old colleague of her father Victor during his time at the Merrimac Chemical Company, based in the state of Massachusetts. Anita is sure that Else had kept in contact with his colleagues after the death of her husband, though it's unlikely that she had met them in person.

Whoever this woman was, Marion would be safe in America. But her mother was still in Berlin, with many documents to get hold of before she herself could leave. The hardest part was to find a country that would take her. In the aftermath of Kristallnacht, America now seemed impossible, despite Marion having arrived there so recently. But there was family in England — a nephew and a niece — and her sister was now in Ireland. So, with great reluctance, Else bent her efforts to what seemed a more attainable goal.

THE GYPSY LIFE ISN'T BEAUTIFUL

The woman in the photographs referred to as *Mutti* is elegant and self-possessed, the product of an affluent background which had cushioned her from the hardships of the Weimar years. Her maiden name was Else Grelling. Her parents were both Jewish: her father, the writer and lawyer Richard Grelling, and her mother Margarethe, whose family, the Simons, were very wealthy indeed. Her parents' marriage had ended in divorce when Else was 10. But, from the evidence of Marion's photos of so many foreign trips in the early 1930s, Else had sufficient income that she and her daughter could afford to live comfortably, despite Else being a single parent with no history of earning a living that Marion ever mentioned. She seems at ease in front of the camera, amused and possibly flattered to be the subject of so much attention. To all appearances, her affluence made the difficulties of life without a husband less of a burden than otherwise they might have been. But the self-portrait that emerges from the few letters of Else's that survive is rather at odds with the air of confidence of the woman in the photos.

Else sitting at a café table, Friedrichshafen, Germany, August 1930. (© Sheri Blaney, Samter Archive)

It may have been the setbacks in childhood, the bitter quarrelling of her parents that ended in divorce; or the body blow of early widowhood and the social isolation of being a single parent at a time when German society was indifferent to the fate of widows: by 1918, war had made so many. Most likely, it was different factors combined that made Else, by her own admission, very awkward in the company of people she didn't know well. And by the early months of 1939, there was also the unavoidable reality that, like every Jewish German, her standing in society had been degraded by six years of Nazi rule. Even living as discreetly as she did, whenever she left the house – whenever she *had* to go out – she may have wondered if her sense of style and the confident demeanour she was able to project was sufficient to conceal her Jewish background; whether she could still come across as a German of the upper middle class. It was something she had hardly had to think about until the Nazis had taken over, since when they had tried to make her think of nothing else. A card in the Berlin archives from the population, occupation and business census of 17 May 1938, in which Else is among those listed, each with a horizontal row of their own, has columns for forename, family name, date of birth, place of birth. But there are also four individual columns under the general heading: *Was or is any of the grandparents of the Jewish race (yes or no)*.[1] In each of the four columns in Else's row, the answer is *yes*. So, in early 1939, whenever she went to the shops or took the S-Bahn into central Berlin, to speak to lawyers or bureaucrats about her plans for emigration and the sale of the house, appearing to be what she had never had to think that she was not may have taken an effort of will that one dark look or a pointed remark could have quickly undone.

The sense of jeopardy was never easy for anyone to cope with, even less so when you had suffered the losses that Else had known. Her parents' marriage had been unhappy, but, as a young woman on the threshold of adulthood, Else would have hoped her own life would be different. In her teenage years, after her father had left, and then once her sister and brother had gone, she had lived with her mother and stepfather, the banker Richard Landsberger, and Eva, her stepsister, the offspring of that marriage, who was very much younger than her. Then at some point around 1910, when Else was 20 years old, she met Victor. Marrying him should have been her route to a bigger world and perhaps a lasting happiness. In the photo of her grandparents that Anita still has, Victor and Else certainly look the part. But like those of so many women of that generation, Else's hopes would be dashed.

Left: Victor and Else Samter, 1912; Right: Victor with baby Marion, 1913. (Courtesy of Anita Savio)

Victor Samter was more than ten years her senior, an experienced research chemist with a growing reputation. He had trained in Germany, spent several years at Merrimac in the USA, then returned to Berlin in 1907, expanding his knowledge of patent law and writing books on aspects of industrial chemistry inspired by the more dynamic methods of production and vocational training he'd encountered in America. Anita recalls her mother telling her that Victor had been involved in the development of early plastics, namely Bakelite, invented by a Belgian called Leo Baekeland. This almost certainly referred to the job that Victor took in 1911 with the Berlin firm of Rütgers-Werke, which had gone into partnership with Baekeland's firm. That same year Victor married Else Grelling. The couple had soon moved to an apartment in the Schöneberg district of south-west Berlin. It was here in 1913 that Marion was born, as a photo of Victor holding his baby daughter confirms.

Then war broke out. Else always told her daughter that Victor didn't support it, but like so many Jewish Germans – around 100,000 who saw themselves first and foremost as Germans – he felt it was his patriotic duty to fight. He enlisted as an ordinary soldier and was sent to the Eastern Front, where the Russians had attacked in the weeks after war was declared. Victor was unlucky to be wounded in the opening battle, at Stallupönen, a place in East Prussia just 7 miles from the village where he was born. He appears to have lingered on for some time in a hospital

Grelling family photos on a sideboard, Berlin, undated. (© Sheri Blaney, Samter Archive)

in Königsberg (today's Kaliningrad), but on 13 November 1914 he died, leaving Marion without a father or even memories of a father.

At 24, Else was a widow with a 1-year-old daughter to raise in a society that would soon become more liberal but also more volatile, more combustible, than she had ever known it. She never remarried but brought up her daughter by herself, albeit with financial support she almost certainly received from her mother, to supplement the war-widow's pension she was paid by the state. Anita recalls Marion, her mother, telling her that she and Else had lived for many years in an apartment in a multi-storey block on Landshuter Strasse in Schöneberg; it may have been the same home her parents had moved to before she was born. Marion had memories of standing on the balcony as a girl of around 12 years old, dropping stones onto the hats of people coming into or going out from the block. One visitor subjected to this treatment was her own aunt Charlotte. Luckily, everyone wore hats in those days!

Another memory Marion often mentioned was of Albert Einstein. From 1917 until his exile in 1933, the great physicist lived in an apartment in Haberlandstrasse, just across the street from Else and Marion. Young Marion would watch him every morning as he walked along Landshuter

Strasse on his way to teach at Berlin University in the centre of the city. By 1925, the Jewish population of Berlin numbered 170,000, around a third of all German Jews. Einstein was one of many German-speaking Jewish intellectuals drawn to the heart of the German-speaking world. During the 1920s, the city was perhaps the most vibrant in Europe, with a culture of licence and experimentation that only Paris could rival. But these qualities were also a measure of political instability, which often led to violence, especially toward Jews. Even before the terrible outcomes of the First World War, Einstein had always been alert to the undercurrents of nationalist feeling and where they might flow. As a prominent pacifist he had opposed the war from the start; in 1913, when the Prussian Academy of Sciences had approached him to give up his position as the newly appointed professor of physics in Zurich and come to Berlin, he agreed, but only on condition that he could keep his Swiss passport. And by the time that Marion Samter was old enough to fully appreciate who the great man was, the sight of whom so thrilled her every morning, perhaps she had her own misgivings about the way things were going.

The young may have more natural reasons than the old to be optimistic, but, even as a young person, like every other Jewish German Marion would instantly have been affected by the Nazis' rise to power. The ban on Jewish students in higher education was just the most obvious example. But anyone looking at the photos she took would never guess at the growing threat. Perhaps, for all sorts of sensible reasons, she tried to ignore it; she certainly avoided taking the kinds of exterior shots of German cities she seemed to revel in abroad, perhaps wary of drawing attention to herself as a Jew. Her German images are mostly of domestic interiors and of people she knew well.

In later life in America, Marion's political awareness expressed itself through volunteering in support of women's right to vote. But, even before the Nazis had come to power, at the age of 18 or 19, she spent a summer in the mining valleys of South Wales, delivering a programme of education for the benefit of the people who lived there. Long before that, her own education would have been partly a lesson in moral survival in a climate of unrest in which every new upheaval – the humiliation of defeat in war, the revolutionary violence of the winter of 1918–19, the punitive conditions of the Versailles Treaty, the hyperinflation of 1923, a further economic collapse and the huge rise in unemployment that followed the Wall Street Crash of 1929, and the chaos that followed – was blamed on the Jews.

From as early as 1920, Einstein himself, the man whom Marion had watched from her window every morning, had had to put up with anti-semitic students at Berlin University disrupting his lectures with racist harangues. Thirteen years later, Einstein was among the first of the thousands of Jewish intellectuals who sought refuge in America, including many who feature in this story. He was in California when the Nazis seized power and would never go back to his native land. But after he had dared publicly to criticise the new Nazi government, a bounty of $5,000 was placed on his head. In March 1933, returning to Europe, he settled on the Belgian coast. But by the end of the summer, credible threats of assassination had forced him to flee to Britain. He would soon return to America.

Einstein's books were among those burnt in a pyre in Bebelsplatz in central Berlin on 10 May that year, having already been banned from the curriculum at German universities, dismissed as 'Jewish physics'. The same banning order was slapped on the works of all other Jewish intellectuals, but the Nazis also targeted every other aspect of German public life in which Jews had an influence or a stake. Jewish public servants were forced to retire from state employment in April 1933 under the so-called Law for the Restoration of the Professional Civil Service; among them was Else's brother, Kurt Grelling, who was forced to resign his job as a teacher. Later, after the enactment of the Nuremberg Laws in September 1935, the range of professions open to Jews was drastically reduced. This reversed a century or more of liberal reform, including more than sixty years since full emancipation, which had seen Jews find their place in many areas of German life from which they had long been excluded.

Boycotts of Jewish businesses had been a tactic of intimidation since the action carried out nationwide in April 1933. But in late 1937, the Nazis moved to expropriate those Jewish firms, including some of the biggest success stories of the German economy of the early twentieth century. This state-sanctioned theft directly affected Else's nephew, Werner Sachs, but also Else and her siblings, too. Else's stepfather, Richard Landsberger, was a banker whose business was based at 41 Jägerstrasse in the prestigious Mitte district of central (later East) Berlin; the property was finally restored to the family after the Reunification of Germany in 1990, a long, drawn-out process chronicled by Else's great-nephew Peter Sachs. In 1906 Landsberger and Margarethe, Else's mother, had purchased two properties in the same city block, including No. 40 as well as its numerical neighbour, and also two more around the corner at Oberwallstrasse 12 and 13. Margarethe died in 1934, some six years after Landsberger, and the buildings passed to her children: Else, Charlotte, Kurt, and their half-sister Eva Landsberger. This was done through an *Erbengemeinschaft*, an association of inheritance, similar to a trust, which was set up for their benefit. But in 1937, the buildings were commandeered by Himmler's *Kriminalpolizei*, and the family was forced to sell them for 450,000 Reichsmarks. This may have been a fraction of their true value, but the issue in any case is largely academic: despite the veneer of legal process, no money was ever paid them for this fraudulent sale.

Dispossession, the legalised theft of everything they had, from employment to property to wealth; an erosion of ordinary freedoms and of any kind of normal social status that with each new measure seemed to have reached a new low of brazen contempt until the Nazis found yet another, deeper indignity to heap upon the Jews. After Kristallnacht, it seemed clear that there would be no low, no floor beneath which they couldn't sink, though even the Nazis themselves did not yet know where that would lead. Aside from staying put, there was only one option for those with the means to take it. Else Samter's surviving correspondence with her brother-in-law Hans Sachs, her sister Charlotte's husband, dates from the early summer (May to July) of 1939. By then Hans and Lotte were living in Dublin, having managed with great difficulty the previous year to escape to England themselves. In these letters Hans urges Else to take the steps that would enable her to join them.

Else's German passport from the time has not survived, but a document Anita does possess is the *Kennkarte*, the identification card with which, from July 1938, every German Jew was issued. Else's is dated 5 January 1939. Its left-hand page is emblazoned with a big red J, and on the right, beneath the photo, she has the middle name of 'Sara', and not Clara, the middle name her parents had given her. The same name, 'Sara', in Nazi thinking a typically Jewish name, was imposed on every German-Jewish woman, just as the middle name 'Israel' was forced on every German-Jewish man. This decree on Jewish names became effective on 1 January 1939, just four days before Else's *Kennkarte* was issued. A person's name is perhaps the ultimate marker of who they imagine they are. Imposing a name in this way, like the big red J, was intended to emphasize to any German Jew that their personal identity was of far less importance than what the Nazis saw as their race. It was part of an escalating process of racial branding, and shaming, that would later be more publicly expressed in the odious yellow stars. By any standard of civilised behaviour, it was madness.

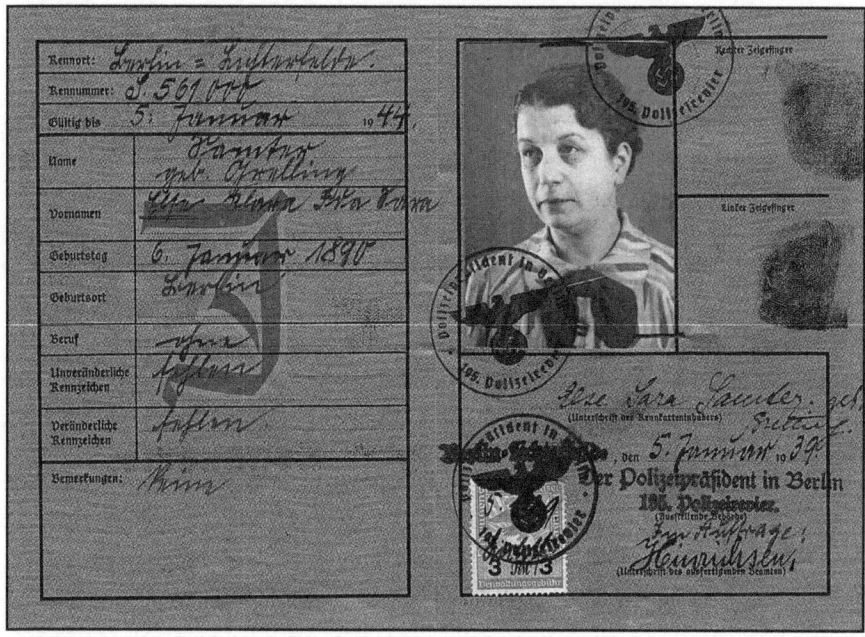

Else Samter's *Kennkarte*. (Courtesy of Anita Savio)

The imposition in the *Kennkarte* of a racial middle name would also be applied to the passport Else needed to emigrate. It was a crude reminder of a kind of identity that, for the generation of secular Jewish Germans that Else and her siblings were part of, was of less significance than for any who had come before them. As a child, Else's brother Kurt had even been baptised into the Protestant faith, just like his Jewish father Richard. The Grellings' cultural milieu was one they shared with many other Germans of the upper middle class, whether Jewish or not. The family had long intergenerational memories of a style of life that was affluent and secure. Else's maternal grandfather, Louis Simon, had become wealthy through cotton manufacture, a family business jointly owned with his brother Isaak. In the next generation, under the stewardship of Margarethe's cousin Henri James Simon, known as James, and his brother Louis, it became the most important cotton-trading company in Europe in the decades before the First World War. As a mark of how comfortable the family felt among the well-to-do of German society, around the turn of the century James, by then a generous patron of the arts who funded archaeological digs in Egypt and the Near East, became a close confidant of Kaiser Wilhelm II.

In old age, James's mother Ida was drawn by the German artist Ismael Gentz. John Cooke, Else's great nephew, possesses a photo of the drawing and remembers asking Else about it in the 1960s. He recalls that *she* at once said that the picture was of Ida Simon in the sitting room of her apartment overlooking the Tiergarten in Berlin, and that when Kaiser Wilhelm II rode by, he would look up to her window and salute her, because the Simon family were so-called 'Kaiserjuden', acknowledged by the Kaiser for their good works in Berlin.[2] This munificence extended beyond her death in 1906 through the Ida Simon Stiftung, *a medical charity for chronic women's illnesses, 'without regard to belief'*, as described by John's cousin Peter Sachs.[3] It led in 1911 to the building of a maternity hospital, the Universitäts-Frauenklinik, overlooking the River Spree in Berlin, constructed with funds from the foundation.

The term *Kaiserjuden*, to describe the group of assimilated Jewish advisers to Wilhelm II in the years before the First World War, was apparently coined by Chaim Weizmann, the celebrated chemist and prominent Zionist who later became the first president of modern Israel. Weizmann was originally from Belarus and thus his status, even among German Jews, during the seven years he lived in Germany,[4] was as an *Ostjude*, or eastern Jew, of whom large numbers had only recently arrived in the country, fleeing pogroms in the east. Informed by this experience, the term *Kaiserjuden* is laced with mockery. But perhaps for a time, both before and after the war, the assimilationists seemed to be winning the argument. Among the other *Kaiserjuden* were Albert Ballin, the Hamburg shipping magnate whose wealth enabled millions of eastern Jews to emigrate to America in the early years of the century; and Walther Rathenau, the wealthy industrialist who as foreign minister became a key figure in the Social Democratic government at the start of the Weimar Republic. But then in June 1922, in a sign of what was to come, Rathenau was murdered in broad daylight by antisemites in a drive-by shooting in a Berlin suburb.

So, the signs may have been there in the 1920s, but Germany was not alone in that decade in unabashed expressions of antisemitism. After all, America's leading industrialist, Henry Ford, published his own weekly newspaper, the *Dearborn Independent* (aka the *Ford International Weekly*), which openly promoted conspiracy theories about Jews.[5] At the height of its popularity, in 1926, almost a million people bought it every week. Among European countries, Germany was in many ways less hostile to Jews than others, especially those in the east. Even Einstein, who had counted Rathenau as a friend, had remained in Berlin until emigration was forced upon him.[6] Eventually, he had made it to America; a man of world importance, he could pick and choose from the many countries that tried to entice him to come. But few among even the most professionally accomplished had that kind of bargaining power. In the mid-1930s, Victor Klemperer, a professor of French literature in late middle age, felt that he had little to offer to anywhere new and above all was too old to start again. Until Kristallnacht, tens of thousands of older Jews had taken the same view; afterwards it was almost too late.

By the end of 1938, Else was approaching 50 herself. At any age, the process of emigration is a practical and emotional challenge, as the letters exchanged between Else and her brother-in-law, Charlotte's husband Hans Sachs, make clear. In one, dated 12 June 1939, Hans addresses the anxious questions about her future that Else must have raised in a letter that doesn't survive. With the benefit of having already endured the same ordeal, he takes her through the options she has for sending her luggage ahead: which port she could send it to – Southampton, Dover or Harwich – where she could pick it up, how long she could expect to wait to retrieve it or where she might store those pieces for which she doesn't have immediate need. But he cautions her over plans she must have mentioned in a previous letter for how she might earn a living in England: by buying a machine on which to make *Baumkuchen*, a ring-shaped cake, baked on a spit, which Hans is certain that the English will not find to their liking. But with no spouse to provide for her, no war-widow's pension after emigrating, no income from the stolen Berlin properties and almost nothing of her own money that she was allowed to take out of Germany, she was worried about how she would support herself in the new country.

These logistical headaches are one reason why uprooting yourself, unwillingly as a refugee, is one of the hardest choices that anyone might ever have to make, never mind the emotional heartbreak involved. For German Jews, even after the legal alienation, the internal banishment of the previous few years and the threat to personal safety after Kristallnacht, cutting the few ties that remained was an agonising wrench – particularly if, like Else, you were no longer young and your country was the only one you had ever known. So, it's not surprising that she was still so ambivalent about her imminent departure even in late spring 1939, when the extant correspondence between Else and Hans begins.

In a letter dated 25 May, Hans tries to soothe his sister-in-law's worries about what lay ahead, acknowledging that she will have to leave a lot behind, as he and Lotte had done at the end of the previous year. Else is especially pained at the thought of leaving her dog; rather missing the point, Hans asks her why she can't just sell the dog or give it to someone as a present. He adds that for him, *the most difficult thing was the irretrievable separation from people, as we still had a large circle of friends.*[7] In the end, for most of us these bonds of emotion to people or pets or a present anchored in the past are what bind us to the places where we live.

Else Samter with her beloved terrier dog, 1930s. (© Sheri Blaney, Samter Archive)

Nonetheless, Jews were also required to give up almost everything else. Every German Jew who left the country had their wealth confiscated as a condition of departure – in effect, it was stolen – through wealth levies and taxes and racially targeted foreign exchange controls. There was nothing whatsoever that they could do about it. On 26 April 1938, an edict came into force called the Decree for the Reporting of Jewish-Owned Property, a register of the assets and property worth over 5,000 Reichsmarks (RM) (less than £500) of all German and Austrian Jews. It was also stipulated that Jews would have to surrender 50 per cent of their wealth in order to obtain permission to emigrate. At this point, it was the explicit policy of Hitler's government to empty German lands of their Jewish populations by encouraging the Jews to leave; unsurprisingly, the threat of being dispossessed deterred a good number from doing so. As the months went by, things would only get worse. By the time that Else was actively trying to get out, Jews were allowed to keep almost nothing of what they owned. The goalposts were always shifting, and always to the growing disadvantage of the Jews. The letters between Else and Hans offer detailed insights into how this process worked.

Else knew she would have to leave the house she had jointly bought with her brother in Lichterfelde-Ost. Kurt had lost his job as a *Gymnasium* or upper secondary school teacher in 1933, and with their income from property an uncertain prospect, the families – Kurt's and Else's – had hoped to secure themselves a place to live from which they couldn't easily be evicted. Else lived upstairs, with Kurt's family in the downstairs flat. But, by the time these letters were written, the house was being sold and the flat was vacant, awaiting new occupants to be installed by the new owner of the building. The letters contain long passages in which Hans and Else discuss the conditions of sale, which by the date of the first letter seems already to have taken place. For the oversight of this process they were indebted to Frau Gertrud Brenning, the family banker, who was also Jewish. She engaged the firm of Wunder, von Wendland & Co. of Bamberg to take general power of attorney. Previously a Jewish-owned bank called A.E. Wassermann, like other Jewish businesses and banks it was subject to compulsory sale on deleterious terms to a new 'Aryan' ownership, with Herrn Wunder and von Wendland appointed by the Nazis to run it. The bank held numerous *Auswanderungskonten*, escrow accounts for Jews who were emigrating, into which they were obliged to deposit the lion's share of their remaining assets – all but 5,000 RM – before they were allowed to leave. In his letter of 12 June, Hans writes that, in his own case, the bank had had to place the money into a locked intermediary account before obtaining permission to transfer it to his and Lotte's account. They were still hoping to obtain access to this money from outside Germany, but the hope was baseless. Even if Else and her siblings had not been Jewish, once the war had started, it was impossible to remove any money from the country.

Hans and Lotte's position was therefore hardly any better than Else's, but at least they had found themselves a comfortable apartment in the Irish capital. They invited Else to come and live with them, and in Hans's letter to Else of 7 June he discusses the lack of border control between Britain and Ireland – a common travel area that still exists – which he assures her will make it easy to reach them on an English travel visa. In the first letter of Else's that survives, dated 1 July, she makes it clear that an organisation she calls the *Wob. House* has sent her a cable, followed by a letter, regarding an immediate application for a visa that they were making to the Home Office on her behalf; this had been promised to her by mid-June, and, according to Else, they had a bad conscience over the subsequent delay. That may have been true, but the organisation she refers to, Woburn House in central London – the name of a building that was home to the

Board of Deputies of British Jews and various Jewish aid organisations – had been overwhelmed by demand since 9 November the previous year. In March, they had been forced to move to larger premises nearby, but for desperate German Jews, the name persisted as a symbol of hope.[8]

Else says that until she receives the visa, she won't be able to contact the Irish consulate (about her intention to travel to Ireland), but that if she does receive it and is allowed to travel, she hopes to leave on Tuesday, 11 July. She asks to stay with them for fourteen days. She is still trying to register the sale of the property at Wilhelmstrasse 13, and in this regard, Frau Brenning had spent a week negotiating with the Nazi bureaucracy until the permits Else needed were issued. Now Frau Brenning had gone on holiday, along with the judge from the land registry; the official left in charge *is so overworked*, as Else puts it, *that he keeps promising it every day and apparently hasn't done it yet.*[9]

The picture Else paints would seem like the inefficient grind of any normal bureaucracy were it not for the sense of panic that colours her clear frustration. *My nervousness gets worse every day*, she confesses, *as I don't know if my papers will be sufficient to let me leave.*[10] The stress has begun affecting her physical health in the form of hives, exacerbated by the straitened circumstances in which she was living. Still in the apartment in the house on Wilhelmstrasse, despite the near-completion of the sale, if she would not be able to emigrate in the very near future, she faced eviction whenever the new owner took possession of the property. Even the chattels she was able to take with her brought anxieties of their own; *most of all*, she writes, *it's a horrible feeling knowing that I won't see these things again for many years, and that if I do, half of it will be missing and everything broken.*[11] But, above all, she had no illusions about the predicament in which she found herself and the scale of upheaval to come. *Now I'm in a borrowed bed, with a table, three chairs and an empty flat, as if I am a young girl again. But the gypsy life is not beautiful.*[12]

A week later, she writes that she will soon abandon her attempt to emigrate, as *new difficulties materialise on a daily basis, and that's aside from the fact that I still haven't got a visa.*[13] Once again, the difficulties lay with the Home Office in London. She was still thinking of getting to America to be with Marion, and to that end, acting on Hans's advice, she had been to the Berlin offices of the United States Lines; but, as she puts it, they *scornfully explained to me that it's unthinkable that I could use an English visa to reach Cobh.*[14] *It would cause a lot of difficulties, and I would need to have a lot of proofs for the Irish consulate. I don't know what they mean by this. Would you be able to send me something if it isn't too much trouble? I will go there on Monday and they will send you a letter-telegram, in the event that they are able to tell me what I need.*

I have also found out that a German freight steamer goes to Dublin every 14 days, and I can send my luggage with them. That would be very good for me, as it wouldn't be moved around so much and it wouldn't be left standing and therefore there would be less chance of things being left behind.[15]

Here Else reveals a predicament that is common to all refugees, in being so utterly dependent on the kindness of others, even members of her own family – that is, Charlotte and Hans and their daughter, her niece Ilse, based in Oxford. All had been refugees themselves, to differing degrees, and they could well understand how she felt. But, despite Hans's offer of sanctuary in their Dublin home, Else did not have any sense of where she would live, an insecurity she refers to several times in the letters. *You write to me that I should aim to address the luggage to the place where I will spend most of the time during my intermediate stay, and to that place I should send the main part of my luggage. I have asked both you and Ilse that same question and have always received the answer that this could only be decided once I am there, and that I shouldn't break my head over it. But, of course, I often think about what's going to happen to me in the years in England. It is truly an awful feeling to enter the unknown.*[16]

This insecurity affected every decision she took, albeit what they could bring in their luggage was a question that Jewish refugees were still in a position to decide. In the light of what came later, this seems something of a problem of affluence, though it was hardly an embarrassment of riches: by this point, with wealth and property effectively stolen, ordinary chattels were more or less the sum total of what Jewish emigrants could hope to take with them, the last material connections to their former lives. *I couldn't organise my luggage like that,* she frets, *as I had to pack according to the lists, and the packers, the customs officers and I would never have finished it if we had put all my belongings in several suitcases. You didn't experience this. For example, I have all my shoes in one suitcase; in another I have all my bed linen and towels; in the next I have all my books, a hairdryer, an electric cooker, medicines; in the big wardrobe suitcase I have my clothes, underwear, etc. So, therefore, in England I would need to calmly rearrange everything and put some items in storage. As you know, various suitcases have been sealed since 23rd June, and I can only rely on my few pieces of hand luggage, and for this I had to obtain a permit from the foreign exchange control office, and they had to take into account how long the journey would be. Naturally, I didn't factor in that I still had to live for many weeks in Berlin, and I couldn't have known that anyway.*[17]

The mental exhaustion evident in this passage was made worse by a sense of isolation that now afflicted every German Jew, with no one she could turn to, aside from Frau Brenning, for detailed, meaningful advice.

Then two days later, on 10 July, Else sent her brother-in-law a cable that is full of alarm (admittedly, a quality inherent to the medium): *LANDING IRELAND IMPOSSIBLE WITHOUT SPECIAL VISA. URGENTLY REQUESTING APPLICATION DEPARTMENT EXTERNAL AFFAIRS.*[18]

This was a further example of what Else had already described as *new difficulties* that *materialise on a daily basis*. She confirms as much in a letter written two days later, after another pro-forma letter from the UK Home Office had arrived. *If only one could have foreseen that maybe it would have been easier to get an Irish visa than an English one. The people at the Irish consulate were very dismissive because I was a refugee. Of course, they think that you could get a visa for me there in Ireland. How quickly that would happen, they didn't know. They also told me I could travel from Hamburg to Dublin with my luggage on a freight steamer, and they gave me the address of a shipping company. They wrote to me today that a steamer will leave on 20th July and then another one on 3rd August. That would be very appealing, and would mean that I arrive with you after you are back from Oxford.*[19] *But just now another company phoned where a few days ago I made enquiries about transport to Dublin for luggage and passenger; but they say again that they have been told today by Hamburg that emigrants cannot be transported on the ship.*[20] This was typical of the bureaucratic chaos in which Jewish refugees were continually caught up, as ever more cynical measures applied by the Nazis combined with growing reluctance on the part of foreign governments – in this case the Irish – to accept the victims of Nazi terror.

There seems to have been a certain amount of confusion about where Else would be staying: whether she wanted to stay with Lotte and Hans and whether they were happy to have her. Family meant bonds of loyalty, and therefore safety, but these same bonds also brought tensions that were hard to hide. This added to her stress, a matter that she finally addressed directly in the letter of 12 July. *About me coming to you*, she writes, *unfortunately we are talking at cross purposes. I have always said that I'd like to come. The limitations about when I should come, the flat being too small, etc. have only ever come from your side. I have concerns only if I am there by myself alone because I am very awkward with acquaintances. […] Lotte asks whether I will be looking for a room or whether I'm thinking about [staying with] a family. These are questions which again and again I have addressed to both you and her and to Ilse, and I have always received the answer: 'That can only be decided once you are in the country. Don't break your head over it.' But even as I have broken my head, I have not come to a conclusion, because I don't have enough to go on to weigh up the possibilities there.*[21]

This state of emotional paralysis was not unusual among Jewish refugees. It was a direct consequence of their powerlessness, the sense that life was not theirs to command; that any plans they made were subject to the indifference, the cynical whims or the casual or deliberate cruelty of state power, whether Nazi or, to a far lesser but not trivial extent, those of another government. The same was also true of Else's brother Kurt and of other refugees whose stories are even briefly connected with his own. This sense of powerlessness had physical as well as psychological effects. Else describes the miserable state she is in, with a terrible toothache whose potentially lengthy treatment she does not have the time to contemplate, as well as the hives she had written about in an earlier letter. *You can see how important it is for me that I finally find peace*, she writes. *I cannot endure this situation for much longer.*[22]

Luckily, she wouldn't have to. Hans's last two letters to Else are dated 16 and 18 July. In the latter he insists that with the Irish government issuing just three permits a month, the time she would have to wait would be much longer than for an English visa. He advises her to wait patiently for news from London, reassuring her that *it has been confirmed to me again that one can travel* [to Ireland] *with an English permit.*[23] And here again he reveals yet another insecurity that is fundamental to the experience of all refugees: the justifiable anxiety over how long the country that takes them in will allow them to remain. Hans has reminded her in the earlier letter, from the 16th, that her situation is tied to the uncertainty of his and Lotte's: that *our own long-term presence here is not secure, that our permit is valid until the end of the year, but my grant runs until 1st May next year, so we can anticipate remaining here until at least that time.*[24] It was as much certainty as he could offer, though he also chose to take a positive view of the leniency of the Irish authorities, albeit every visa was a temporary measure that was destined one day to run out. *The term 'visit'*, he writes on the 18th, *is interpreted generously here. But it would certainly be limited to the timeframe of the English permit.*[25]

And then there are no more letters between them. On 2 August Else was issued with a British visa. According to a record card held by the German-Jewish Aid Committee (Woburn House), she had already registered with the American consulate in Berlin, with a view to joining her daughter. This prospect, but also her sister's residence in Ireland, as recorded on the card, may have persuaded the Home Office that her time in Britain would be a brief one, that she would soon travel on to Dublin, if not to America, and would not be a burden on the state. Whatever the reasons, about a week later she was boarding a ship, which arrived in Southampton on 11 August. It was just in the nick of time. On 3 September, Britain declared war on Germany, and the escape route she had taken was closed.

AN IRRETRIEVABLE SEPARATION

By the time that Else had got to Ireland, Lotte had restored a sense of order; not only in the generous apartment that she and her husband had rented at 3 Palmerston Villas, a quiet cul-de-sac in the Upper Rathmines area of south Dublin, but also through a growing network of new friends and acquaintances, a group of fellow German-Jewish exiles and others to replace the large circle they had had to leave behind. Lotte had always been the prime mover in her husband's social life. She loved people. With her gift for human contact, especially among the wives of Hans's academic colleagues, she had soon forged new friendships with the same natural ease as, in later years, she would gather up the scattered threads of her wide and complex family. As her grandson John Cooke recalls her saying, with a clear emphasis on the final word, *Man soll sich kümmern über die* Leute: You need to care about *people*. It was a maxim she always lived up to.

Hans and Charlotte Sachs. (Courtesy of John Cooke)

In Heidelberg they had enjoyed a prosperous life on the north bank of the River Neckar in the Neuenheim district, a neighbourhood of generous Jugendstil villas from the turn of the century. Like Lotte's, Hans's upbringing had also been one of considerable affluence. By the age of 40, his father Elias had made a fortune as the 'Coal King of Upper of Silesia', as he was known, before retiring to raise his family. The family home in Kattowitz, now Katowice in Poland but then an integral part of Germany, was the size of a small palace and later became a bank. Unlike his son, Elias was also a practising Jew, who endowed a synagogue in the city, which the Nazis later destroyed. Hans exuded a quiet confidence, in part a product of his comfortable childhood but also from a steadiness of character that helped to convince Charlotte Grelling of his merits as a husband, even if her mother at first did not approve. As the eldest child in one of the grandest of the Berlin Jewish families, and as a girl of considerable beauty and charm, she knew that Margarethe, her mother, had felt that she could make a better match. But times were changing even before the First World War, and Hans, a young researcher at the cutting edge of science, was a coming man. By the time they married, in 1905, he had attached himself as research assistant to the famous immunologist Paul Ehrlich, who three years later would win a Nobel Prize.

Hans rose quickly to full professor, first in Frankfurt then, from 1920, in Heidelberg. But even after emancipation, German Jews had found themselves barred from many professional fields. Within medicine, Hans found his own niche in one of the new sciences, serology, that was not already a preserve of the non-Jewish elite. Undeterred, German-born and German-trained, in his own mind his successes only added to his country's prestige. In the decade before the First World War, he developed reliable tests for the diagnosis of syphilis, which brought him international acclaim. But when war broke out, his public writings cast his own field – the fight against disease – as a part of the war effort every bit as integral as the fighting at the fronts, exhibiting an unquestioning love for the fatherland in its hour of need. Despite the international contacts he had made and would continue to make through his work, in a time of national struggle he could not imagine that he was anything other than German.

The 1920s, for Hans, were years of achievement and growing professional esteem set against the backdrop of political crises that left prosperous university cities like Heidelberg less affected than other parts of Germany, though not untouched. After the crisis of 1929, political unrest could be felt across the country. By that point, the Nazis were well organised and had set about recruiting disaffected Germans in every town and from all strata of society, turning an economic malaise to their own malign advantage. In Heidelberg in October 1930, a furore erupted at the university over the appointment of Dr Emil Julius Gumbel as professor of statistics, an episode recalled many years later by Thomas Mann's son Golo, who was a student in the city at the time. Gumbel was Jewish but also a pacifist with a history of polemical writing in support of those beliefs. But pacifism was a dirty word to those, like the Nazis, who could not see past the defeat of 1918 and the crippling humiliation that followed. It didn't help that Gumbel had supported the failed revolution of 1918–19, so his pacifism was seen as a betrayal of his country. Linked to his Jewish background, it gave succour to the myth of a 'stab in the back', which the Nazis had long exploited to sow hatred against Jews, the blatant lie that Jews were involved in a grand conspiracy to undermine the German state. As in other universities across Germany, a large number of professors and a sizeable part of the student body had nationalist leanings laced in many cases with antisemitism. The result was a campaign of harassment so relentless that Gumbel was soon obliged to step down.

There's a natural tendency to hope that periods of political turbulence will blow themselves out, even when in hindsight there is overwhelming evidence that the conflict was getting worse. When several outcomes are possible, the view we take of the present and the future will reflect our experience of the past, which in the case of the Sachses had been happy and fulfilled. So, no matter how bad the signs may have been in the previous few years, Hitler's seizing of power in 1933 would certainly have shocked them. Within weeks, as in every city, signs began appearing all over Heidelberg – *Die Juden sind unser Unglück*: the Jews are our misfortune – to intimidate the Jewish population, reinforcing the official steps that would soon begin excluding them from all aspects of German life. In May 1933, as in so many cities, books by Jewish authors were burned by students in the main square, whose name, Universitätsplatz, spoke to the importance of higher learning in Heidelberg's civic identity. The previous month Jewish state employees, including university professors, had been summarily dismissed from their posts. Though the intervention of colleagues would see him reinstated in July on account of his long and distinguished service and his importance in a vital field, Hans must have realised it would only be a temporary reprieve. His daughter Ilse had completed her medical studies that summer but, as a Jew, was not allowed to take the state exams that would enable her to practise; and two key Jewish colleagues were expelled from the country, despite the representations that Hans had made on their behalf. So, he went on working with a cloud of racial stigma hanging over him and, for a time, he continued to publish. His output of newspaper articles as well as academic papers had always been prolific, but a ban on the work of Jewish intellectuals would soon bring that to an end; his last article in a German publication, the *Münchener Medizinische Wochenschrift*, appeared the following year.

Sachs continued to give lectures, though the number of students who attended them dwindled considerably after the Nazis came to power. He retained his position as director of the prestigious Kaiser Wilhelm Institute for Medical Research, based in Heidelberg, and at first was not prevented from travelling to academic conferences abroad. But there must have been an air of unreality to all of it – a palpable sense that his professional influence and freedom were being slowly whittled away. Then in September 1935 came the confirmation of what was already the clear direction of travel – the Nuremberg Laws – and the following month a letter dismissing him from his post, in accordance with the new legislation. He was also removed from the editorship of a leading journal, the *Zeitschrift für Immunologie und experimentelle Therapie*, and this time from the directorship of the Kaiser Wilhelm Institute he headed. Retired on a pension, which at least would be enough to allow the Sachses to continue to live comfortably in Heidelberg, Hans's career as a scientist in Germany was officially at an end.

It was obvious that he should try to find a position abroad while he still could. Given his extensive network of contacts, surely that would not be impossible. He was not at Einstein's level of world renown but in his own field had done groundbreaking research and served international bodies like the League of Nations, one of the first German academics to be invited to do so after the end of the First World War. His preferred destination was Britain, whose language he spoke well and where there were colleagues with whom he already enjoyed a warm professional relationship. He wrote to one of these men, the American-born bacteriologist George Nuttall, by then emeritus professor at Cambridge, whom he hoped would be able to arrange a suitable position at a British university. The following year saw travel restrictions eased in the run-up to the Berlin Olympics, which in the original example of sportswashing the Nazis deceitfully exploited to show their barbarous regime in the best modern light. Those who wanted to be fooled allowed themselves to be fooled. Hans, like Lotte, was not, as no Jew could be or was. But he did make use of the temporary thaw to travel to Britain to explore whatever opportunities there might be – in London, Cambridge and Glasgow – though nothing materialised with a salary sufficient to their needs. He looked at other potential openings in places that, on the balance of probabilities, ought to have been safe in the years ahead: in Switzerland, in Sweden – countries whose ambivalent neutrality in the coming war would indeed be respected – and also in the USA. But nothing came up, even for someone of his stellar reputation. It may well have dawned on him that, at 57, he was yesterday's man, whose greatest successes had come early in a field that had now moved on from the areas in which he had made his name.

Seeing her father's difficulties and being blocked in her own career, in 1934, his daughter Ilse had taken the route to professional advancement that Marion Samter would choose the following year. She went to Switzerland, to the city of Basel, and studied for the summer term at the university, passing the medical examination for foreigners at the end of June. In October, she took up a temporary research post at the Istituto Sierterapico Milanese in Milan, working in the same field as her father, before returning to Germany in August 1935. Then in 1936, she became the first member of the immediate family to emigrate, travelling to England at a time when this was still a fairly straightforward process for German Jews. She was also young enough to do so without material loss, with no assets the Nazis could steal and no career prospects to abandon; in fact, nothing to lose besides the proximity and support of her parents, brother and friends.

That same year, Eva, Lotte's much-younger half-sister through her mother's second marriage, and her second husband, a man named Felix Oppenheim, left for Portugal, where they thought they would at least be safe. But Hans and Lotte remained in Heidelberg, surrounded by their many friends, some of them – those who were Jews – in a similar position, clinging to a life of precarious affluence and dwindling legal rights as they tried to look for a way to leave that would not reduce them to penury as fugitives in a foreign land. Hans knew that emigration was likely to mean the loss of his pension, along with most of their assets. Having not been able to obtain an academic post, despite the efforts of 1936, he continued to look for a way to stop the Nazi state from stealing all they had.

Things would soon take an even darker turn. The actions and abuses of the previous few years had widened the window of what it was acceptable to say, allowing an ancient animus that in some ways had seemed to be dying to reawaken from what had turned out to be merely a sleep. In the first six months of 1938, in echoes of what had already happened in Germany, laws were passed in Romania and Hungary, curtailing the rights of Jews in those countries, and pogroms in Poland during the same period resulted in the deaths of Jews. Vienna was among the most civilised of

European cities, but even before the dismantling of the Habsburg Empire at the Versailles Peace Conference, and the loss of status and economic hardship that followed, blatant antisemitism had always been a staple of daily life. In April and May, following the Nazi annexation of Austria, known as the Anschluss, in March, Jews in Vienna were forced on their hands and knees by mobs including their own neighbours to scrub the streets with small brushes or to eat grass. Some suffered heart attacks at the shock and humiliation; others took their own lives, overwhelmed by the storm of hatred which had suddenly descended with a force that almost no one, perhaps not even the perpetrators, had foreseen. The Sachses would have been alarmed to hear or to read of these events, which were gleefully reported in the Nazi press. But while they must have hoped the dark angel that was swept across the continent that year would overfly their unassuming life, at the same time Hans redoubled his efforts to secure both their visas and as much of their fortune as he could.

In June 1938, the Munich synagogue was burnt to the ground and, in the same month, all remaining Jewish-owned businesses across Germany were forcibly 'Aryanised', commandeered by the Nazi state, a measure that directly affected the Sachs family. Hans Sachs's younger sister, Grete, had married her cousin from Kattowitz, Paul Grünfeld, founder and owner of the Gesellschaft für Metallurgie (GfE), the company for which Hans and Lotte Sachs's son Werner was working. In his book *Berlin Mitte: A Tale of Restitution*, Hans and Lotte's grandson, Werner's son Peter Sachs, wrote of the forced sale of the company that year, that, *with the resignation of industry minister* [Hjalmar] *Schacht*[1] *the full 'unholy' weight of the Nazi machine (my father's words) fell on Jewish industry. GfE was refused foreign currency to import metal ores, essential to its work, unless it was 'Aryanised', and by the end of 1937 negotiations had started to sell the company to an Aryan organisation.*[2]

In fact, the Nazis did not have things all their own way, even when their grip on power was nearing its height. In November 1937, Paul Grünfeld had died and leadership of the company had passed to Herbert, his eldest son. Nazi Germany pursued an official policy of self-sufficiency, but complete autarky for a complex modern economy is next to impossible. Companies like GfE still needed to obtain vital raw materials from overseas to be able to produce the kinds of specialised alloys demanded by their customers. To meet those demands, the company bought nonferrous metals such as cobalt from the Belgian Congo. But the growing antisemitism in Germany tainted the case for doing business that would benefit the Nazis, even in places like the Congo, where in living memory unspeakable atrocities – amounting to a genocide – had been a routine occurrence for millions who had lived under Belgian colonial rule. According to Sachs family lore, the Belgian management of the Union Minière de Haut-Katanga, the mining concern in the Congo from whom GfE bought cobalt, was so disgusted at the Nazis' treatment of its Jewish clients that it threatened to withhold from Germany any further supplies of cobalt unless the Grünfelds (and, presumably, the other senior Jewish employees) were allowed to emigrate. In a memoir of GfE written late in life, Werner Sachs recalled that Grete Grünfeld was also able to retain her Swedish shares when she emigrated to England. This may have been crucial to the Jewish staff's own future prospects, but in any case the Grünfelds were so well loved that, when Grete and Herbert left Berlin by train in August 1938, they did so in a private compartment full of flowers sent by well-wishers. GfE was quickly re-established in Zurich and London, with the latter firm named the London and Scandinavian Metallurgical Co. Ltd.

In July 1938, after the Grünfelds' German business had been transferred to the Vereinigte Stahlwerke and the Reichswerke Hermann Göring, Werner left for England with his wife Emma. To secure their British passports, their two young children, Peter and Ursula, had been born in England in the previous few years, after Emma had travelled there for that purpose. But the children were now obliged to remain with their grandparents in Heidelberg for six more, anxious weeks. In the same month of July, at a conference of thirty-two nations that took place at Évian-les-Bains in France, the world's leading democracies, including Britain and France and the USA, refused any increase to the insignificant numbers of Jewish refugees that they were willing to accept. For Hans and Lotte, it must have deepened a sense that they were powerless in the face of a rising tide, no matter what they did.

Nuremberg, a city just a few hours' journey to the east of Heidelberg, had been linked with the *Meistersinger* of Wagner's opera – historical, archetypally German figures – since long before the Nazi rallies and the racial laws for which it later became a byword in infamy. Hans shared his own name, both first and last, with the most celebrated of these musical heroes, a central character in the opera. In August, the city's Grand Synagogue on Hans-Sachs-Platz was destroyed. In the same month, the Swiss authorities began refusing entry to Jewish refugees, as Marion Samter would soon discover, almost at the cost of her freedom. But still the Sachses could not leave without giving up almost everything they had, so they clung on despite the visceral fear they must have felt by then.

Hans Sachs with his grandchildren, Ursula and Peter Sachs, 1938. (Courtesy of Ursula Owen)

In September, Jews were barred from attending public cultural events. At the end of the month, the British prime minister, Neville Chamberlain, gave in to Hitler's demands over the Sudetenland, waving a white piece of paper, like a flag of surrender, and hailing 'peace for our time'. There were many who believed him, or wanted to, despite evidence of Hitler's ambition that now seems all too apparent. By then, Hans had brought his grandchildren to the Dutch border by train; in old age Peter Sachs still remembered his grandfather smoking cigars in the carriage along the way. There they were handed to a go-between, who brought them to an airfield in the Netherlands and may have come with them on the plane. A few hours later, they had landed at Croydon aerodrome, south of London, where their worried parents were waiting.

Then in early October, just days after the Munich conference, the Polish government revoked the citizenship of any Polish Jews who had lived outside Poland for more than five years. When later that month the Nazis expelled to the Polish border 17,000 Polish Jews who were living in Germany and, true to its word, the Polish government refused to take them in, even then Hans and Lotte might still have hoped, despite there being no reason to, for some kind of dignified exit. But the pace and ferocity of events across the country and beyond would also have left them reeling – knowing what they had to do but facing options that were invidious at best and obstacles that may have seemed insurmountable. And then, on 9 November, any hope that remained was shattered by the sound of breaking glass.

More than ninety Jews across Germany and Austria were killed in the course of that one night and the following day, and many times that number died by suicide. Some 30,000 Jewish men, around one in six of those who remained in Germany, were arrested and sent to concentration camps at Buchenwald and Dachau and Sachsenhausen. Almost 1,400 synagogues were destroyed and thousands of shops and businesses were looted once their windows had been smashed. No town or city where Jews were living was spared. Heidelberg's main synagogue on Lauerstrasse was burnt to the ground, with the fire brigade being allowed only to make sure the flames didn't spread to neighbouring houses. Other synagogues in the city suffered a similar fate, while at least seventeen Jewish businesses, including the premises of lawyers and the one remaining Jewish doctor, were ransacked and then demolished. A similar number of private houses was also violently attacked and destroyed. Among the small Jewish community in Heidelberg, seventy-five men were arrested and deported to Dachau.[3]

As in every other place, the Nazis knew exactly who to target and where they lived. The Sachses' home would also have been attacked had it not been for an SS officer named Otto Westphal, one of Sachs's former students, who by then held a position at the Kaiser Wilhelm Institute that Hans had once led. Westphal had joined the Nazi party as an impressionable teenager, but by 1938 was deeply disillusioned with Nazi rule. As he later described at his denazification trial after the war, in testimony that Lotte herself corroborated, on Kristallnacht he had stood guard in the street 'to protect the esteemed professor from spontaneous attacks';[4] as a result, the Sachses escaped the fury of the mob. The following morning, according to Lotte's written testimony, Westphal *offered his help in protecting my husband from being taken to a concentration camp in the course of the general action taken in those days against the Jews in Germany. He told us he had seen to it that my husband's name was struck off a list prepared by the SS.*[5]

In fact, the violence, which was carefully choreographed across Germany and Austria to appear spontaneous, had followed a pattern of instructions drawn up by SS *Gruppenführer* Reinhard Heydrich. Westphal's support for the couple, a rare exception to the rule of Nazi terror, included mailing them in England the following year the gold watch that Hans was not allowed to take out of Germany. The Sachses, apparently, were not the only Jewish household that Westphal managed to warn that night; at some personal risk, while not actively opposing it, it seems that he continued to help both Jews and non-Jews who were hounded by the Nazi regime.

But if they may have had reason to be grateful to Westphal that nothing had happened to them when the pogrom had affected so many, it was also clear that they could wait no longer, no matter what the cost. Though their own home had been spared – for now, at least – the sound of shards of glass from Jewish-owned shops and houses being swept from the streets over the next few days, and the news that reached them over the coming weeks of men they knew, or knew of, being rounded up and carried off to Dachau, would have left them in no doubt about the danger they faced. Could they even venture out to buy provisions or would they be set upon and Hans arrested and sent to a camp, like so many others, regardless of his age or former social status? In any case, what status did they now enjoy? They were Jews, no longer Germans, since 1935 no longer citizens but subjects of the state, wholly at the mercy of its sadistic whims. After Kristallnacht, it was clear that the law would not protect them, as the law was now an arm of the Nazi regime, an expression and an agent of those whims.

In a state of individual and collective panic, tens of thousands of Jews now petitioned the embassies and consulates of whichever governments they hoped might take them in. Hans gave up his efforts to leave with at least some of their assets intact. Lotte would later write that Westphal had used his personal authority to order the police to issue the Sachses their passports, and this was duly done. But they also needed visas from the British government. As was true in Else's case, the Home Office was then as slow, as reluctant to react, as it often is today, the more so after the failures at Évian in July. In the end it was the consul-general in Frankfurt, Mr R.T. Smallbones, who made the difference. A man whose sense of ethics had not been swallowed by his job, he possessed sufficient independence of thought and judgement to see a clear humanitarian need that his government refused to acknowledge. In a letter to Hans dated 24 November, he admitted the bureaucratic failures – that *the organisation within the Home Office has broken down and there is no hope of getting a decision from them about your case within a reasonable time.*[6] He issued the visas himself.

The following day, the local tax office took the exorbitant sum of 48,500 RM as payment for the right to flee the country, an emigration tax known as the *Reichsfluchtsteuer*. By the middle of December the extortion process, comprising a number of spurious levies – including a special Jewish property tax, the so-called *Judenvermögensabgabe* – was complete and they could leave. Even after so much state-sanctioned theft, they were still obliged to pay their own travel expenses from the 5,000 RM that was all they were allowed to take with them. The remainder of their assets had to be deposited in accounts with the Prussian state bank, which would then be at the disposal of the Deutsche Golddiskontbank, a division of the

Reichsbank; Jewish wealth would fund the killing machine that had already begun killing Jews. It was a modus operandi whose perversity became ever more grotesque the longer the Nazis were in power. Lotte also had to hand over her jewellery and Hans lost his annual pension of 10,000 RM, as he had feared would happen. Perhaps worst of all for a man of learning, he was forced to accept that they could not bring with them each and every volume from the huge personal library they'd accumulated over time. But the process of selecting which to take and which to leave behind, for such a cultured man, was like trying to choose between favourite children. As his daughter Ilse later recalled of her last visit home in 1937, her father, usually so unflappable but now fearing the upheaval to come, would run from room to room as he made his selection, crying out in French, '*Écrasé! Écrasé!*' ('Crushed! Crushed!'), in giving vent to his distress. No one can say why his lament was in French; perhaps German had already become so tainted that to use it for this purpose would have seemed to him absurd.

Once all the necessary sums had been paid, they were given a clearance certificate and then their passports. Leaving behind the furniture they hoped would follow, it must have been around *Heiligabend, Weihnachtsabend*, Christmas Eve, a day they had always celebrated along with every other German, that they travelled by train to the Netherlands. From there they went by ship to Harwich, arriving on 27 December, and then to London on the train. They stayed for a time with Grete Grünfeld, Hans's younger sister; following her departure from Berlin the previous August, she was living at 3 Hyde Park Place, on the north side of the park.

In the early part of 1939, Hans tried once again to find a position in England, but with even more refugees newly arrived in the country, some as well-qualified and far more cutting-edge than him, he must have known that his chances were slim at best. Only one option turned up, a position in neutral Ireland, a young country still trying to establish institutions of its own after the Irish Free State had detached itself from Britain less than twenty years earlier. The Irish Medical Research Council (IMRC) had been set up as recently as 1937. After the intervention of the Society for the Protection of Science and Learning (SPSL), a UK body with strong links to Ireland, in February the IMRC offered Hans a full-time research post at Trinity College, the most prestigious university in the country. It came with a grant of £500 p.a. or slightly more than half the amount in pension income he had received in Germany. It would still be just about enough to live on; but Ireland was then a backwater in scientific terms, as in others, and Hans was reluctant to accept. It was only in early March that he did, after the General Secretary of the SPSL had made it clear that there were no other options. In truth, given the extreme resistance of the Irish to admitting Jewish refugees – especially doctors – in their hour of need, he was lucky to be given even this chance.

A reconnaissance trip to Ireland in March preceded their move in April, though how permanent that would be, neither Hans nor Lotte could tell. But within a very short time, once their furniture had arrived there in May, the large library they had still managed to bring with them was lining the bookshelves from floor to ceiling in the drawing room of their Dublin home. A happy surprise, this partial restoration of their former life was a great source of comfort. In a letter of 20 May to Frau Brenning – who remained in Berlin despite herself being Jewish; nothing is known of what happened to her – Hans admitted that, while they were still getting used to a country where people did not speak German, *we are at least glad to be living again amongst our own furniture, although much of it was damaged during its long journey.*[7]

The trappings of that former life, the high cultural milieu they spoke of, along with what their granddaughter, Ursula Owen, has described as a 'social cocoon of educated people'[8] who gathered around them, including the physicist Erwin Schrödinger and his wife, lent the Sachses' apartment at Palmerston Villas an atmosphere of Middle Europe that was quite unlike anywhere in the Irish capital. It helped that, in the recollection of their daughter Ilse, the apartment was in fact larger than the one they had left behind. But despite the sense of continuity and reassurance they had managed to re-establish in their new home, the shock and upheaval they had been through would not yet have settled down when Hans wrote that first extant letter to his sister-in-law Else on 25 May, just weeks after they had disembarked in Dublin.

He was almost 62, exhausted not only by the trials of their escape but by what they had escaped to: a new home in a new neighbourhood in a new country; a new position and the demands it imposed to converse with new colleagues in a language with which he was familiar but had never had to speak every day as a personal and professional need. That was a lot of novelty, all of it unsought, for a man of his age and habits. Still, it would have been a source of relief to have colleagues again who regarded him with the respect his achievements deserved, who treated him as the 'esteemed professor' that Westphal would later describe. After years of assaults on his personal and professional dignity, he could enjoy rights and status once more, even if the one-year term of his contract and the time-limited visa they'd been granted meant that any rights in their case were always contingent, never inalienable, never completely secure.

But at least he could breathe again without immediate fear, and this freedom of time and space, having reached the safety of Ireland, alerted him to the essence of what he had lost. As he wrote to Else, *the most difficult thing was the irretrievable separation from people.*[9] Of course, safety was no more than a consolation for someone who was used to challenge and stimulation as a routine aspect of his working life. The research he did in Dublin was not on the same level as before, and with no teaching to do, the lack of contact with students was an absence he felt keenly. But by early June he was clearly adjusting to the disappointments of this new existence, writing to Else of the small comforts he had found. *We have to be content that we can live in peace and take pleasure from the landscape*, he says. *Otherwise, it would be very lonely.*[10]

They returned to England for a week at the end of July to attend their daughter Ilse's wedding to her fiancé, Arthur Cooke. After that, they had plans to travel on to New York for a scientific congress at the end of the following month, though without visas this later trip almost certainly could not have happened. But he also hoped that a position might arise at an English university that would better meet the professional expectations he still entertained.

Then, in the days or weeks after 11 August, Else arrived in Dublin and moved into the spare room in the apartment at Palmerston Villas, where she would live for most of the next two years. Now both Else and Marion were safe, as well as Lotte and Hans and their children and grandchildren, too. But Else and Lotte's brother, Kurt Grelling, and his family were still in mainland Europe, after a holiday at the seaside that was comforting and necessary but overshadowed by fear. The story of the trials they faced will take up the rest of this book.

BELGIUM

A MAN OF LETTERS

On the day that Else Samter was issued with her British visa, her brother, Kurt Grelling, was nearing the end of a three-week stay with his family in Oostduinkerke, a resort town on the Belgian coast. With the forces of the Wehrmacht massing along the border to the east, it seems a strange time to have chosen to go on holiday. It was almost two years since Grelling had first begun travelling to Belgium. Robbed of the ability to work in his homeland and then, in the summer of 1937, of the income he had earned from the properties in Mitte in central Berlin, he had taken up the offer of paid employment in Brussels, in spells of several weeks at a time. The man who employed him, the philosopher Paul Oppenheim, hailed from a background as wealthy as Grelling's. But, in recent years, his financial position had been far more secure. For Kurt, the friendship with Oppenheim was a lifeline, a piece of good fortune at a time when you needed to count your blessings. On his fourth visit, in November 1938, the move became permanent when Kristallnacht had banished the thought that he could ever go back to Germany with the Nazis still in power. He confirmed this a week later in a letter to his old friend Otto Neurath, the Viennese sociologist who by then was living in the Netherlands.

It goes without saying that after 10th November I won't be returning to the promised land, he writes. *In all my misfortune, once again I had some great good luck that just in the nick of time I managed to evade my pursuers. Who knows what kind of trench-digging they would have used me for. Most middle-aged male Jews in Germany of whom people here know something have been arrested. The police came three times to my wife to get me. On at least one occasion a nice police superintendent was glad that I wasn't there, of that I'm sure. I believe I can state that, to the honour of the German people, only a small part of those who know what's going on aren't ashamed. But I don't dare to put an estimate on it. Unfortunately, most of them only find out a small amount. I assume that 90% of what we hear or read here in Brussels is true, but I wish that it would only be 10%. In these days, and particularly since March, I've had to think about the German-Jewish nationals in Vienna, to whom*

Kurt Grelling working at home in Berlin, 1934. (© Kurt Grelling Archive)

the saying, 'Better a small pogrom than a massive confiscation of property' seems to apply. I hope they got out of there in time; otherwise, now they would suffer both at once. Only the pogrom isn't a small one.[1]

Grelling's faith in his compatriots' sense of honour, in what he assumed was their revulsion or lack of awareness of what was happening, was coloured by not having personally experienced the wanton violence of Kristallnacht. But, at least until the events of that night, it was not uncommon for German Jews to take that view. For Kurt, to think otherwise – to imagine that anything more than a fanatical minority condoned or even welcomed the lies, the persecutions, the thefts, and would readily accept the spoils of terror, with what that would say about human nature or the people he still thought of as compatriots – was almost too much to take in. Not since the Middle Ages had Germany seen anything like the level of violence against Jews that was then taking place. But, if that was any guide, then things would surely calm down again, once the bloodlust had been satisfied and the booty seized. And if it wasn't a guide, what historical precedent could be looked to for a glimpse of what was coming?

Grelling would have known that most of our thinking about the future is based on past experience; that our attachment to the past, upon which, the more we age, our sense of who we are depends, is a habit we're reluctant to give up. It was exactly 200 years since David Hume, the father of positivist philosophy, had first identified the problem of induction, which positivists ever since, including Grelling, Oppenheim and Neurath, had wrestled with but had not overcome. It framed the unthinking assumptions by which all of us live as the belief, based on nothing more than habit, that the future would resemble the past, when there was no logical method and no empirical proof to show beyond doubt that that would happen. The future was largely unknowable. Even if, based on our experience of the past, some events seemed far more likely to occur than others, they were never certain. Even now, when war seemed the inevitable next step, there was still a chance that it would not be. And if it was, why should it be like the last one? That it would be was something the French had assumed, with their long line of underground forts to defend the country's border with Germany. But the possible outcomes are always too many to fully comprehend and the only ones for which we have any evidence have already happened and are thus unlikely to recur exactly as they have in the past.

So, there was little comfort to be had, apart from what arises from comparing your own misfortunes with those of others who are suffering more than you. No matter how badly things were going, everyone knew someone in more difficult conditions than their own, whether trench digging or worse. Neurath's son Paul was one of them, rounded up in 1938 and sent to the camp at Dachau, before being transferred to Buchenwald, where conditions were equally hellish. Almost the only thing that anyone could do was try to help. In a letter of 24 June 1939, just a fortnight before he had left for the coast with his family, Grelling had asked Neurath for assistance in the case of Luise Rothstein, a young philosopher he had known in Berlin. *Like most Polish Jews,* he writes, *she cannot go back to Poland and is not allowed to stay in Germany. I met her in Berlin because she took part in my private logic circle for a while.* [...] *She wrote to me some time ago because she wanted to try to come here to continue studying, which is not entirely out of the question, although it is associated with the well-known difficulties. She has a quota number for the USA and has been told that she has to wait at least another year and a half for the visa. She probably cannot stay in Berlin for that long, and there is a risk that she will be deported to the Polish border. In the event that she doesn't have an entry permit to Belgium or doesn't get it in time, she asked me to help her get to England.*[2]

The previous October, the Nazis had deported 17,000 Polish Jews to the German–Polish border. The Polish government refused to take them back, leaving them stranded in desperate conditions. Among that number were the parents of a young Polish Jew called Herschel Grynszpan, who was living in Paris. His reaction to the outrage was to shoot and kill a junior diplomat, Ernst vom Rath, who was working at the German embassy in the French capital. The assassination had lit the fuse for Kristallnacht, though by then almost anything might have. In the case of Luise Rothstein, Grelling wanted Bertrand Russell to intervene. In the late 1920s, he had translated four of Russell's books into German,[3] and the previous summer, at Kurt's request, the Englishman had written him an affidavit to help his job-finding efforts in America. It seemed reasonable to hope he might also do his best for Rothstein.

So, there were many people in predicaments worse than Grelling's. But he also knew he should step up the efforts that were needed for himself, given the difficulties that others had found in getting to America and his own failures until then in that regard. He hadn't seen Greta or his children since travelling to meet them all for Easter in the village of Gland on Lake Geneva, where the children were at school. Together again for a long summer holiday, they had taken rooms at the Hotel Gauquié in Oostduinkerke, a few miles from the French border. According to one of Kurt's letters, Oppenheim was also on holiday nearby.

The Grelling family in Gland, Switzerland, Easter 1939.
(© Kurt Grelling Archive)

Kurt's grandchildren possess a couple of photos of a day trip to Ostend that the family took in the course of that holiday in July and August 1939; one with Kurt and another with Greta, each one standing in the street with the children, 12-year-old Karin and 9-year-old Klaus. It seems reasonable to assume that Kurt took the photo in which Greta appears and Greta took the one including Kurt. There is no photograph of the four of them together on this holiday; it would have meant asking a stranger to take it. Perhaps they didn't think of doing that or perhaps it was a step too far, one that could draw attention to the fact that they were not Belgians, despite the beret Kurt is wearing to protect his bald head from the sun. Though no one spoke Dutch, the local language in that part of Belgium, Kurt's spoken French was very good, while the children's would have been more than passable after six months at a boarding school in the French-speaking part of Switzerland. But, as soon as they opened their mouths, many would have realised that they were Germans, like tens of thousands who had lived as refugees in the country over the previous few years. The numbers had grown steadily until the surge that followed Kristallnacht a month after Kurt had returned. Many of those who came had no friends or family in the country, and no means of support. They were put into camps managed by Jewish refugee organisations, principally the Comité d'aide et d'assistance aux victimes de l'Antisémitisme en Allemagne (CAAVAA). Those Jews who had the means to do so, such as Oppenheim, helped others financially through bodies like CAAVAA, knowing that if they didn't do it, no one else would. Kurt was one of the lucky ones, having emigrated with the knowledge that paid work with Oppenheim awaited him; not only paid but dignified, because it paid him to do what he was good at. Dignity was a rare privilege in difficult times.

In each of the photos, Kurt and Greta look solemnly at the camera, while the demeanour of the children could not be more contrasting. In both images, Karin looks at the ground; while in one, her brother beams at Greta behind the lens, in the other, taken by his father, he pulls a face. It is always unwise to read too much into a single image, which is never more than a fleeting moment frozen in time, though also never less than that. By July 1939, it was three months since Karin and Klaus had seen their parents. By January that year, Greta had managed to find places at a school in Gland called Les Rayons. Conditions for the children of Jews in Germany had become increasingly difficult. On 15 November 1938, a few days after Kristallnacht, Jewish children were expelled from German public schools, though, being *Mischlinge*, a pejorative term meaning 'mixed breeds', Karin and Klaus may not have been officially excluded. But the stigma of having even one Jewish parent was now enough to affect them in the most brutal ways. On coming to America in 1947, Klaus would change his name to Claude, so as not to be taken as a German. In an unpublished memoir written late in life, Claude remembered as a young child in Berlin being set upon by some boys from his school, who wrestled him to the ground. When the beating was over and Klaus got back on his feet, he discovered that the gang had emblazoned a big red J on his rucksack. Whether *Mischling* or not, the Nazis and their offspring didn't give a damn. Whether it happened before or after Kristallnacht, the incident was a clear demonstration that Karin and Klaus were no longer safe from the general persecution of Jews which had now become a routine fact of life. By the end of 1938, Greta had found them places in the school in Switzerland. Kurt was no longer in Germany, so Greta was alone in dealing with the children's move abroad. It didn't help that, as Kurt spells out in the letter to Otto Neurath, dated 18 November 1938, even those who could assist them were vulnerable. *Unfortunately [...] my lawyer, who knew about all of these things, has been arrested*, he writes. *I am trying from here to mobilise various Aryan friends to help her. It's lucky for us that my wife is a pure-bred Aryan and at least the children are only mixed-breeds. Because of that, my family is protected from much of what others have experienced so terribly.*[4]

Greta Grelling with Karin and Klaus, her two children, in Ostend, Belgium, July 1939. (© Kurt Grelling Archive)

Kurt Grelling with his children, Karin and Klaus, in Ostend, Belgium, July 1939. (© Kurt Grelling Archive)

Happily, places were found at Les Rayons, and by all accounts, when the children arrived there in January 1939, they were instantly made to feel welcome. Klaus would soon be thriving in the liberal environment at the school, but separation from her parents weighed heavily upon Karin. Years later, she told her second cousin, John Cooke, that as the elder sibling in those years at the school she had always felt responsible for her brother's welfare. So, her downcast eyes in both photos, which may have been a matter of temperament, quite different from Klaus, may also have reflected both the weight of an adult burden for which she wasn't ready and the pain of being parted then reunited with her parents, knowing that the latest reunion would soon have to end.

In both photos, there's a certain formality, even awkwardness, despite Kurt holding a protective arm around each of his children, while staring with great deliberateness at the camera, determined to make the most of the short time they had. To an extent, the formality was also a product of the age, of class and of culture. As an old man, Claude, by then thoroughly American, recalled that in the world of his Berlin childhood, children ate some two hours before the adults, as was normal for people of their class. In Karin's reminiscence late in life, she recalled that her parents had always been a little distant, never openly loving toward her. She remembered her father as he appears in a photo that she later received, *one elbow on the table with a hand on his high domed forehead, always reading and studying.*[5] Claude had fonder memories of intimate contact with his father, of hugs and kisses and expressions of affection, confessing that he had always adored him.

So, there was clearly a difference in how the siblings remembered their childhood, though on certain things they agreed. One was the benefit they had gained from their father's wide intellectual culture. Confined at home after the shock of being dismissed from his job at the *Gymnasium*, Kurt spent a lot of time with his children, entertaining them in a way that felt most natural to a serious man, a teacher, by sitting in the kitchen reading aloud as they ate their supper. As Claude recalled, there were selections from Greek mythology and *The Iliad* and from the journals of adventurous Europeans from the late nineteenth century, such as the great Norwegian polar explorer Fridtjof Nansen and Heinrich Schliemann, the German archaeologist who had discovered the site of ancient Troy.

But this instruction of his children was never enough for a man who had always relished the challenge of work. To relieve his boredom, Kurt would sometimes make trips to academic conferences abroad, until this became impossible. The first was in Prague in early September 1934, the first meeting (a pre-congress) of the International Unity of Science Movement, organised by Otto Neurath. In their letters, Grelling and Neurath discuss the meeting at length, both before and after the event. In Karin's later recollection, Greta went with him on these trips, putting Karin and Klaus into children's homes rather than with relatives or friends. This, too, was not unusual for people of their class at the time; it was just how things were done.

On the other hand, family holidays were frequent, at least one a year through the mid-1930s, keeping up the appearance of a normal bourgeois lifestyle despite it getting harder to do so. In those later recollections, Claude had vivid memories of trips to the North Frisian island of Amrum, close to the Danish coast, most likely in the summer of 1936. The following year they had travelled by paddle steamer north along the Rhine. One of Claude's earliest memories, from December 1935, was of falling over in the snow while his mother was teaching him to ski. His father confirms it in a postcard with the photo of an alpine vista he sent to Neurath at the time. *I have run away with my family to the Tatra Mountains for 14 days,*[6] he writes, as if truly running away was as easy as taking a holiday. At that stage, it was still possible, even necessary, to laugh at the absurdity of the Nuremberg Laws; the oppression was not yet total. But, even then, he would only write such things from foreign countries to friends who lived abroad. Nothing that suffered the gaze of a Nazi censor could ever sound so bold.

Neurath was one of the most energetic men of his time. A socialist and a Marxist in the loosest sense of what that means, he was an intellectual polymath, someone with whom Grelling, in their long correspondence, seems most at ease in giving voice to the full range of his interests and worries. Neurath's voracious reading was notable even among his peers, and his hunger for knowledge was more than matched by his drive. In all the visionary projects he conceived and then delivered, the broad aim was to improve the lives of ordinary people through a range of practical measures in education, economic or social policy. He was a leading light in the social experiment known as Red Vienna, the period, roughly corresponding to the Weimar Republic, when his home city was an island of left-wing social ambition in an otherwise conservative, Catholic country. He helped develop schemes for social housing that were so successful that the basic commitment to secure, affordable homes is still a foundational aspect of Viennese civic identity. But, despite having no formal training in philosophy, he was also an abstract thinker with an unshakeable faith in the objective truths of science. Before the First World War, with the mathematician Hans Hahn and the physicist Philipp Frank, he'd been a founder member of what would later be known as the Vienna Circle. In the 1920s, the group's membership expanded and its focus narrowed, culminating in 1929 in a famous manifesto that Neurath himself composed, along with Hahn and the philosopher Rudolf Carnap. In their radical prospectus for the discipline, philosophy was in fact a science capable of explaining the other sciences, with almost no role to play besides that function. Neurath would be the greatest proselytizer of this vision, and the vigorous efforts he made in this regard are a consistent feature of the letters he exchanged with Grelling.

By the 1930s, the leading figures in the Circle were Neurath, Carnap and the philosopher Moritz Schlick. Inevitably, there were tensions within the group. Staying true to the manifesto, Neurath, a down-to-earth sociologist, had a tendency to dismiss much of earlier philosophy as unverifiable nonsense. But he reserved particular scorn for the work of their Viennese contemporary, the aristocratic Ludwig Wittgenstein, blurting out a one-word excoriation – 'Metaphysics!' – in meetings of the Circle whenever Wittgenstein's philosophy came up. Nonetheless, the *Tractatus Logico-Philosophicus,* Wittgenstein's groundbreaking work from 1918, was a sacred text to some members of the Circle, especially Moritz Schlick. Taking their cue from Wittgenstein's ideas about the limits of what language can meaningfully express, the Circle's aspiration to use logic to analyse and explain the raw data of science through propositions that could be empirically verified, known as protocol statements or sentences, earned it the name of logical positivism or logical empiricism or, in some circles, neo-positivism. But Neurath the empiricist, a man of social action quite different from anyone else in the Circle, was never convinced by what logic on its own could tell us about the world or, more crucially, by what it could do to improve it.

His hunger for social engagement led him to take risks in the pursuit of his vision. In 1919, after his involvement in the short-lived Bavarian Republic at the end of the First World War, Neurath was arrested and put on trial. With customary good fortune, he received only a light sentence – others involved were shot – and was soon released and returned to Austria. Back in Vienna, he curated and opened his Museum of Society and the Economy, which used his own idea of pictorial statistics – today a commonplace in public life – to explain how society and the economy worked in a way that anyone could understand, no matter what their level of education. It proved hugely popular with the public. But by the early 1930s, the economic picture was looking worse everywhere and especially in the countries so heavily punished by the Treaty of Versailles. Politics inevitably followed. Neurath's firm belief that with the right information people will make rational choices would soon be tested to destruction or, perhaps more accurately, proved by negative example. In February 1934, when the right-wing government of Engelbert Dollfuss had crushed the Austrian socialists in a brief civil war, ushering in Austria's local brand of Christian fascism, Neurath was forced into a sudden emigration. He was in Soviet Russia at the time, a guest of the Stalinist state, a fellow socialist who, from everything we know about him, would not have been comfortable with the growing repression that bore more than a passing resemblance to what was happening in Germany. Fearing arrest back in Austria, he took the long way round through Scandinavia to the refuge he would claim in the Netherlands. In a letter dated 18 July 1934, addressed to Grelling in Menton in the South of France, where the Grellings were then on holiday, he outlines the situation he had faced, for which he had clearly prepared in advance. *I was outside* [Austria] *when they restructured the state*, he writes, *and was able to arrange things so that, as far as possible, I could further my work from here. Our international centre, of which I'm the director, has always had its base in The Hague, and it is seen as an institute and, according to Dutch law, is unaffected by happenings elsewhere.*[7]

This sounds grander than perhaps it was. Having had the foresight to establish a base for his activities outside an increasingly authoritarian Austria, he had few sources of income for some time after arriving in The Hague. What he did have were a confidence and a vision that never left him, even in the bleakest moments. He was sure that things would work out for the best, because they always did. Induction had never been a problem for Neurath. Not for the first time, he saw a crisis as a golden opportunity to spread the gospel of science, of the recognition of the underlying unity of the sciences; of a set of basic principles, yet to be discovered, that from physics to sociology would underpin them all. A long-held dream within science, a Utopian project in the minds of some of the positivists, the accelerating pace at which the ever-more fundamental laws and structures of so many disciplines had been revealed over the previous century had made the discovery of these principles seem inevitable. The International Congresses for the Unity of Science were Neurath's own brainchild, and he as much as anyone was determined to realise this unity. It was almost an article of faith, whose ecumenical aim was in open defiance of the times.

Already, other philosophers, fellow intellectuals who were broadly of the left, men like Grelling's friend Hans Reichenbach, were either leaving or making plans to do so. By that point, Reichenbach was the leader of the Berlin Group, the Berlin Society for Scientific Philosophy,[8] in which Grelling also played a prominent role. But when the Nazis came to power, despite being the son of a non-Jewish mother and a half-Jewish father who was himself baptised, Reichenbach was dismissed from his post at Berlin University.[9] Within weeks, certain that things would not be getting better, he'd accepted the offer of a professorship in Istanbul. But Neurath, whose pugnacious oratory was yet another of his talents, was determined to stay for the fight; though typically, even the departure of so many colleagues seemed to him to be a silver lining, and he writes of their trials with a visionary grandeur, a view of the future that drew optimistic lessons from the past. *We are scattered all over the world*, he declares. *That's how some ideas in world history are spread. Under all kinds of pain.*[10]

By July 1939, the pain had spread widely and seemed likely to get worse. In Ostend, where the photos of the Grellings on holiday were taken, only young Klaus seems unaffected by the worry it is so tempting to read in the faces of his parents and sister. As an old man, Claude Grelling clearly recalled that holiday on the Belgian coast. But he would have been a bit too young to remember the one in Menton five years earlier, the point at which the correspondence between Neurath and his father begins. In February the following year, 1935, when his parents made a grand tour of Italy lasting several weeks, from Sicily to the South Tyrol, both he and Karin had again been left behind in Berlin. At one point on that trip, the Grellings paid a visit to the Villa Incontri, the large country house on the outskirts of Florence, where for many years Kurt's father, Richard Grelling, had raised his second family. Hans and Annemarie, his grown-up children from that later marriage, had continued living there after Richard's death, though by 1935 both had probably left – Hans for Switzerland and Annemarie for an apartment in nearby Florence. Kurt and Lotte and Else seem to have had friendly relations with these other Grellings, family connections that would prove important to Klaus in particular in the years to come. Marion and Else may have joined the Grellings for at least a part of that holiday. In March or April 1935, Marion took many photos of Florence and the surrounding area, including a few at the Villa Incontri. Others were also there: their cousin Ilse Sachs, who had

Ilse Sachs and Else Samter at the Villa Incontri, near Florence, Italy, spring 1935.
(© Sheri Blaney, Samter Archive)

come down from Milan, where she was working at the time, and Grete Grünfeld, the Tante Grete described in the notebooks, with whom Ilse's family was so closely linked.

For a few years in the mid-1930s, Kurt Grelling, unable to find productive employment in Germany, had both the wealth and the free time to make these diverting journeys. But, for a committed intellectual, a life of leisure was not a happy existence, as he hints at in a letter from Menton, dated 21 July 1934. *I receive a pension which, together with the income from my assets, enables me to lead a middle-class lifestyle. I read a lot of newer scientific literature, write reviews for 'Erkenntnis'*[11] *[…] and spend time with my family, especially my two children, now 4 and 7 years old, who are my comfort when I get too wound up about the stupidity of mankind.*[12]

In July 1934, during the month at Menton, Kurt Grelling was 47 years old. The enforced inactivity had been hard to adjust to. Despite his daily attempts to stay mentally alert, the climate of fear which had settled over Germany had made thinking itself a demanding act of resistance. But at least from the following year, when his mother's estate had been settled, Kurt and his family could live discreetly and in relative safety in the house he bought with his sister at Wilhelmstrasse 13 in Lichterfelde-Ost. Else

Karin and Klaus Grelling as young children, Berlin, c.1935. (© Sheri Blaney, Samter Archive)

The house and front garden at Wilhelmstrasse 13 in Lichterfelde-Ost, Berlin, where the Grellings and Else Samter all lived in the mid to late 1930s. (© Kurt Grelling Archive)

lived alone in the top-floor apartment after Marion left for Switzerland that year. Kurt and his family occupied the ground floor. There was a big garden for the children to play in, with a lot of trees. In Claude's recollection, he and Karin set up a 'teepee' and pretended to be American Indians. It sounds implausibly idyllic and, for a couple of years, the Grellings were luckier than many Jewish families whose breadwinners had been forced to retire. As Kurt indicates in his letters to Neurath, after buying the house there was enough left over from the wealth inherited from his mother, and enough income from the Mitte properties, to support a comfortable family life. As Claude remembered it, for a brief period conditions were ideal for a young boy at the age of incipient conscious memory, who wanted only to run around and play with the toys his parents could now afford to buy him. The Grellings took on the trappings of a bourgeois lifestyle, with a cook, a cousin of Greta's, to prepare the meals. But Kurt's hunger for knowledge could not be assuaged; his sense of frustration at the limits that were placed on his life is a palpable aspect of the letters from this period.

By 1936, first Reichenbach and then another prominent member of the Berlin Group, the logician Walter Dubislav, had left Germany and would not return. On a few occasions over the next year or so, Grelling seems to have held meetings at the house for those members who remained. Unlike the Vienna Circle, the Group never kept any minutes. But no matter how abstract their discussions may have been, the philosophy of logical empiricism was linked with the socially progressive politics that was crushed in 1933; many of the leading social democrats had been rounded up in the early months of Nazi rule, including men whom Kurt knew well. So, the meetings would have had to be carefully arranged.

Even before they had moved to the new house, when the Grellings were still renting an apartment in Charlottenburg in the west of the city, harassment by the Gestapo was a routine experience, as it had been from the start. In the same letter from Menton, a year after his forced retirement from teaching, Grelling gives a clear picture to Neurath of how difficult his life had become. *Since March 1933, I have had to endure four house searches, the last one the day before we left. I was suspected of intending to fraternise with enemies of the state. I'm sure you don't undertake action personally against our famous state, but of course as a Marxist you are under suspicion. If you want to write to me in Berlin, please write through another person who is not suspected. I am very good at reading between the lines and, in the war, I learned how to decipher codes.*[13]

He refers here to the period from early 1916 when, in the later recollection of Arthur Rosenthal who had known him during those years, after a spell as an unskilled worker in the Foreign Office Grelling had been drafted into the army as a non-commissioned officer in France and Belgium, as part of a unit monitoring enemy radio and telegraph communications on the Western Front.[14] It would have been a good fit. A mathematician and logician with an excellent grasp of foreign languages would have had the right skillset for the role. At the start of the war, he was 27 years old and had already made notable contributions to his field. He completed a PhD in mathematics at the University of Göttingen in 1910, at the age of 24. In the same year he published a paper on probability, which he linked to the problem of induction; the paper was an influence on Reichenbach's development of his own theory of probability, his most significant contribution to philosophical thought. Soon after completing his PhD, Grelling applied to become a *Privatdozent* – a private, unpaid scholar – at Göttingen, but fell foul of a *numerus clausus*, an informal cap on the numbers of such scholars agreed by the full professors of philosophy at the university. The criteria applied by those professors in their selection of these scholars aren't clear. But, rather than persisting in his efforts to get his foot on the academic ladder, Grelling went to Munich to study national economy for the next few years. Some who knew him later were never quite sure why, though it seems that he was simply following an interest he had in the subject. Returning to Göttingen in 1913, he again became associated with the group around the philosopher Leonard Nelson, for whom he had worked as a PhD student in the years up to 1910. But for the future of Grelling's own thought, it was the close connection with Reichenbach, whom he had first met in Göttingen, that would prove the more indicative link.

Reichenbach was five years younger but developing rapidly. Many years later, in 1928, it was with Reichenbach, along with Dubislav, that Grelling would help establish the Berlin Group. But, in the period before the First World War, Grelling had not obviously been chasing an academic career, even if in other ways he was making a mark. While still in Munich, he began writing regular pieces on philosophy for the *Sozialistische Monatshefte*, a periodical that was closely connected to the German Social Democratic Party, whose politics reflected his own beliefs. But perhaps he had not made the forward strides in a theoretical direction suggested by the brilliance of his thesis, and especially by the notable breakthrough he had made in 1908.

That first success had come in the field of logic, the discipline in which the best of Grelling's later work was done. In the midst of his doctoral research, working under Nelson in Göttingen, he discovered what is still known as the Grelling Paradox. A semantic paradox, it was a version of the famous paradox that Bertrand Russell had discovered in 1902, which, along with other paradoxes discovered in that period, had found new limits to the exercise of formal logic – points at which logic seems suddenly absurd. Following the same pattern, the logic of Grelling's paradox reveals a basic contradiction – it might be called a confusion – in its core identity, in what it is at heart. It asks the following question: Is the word 'heterological' (meaning it doesn't possess the property it expresses or describes) either heterological or 'autological' (meaning it does possess that property)? The answer is contradictory whichever is affirmed: if it doesn't express the property, if it doesn't describe itself (that is, it is heterological), then of course it has to be heterological; but that would mean, quite literally, linguistically, that it does express it, that it does describe itself; and if that is the case, then it must be autological; and if that is true, then of course it can't be heterological, which in fact is what it is. Like all paradoxes, it seems impossible to resolve, and for that reason unnerving to contemplate, unsettling our confidence in a world of clear and stable meanings, of secure identities that are not in conflict on the inside and from the outside cannot be undermined.

The world of philosophy was small, of logic smaller, so, even then, Grelling's paradox would soon have come to the attention of Russell himself. The British polymath's monumental three-volume work *Principia Mathematica*, co-authored with his teacher Alfred North Whitehead, had sought to show that, like human language, mathematical language could be reduced to the language of symbolic logic; that, despite the evident contradictions of paradoxes such as Russell's and Grelling's own, logic was the fundamental language by which the world could be explained. In the 1920s and '30s, Russell was still revered by members of the Berlin Group, including Kurt Grelling, despite having moved away from the practice of analytic philosophy many years earlier. By that point, Grelling's connection to the Englishman was well established. As early as 1910, the year in which the first volume of the *Principia* was published, the younger man had written to Russell directly to point out flaws in his theory of types, the solution that Russell had developed to overcome the vicious circles to which the paradoxes gave rise. This may have persuaded the English philosopher that Grelling had a good understanding of his work. In the late 1920s Grelling translated those four books of Russell's into German; much later, if things had worked out, there might have been a fifth. But more closely associated with the Berlin Group, a regular participant at these gatherings in the early years, was Albert Einstein, who had championed Reichenbach's appointment as extraordinary (associate) professor in the physics department at Berlin University. So, the circles Grelling moved in were among the most elite of his time. Despite not having found the academic post his talents deserved, it seemed reasonable to assume that he would not be forgotten if ever he should find himself in need, and that this would make the difference that it should.

J'ACCUSE!

Another photo of Kurt Grelling that the family possesses dates from the same year, 1908, that the paradox had earned him the lasting respect of his peers. It shows an apparently confident young man, flush with the self-esteem that must have come with such a breakthrough. In the following years, he gained experience not just in his own theoretical area but as a writer of articles on philosophical subjects aimed at a broader readership. In 1915, the first full year of the war, he was working as a civil servant in a junior role for the foreign ministry in Berlin. But the confidence he had gained through the many articles that, by 1915, he had written for the *Sozialistische Monatshefte* must have influenced his decision to write the essay that stands out among his works, both for its length and its strongly political content.

A young Kurt Grelling, 1908.
(© Kurt Grelling Archive)

Given the title *Anti-J'accuse, eine deutsche Antwort* (Anti-J'accuse: a German response), this appraisal of the causes of the war from the German point of view is the only book that Grelling would ever write. First published in Zurich in 1916, it was widely read in the German-speaking world, far more so than anything he later wrote. The book was translated into French and Swedish, so his name also became known to a much wider readership beyond his own language let alone his immediate professional field. Superficially, it could be seen as a career highpoint, a potential springboard to new opportunities, despite the context of war in which it was written. So, it does seem odd that Grelling never mentions it in any of the letters from the 1930s, even when the idea of publishing a book to boost his credentials became something of a critical issue.

It's a strange name for a book, a reactive title whose meaning becomes clear when what the book was an answer to and what the 'Anti' was against are understood. Late the previous year, an anonymous author calling himself, simply, 'A German' had published a book called *J'accuse!*. The title was French, but the book was in German and was aimed squarely at the German-speaking world. A fiercely argued polemic condemning German aggression, it put the blame for the outbreak of war wholly at Germany's (and Austria–Hungary's) door. A few years later, at the Versailles Peace Conference, the victorious Allies of the Triple Entente, especially France, would successfully apply the same argument, with disastrous and humiliating consequences for the defeated powers. The title of this book was lifted directly from the famous pamphlet by the French novelist Émile Zola, written less than two decades earlier. Zola's polemic was a powerful indictment of the case against Captain Alfred Dreyfus and those who had brought it. Dreyfus was a Jew, and the attempt to frame him for a crime of treason that he hadn't committed was motivated, infamously, by antisemitism. The long and bitter saga of the Dreyfus Case split French society down the middle, setting child against parent and friend against friend.

The explicit appeal of this new *J'accuse!*, to turn the minds of other Germans against the conflict, fell on deaf ears. In 1915, the war was still a popular cause, even with confirmed social democrats like Hans Sachs, whose international contacts had enriched his working life. For most German Jews, loyalty to the nation state was unquestioning, no matter how illogical or even self-harming it might seem. The anonymous author of *J'accuse!*, who lived in neutral Switzerland where the book was published, was vilified in Germany and soon unmasked. Any return to the country was unthinkable and would remain so for many years after the end of the war.

It is possible that, in choosing his title, the self-proclaimed 'German' never consciously intended a connection to be made to the antisemitic ructions of the Dreyfus Case. It is mentioned only in passing in the book. But there is also a reference to the antisemitism of the Protestant German Empire. So, perhaps he meant more than simply to condemn his country for starting a crippling war and was hinting at something else, however conscious that may have been. The author was anonymous, but if he had been Jewish, given its provenance, the charge of racial animus the title implies would be hard to overlook. In any case, whether Jewish or not, the contents of the book were so inflammatory and one-sided that even the majority of pacifist opinion inside Germany condemned it as damaging to the long-term cause of peace.

Unsurprisingly, *J'accuse!* was immediately banned both in Austria–Hungary and in Germany. Elsewhere, the book was a runaway success, translated into ten languages and selling millions of copies over the next couple of years. Going further than most modern historians, its argument absolves the nations of the Triple Entente – Britain, France and Russia – of almost any responsibility for the outbreak of war. *J'accuse!* must have done the work of Allied propagandists far better than they could ever hope to do it by themselves; 20,000 miniature copies, comprising extracts from the book and entitled *Die Wahrheit* (The Truth), were air-dropped onto German trenches on the Western Front. It was a major coup in the information war, and Grelling's book was far from the only response. So, it's surprising that he never mentions it in any correspondence that survives, albeit little does survive from that period. But the repudiation of its contents he set down in the months after it was published, the brilliant book-length response he called *Anti-J'accuse*, was clearly written with the aim of coolly dismantling every argument the anonymous angry German seeks to raise. The question is, why bother to write such a book in a field, international politics, in which he had little experience, rather than another book on a subject in which his voice would surely have carried more weight?

Grelling was working for the foreign ministry at the time he wrote it, so it is tempting to dismiss his own book as an unlikely piece of wartime propaganda, and in places it almost reads that way. Its worldly, unapologetic argument in defence of his country's actions was that Germany had a right to realise its destiny as a great nation, to take its 'place in the sun',[1] as the common phrase had it at the time. He argues that:

> when *J'accuse!* claims that it already had this, [its author] shows once again how little he is able to recognise the true motives of

German policy. He points to the flourishing of German economic life, which no one disputes, and to the enormous progress that German industrial development has made in recent decades. But he completely overlooks the fact that, despite this unprecedented development, the standard of living of the German people is still considerably behind that of the English, American and French. But if the standard of living of the German people is to be brought to the same level as that of those other peoples, then, if one takes the capitalist organisation of the economy of all European peoples as a given, Germany must be concerned with a constant expansion and securing of sales markets for industry. This striving to expand and secure sales markets is, above all, what has brought Germany into conflict with England.[2]

In this framing, which was not without foundation, Britain and France were actively blocking Germany's aspiration to become a world power at a level that matched its growing industrial strength, denying access to the range of resources it needed and, above all, the markets for its products that those imperial powers enjoyed. Implicitly condoning the existence of the European empires, while also acknowledging the crimes on which those empires had been built, Grelling argues that, to offer the German people a future of increasing prosperity, to prevent them from emigrating (as millions had in the late nineteenth century), Germany had no option but to follow the path it had taken. Directly addressing *J'accuse*'s central charge, he asks the question: 'Is Germany not free to declare war on another state, at its own discretion, in order to enforce its interests?'[3]

Grelling's focus on 'interests' or 'legitimate interests' has echoes of the idea of 'true interests', as developed by his Göttingen colleague Leonard Nelson. This concept formed the theoretical grounding of a long essay (though nothing like as long as *Anti-J'accuse*) that he was also writing around the same time as the book-length work. Published in the *Sozialistische Monatshefte* in October 1916, 'The Philosophical Basis of Politics' is far more sceptical than the book of the motives of politicians. It hints at attitudes towards the truths of 'objective science',[4] separate from the ways that politicians misuse the science, which would inform his later work. But at this juncture, he still feels that 'practical philosophy or ethics'[5] is the best guide for human action and that politics as a philosophical science should be a part of scientific ethics. At the same time, he is also unsure 'whether such a thing as scientific ethics is possible',[6] a question that in the 1930s, as the shadow of Nazism spread across Europe, would become a bitter dispute at the heart of philosophical debates in the German-speaking world.

Anti-J'accuse was already in print by the time the essay was published in the *Sozialistische Monatshefte*. By that point, Grelling had been serving at the front for many months, an experience that must have put his recent writings into a sober context that he could not have imagined in advance. But where Grelling the dispassionate philosopher stands aloof from 'one-sided interest politics',[7] Grelling the polemicist of *Anti-J'accuse* lays out a robust but principled apologia for his country's actions and the motives of its government, and an equally strong critique of the motives of the other side. Of the two approaches, the essay is easiest to square in hindsight with the man of progressive sympathies who emerges in the letters of the 1930s and also in an autobiographical sketch written a quarter of a century after *Anti-J'accuse*. In this two-page profile from 1940, written in the third person in support of a US visa application, he describes himself as *a Jew, a known pacifist and a social democrat*,[8] blaming those three factors for the failure to advance his career. In 1915, the year in which he wrote *Anti-J'accuse*, he would certainly have answered to the third description on that list, that of social democrat. He would also have acknowledged that the first – that he was a Jew – was one aspect of who he was. But pacifist is the identity from which he seems most keen to distance himself in *Anti-J'accuse*, despite being a paid-up member of the German Peace Society at the time. In defence of the actions of the German government, he even suggests that 'the great majority of German pacifists did not find the right position'[9] on the question of the war, and that the 'fault lies in the incomplete development of pacifist theory, and above all the Manchester prejudice[10] in favour of the harmony of interests and the illusory character of all conflicts of interests between nations. This prejudice', he writes, 'leads naturally to the conclusion that every war is folly and that every means must be used that offers a prospect of avoiding it.'[11]

It's a measure of his intellectual confidence that he feels emboldened to make such a critical claim, one that seems at odds with the more high-minded view of the writer of 'The Philosophical Basis of Politics'. But there may also be other reasons why the 30-year-old logician and mathematician felt motivated to make it, and even to write his book in the first place and to give it the pointed title he chose. So, what might have persuaded this cautious thinker, under his own name, to take such an overtly political stance on the most complex and inflammatory issue of his lifetime? What was he trying to prove?

By the time that Kurt Grelling sat down to write his book, the identity of the author of *J'accuse!* was already widely known; it was in fact his own father, Richard Grelling.

Kurt was 13 when his father had abandoned his first family – his first wife Margarethe and their three children, Charlotte, Kurt and Else; Richard had later remarried and moved to Italy, either buying or renting the Villa Incontri close to Florence. But, even if he had not seen much of him once his father had left, Kurt would have known of his views and achievements, not only his political activity on the centre left and his long involvement as co-founder and de facto president of the German Peace Society (to which Kurt himself belonged), but also his work as a journalist and, before that, as a principled lawyer in high-profile cases with a strong political element. The most famous of these was in the early 1890s, when Richard successfully defended the right to performance of Gerhard Hauptmann's *The Weavers*, a play about a workers' uprising in mid-nineteenth-century Silesia, which the censor had sought to ban. But principles are given short shrift in time of war, when a person's nationality, not their opinion – their given identity not their chosen one – becomes the yardstick for their sympathies. In 1915, when Italy joined the war on the other side, Richard, now an enemy alien, was obliged to relocate from Tuscany to Zurich in neutral Switzerland with his second wife, Marta, and their two children, Hans and Annemarie. It was in the Swiss city of Lausanne that his bestselling book was published that year.

When the identity of the 'German' was revealed, at a time when loyalty to the national cause was a social obligation that Kurt would have felt very keenly, the name Grelling would have carried the mark of Cain that no amount of patriotic service could erase. He might have felt tainted by association, not only as a Grelling, a supporter of the same progressive politics as his father, but also, as the open provocation of the title suggests, as a Jew. In fact, to such an extent, perhaps, that, with the rise of conspiracy theories about Jewish collusion with the enemy and stabs in the back – accusations levelled by antisemitic tracts in Germany at the time of its publication at the author of *J'accuse!* – Kurt may even have feared for his own professional future in the country, whether or not the war was won. But is it fair to infer so much in this direction when other explanations are possible? Might he have been assigned the task of writing the book by his superiors at the ministry, not even to prove his loyalty but just because, as a seasoned contributor to the *Sozialistische Monatshefte*, he was apparently well qualified to write it? Might he even have been ordered to do it? There is no way of knowing, but given the cogency of the argument and also that the book was published under his own name, not in Germany but in Switzerland, it seems unlikely that it was written under any kind of duress. Whatever the reason, there is nothing else like it in Grelling's output.

We know exactly how Richard Grelling reacted to his son's efforts, as he set down his by-then-not-so-anonymous thoughts in the first volume of a second book, *Das Verbrechen* (*The Crime*). An exhausting, three-volume, 1,200-page demolition of his many critics in Germany, it is evidence that, whatever the merits of his argument in *J'accuse!* – and there were many – Richard's views had hardened into something of an obsession, bearing out the rueful observation of one of his obituarists in 1929 that the lawyer and journalist had been unable 'to appreciate a problem from a higher point of view than justice'.[12] In fact, Kurt's book merits no more than a mere footnote in *The Crime*, one that is laced with contempt, even vitriol, for his son's temerity. *Anti-J'accuse* he describes as the 'blood-thirsty, amateurish work of a political schoolboy',[13] the 'stillborn child of a callow politician',[14] which in reality was 'merely a tract in favour of the German government, and at whose cradle the gentlemen of the Wilhelmstrasse[15] have obviously stood with hands of benediction'.[16] But, as if this was not dismissive enough, the footnote's peroration draws deeply from the well of anger he felt towards his son; he tells his readers that, 'with a capricious cruelty like that of Salome [...] I will serve for them the severed head of the anti-accuser on an extra plate, that is to say, in a special pamphlet'.[17]

Thankfully, the pamphlet may never have been written, let alone published, but even in this brief passage, and despite the violence of the time, which of course was the subject matter of both their books, the violence of Richard's metaphor would have startled many readers and may well have shocked his son. The previous relationship between them is something that can only be guessed at, but we do know that Richard was so incensed at his son's impudence that Kurt was removed as a beneficiary of his will; he was only reinstated after Marta, Richard's second wife, had managed to talk her husband round. Kurt must surely have read his father's second book as carefully as the first, though there is no record of the view he took of any of the volumes of *The Crime* or, for that matter, by this time, in 1917, of his own book, as the horror of the war became apparent to anyone who was serving at the front, no matter how far back behind the lines. Perhaps the lack of any written recollection tells its own story, a youthful error he would rather was forgotten, one that he himself had put behind him when, at the end of the war, he returned to Göttingen for a time.

It was there that, for a brief period, he took part once again in the group around Leonard Nelson, who in 1919 was finally made an extraordinary professor. Grelling also became involved with a group of intellectuals connected with the *Volksblatt*, a newly founded social democratic newspaper. But his career trajectory, such as it was, had been forestalled by the war. He made a second attempt to become a *Privatdozent* in 1918, shortly before the end of the war, but this also failed for reasons which again are unclear, but which, in that third-person profile from 1940, he attributes to his politics, his pacifism and his status and identity as a Jew. Elsewhere in that self-description, he lays out why there was not to be a third attempt, writing that *financial reasons made it impossible for him to become a 'Privatdozent' and wait for many years before getting a real professorship.*[18] It was an opinion of himself which had not changed since the career questionnaire he had filled out in 1920, in which, in answer to the question, 'Motives for choice of career?', Grelling had written that he 'should rather have become a university teacher'.[19] But it may also be true that, even before the war, despite that first rejection, he did not push for his own advancement in the years after finishing his PhD, preferring instead to move sideways to study national economy in Munich. Looking back from the 1980s, Grelling's friend and colleague Carl Gustav Hempel, known to his friends as Peter, a much younger man who attended the Berlin Group and worked with Grelling later in Brussels, was given to wonder whether Kurt had ever wanted a university post. Claude, Grelling's son, believed that he had, and based on the evidence we have, Hempel's view was clearly mistaken. But it is also the case that Grelling had a breadth of interests that, for a young academic, was quite unusual, in particular a passion for social affairs that was shared with his father.

Gerhard Weisser, who became an important figure in centre-left politics in West Germany after the Second World War, had studied with Nelson in that period of social upheaval just after the first war. More than ten years younger than Grelling, Weisser would later remember him in an unpublished profile written in the 1950s, a copy of which he sent to Kurt's children. In the profile, Weisser writes of Grelling that *his exercises in logic, his seminar about a series of basic questions about the way society is ordered and many very significant conversations are still vivid in memory.*[20] So, in those last years at Göttingen, as he was making up his mind about the future, Grelling was still committed to the practice of abstract thought but was also someone who, after the real-life experience of war, could see beyond the bounds of the academy. Weisser praises his political engagement as both *realistic* and *comprehensive*, adding that he *concerned himself already in the first months of the Weimar Republic with basic questions about the politics of society that we are still dealing with today.*[21]

It is certainly the case that his thinking about political economy, as with other fields of study, continued to develop throughout his life. One strand of his wide-ranging correspondence with the protean Otto Neurath is an ongoing and deeply engaged discussion of modern economic theory. Over several letters exchanged in the mid-1930s, they wrestle with how to devise an economic system that would not be vulnerable to shocks like the Wall Street Crash, which in Germany had led to mass unemployment and the rise of Nazism. These were critical questions, echoing debates that were then taking place across the field of economics, which were similar to those in philosophy. Neurath was the acknowledged expert, a socialist economist *with my long row of theoretical publications*,[22] as he puts it rather boastfully in one letter. His ideas for a planned, moneyless economy, an economy in kind, were characteristically radical, grounded in his long study of war economy, a sub-discipline of economics in which he was a leading expert. In this area, Grelling couldn't match him for practical or even theoretical experience. But, though Neurath's vision of the economy, with its emphasis on happiness and sustainability, contains prescriptions that today seem increasingly necessary, almost common sense, in the 1930s it was far ahead of its time; for better or worse, Grelling's view, with its respect for the basic tenets of the capitalist system, is closer than Neurath's to the orthodoxy that prevailed in the Western world in the decades after the Second World War, as Weisser's testimony seems to bear out. In their arguments going back and forth over a couple of years, despite having published nothing significant on the subject, Grelling just about holds his own, writing of the need to balance meaningful redistribution with the profit-seeking instincts of the industrialist, arguing, somewhat optimistically, that *A bigger profitability, expressed in money, would bring a bigger income for the general population and that would lead to a better average life situation for the individual.*[23]

Neurath is respectful to his friend, acknowledging that Grelling was *one of the few in our circle who is interested in the economy.*[24] But, at the same time, he makes his case with long, theoretical arguments in which the individual is a very different proposition to the one in Grelling's mind. Kurt eventually gives way to Neurath's greater expertise. *You don't make it easy,* he writes. *Sometimes when I read your letters, I feel like I imagine a moviegoer feels watching a futuristic film. [...] I don't know if you expect me to answer your letter point by point. I am choosing those points of which I believe I have some understanding and where I think a discussion is possible.*[25]

These debates make clear that Grelling had pondered in some depth a wide range of social and economic questions as well as philosophical ones. Straying beyond his main area of expertise (as he had in writing *Anti-J'accuse*), he trusted his ability to reason, his skill in logic, to make sense of a field of activity where divining the future was more difficult than in most disciplines calling themselves a science. As he puts it in one letter, *at present even geophysics cannot predict earthquakes, and weather forecasting is still in children's shoes*; but *even so, the theoretical bases of these things are better understood than the economy.*[26]

It came back to the problem of induction, namely, the imprecision of inductive logic when applied to the complexity of historical data involved in a discipline like economics, in which the basic subject of prediction – human behaviour – defied the attempts of logic to pin it down. But the need for a source of knowledge that could be relied upon was a question of vital importance given the turmoil of the time. For the logical positivists, that source was science.

Back in Göttingen straight after the war, it is clear from Weisser's memoir that Grelling had been deeply engaged with the most vital social issues, but he was also grappling with more basic questions. It was during this period of post-war upheaval that he broke with Nelson's group, in part for reasons of intellectual integrity that went to the core of what he believed about the world. The scale of catastrophe in the war had emphasized the fallibility of human judgement, and perhaps the fallibility of his own, undermining confidence in any philosophy that relied upon it. But pre-war theoretical developments in many fields, including psychology and above all physics, had also called into question the standard explanations of the physical universe and the integrity of the human mind that perceived it. For philosophers, it was Einstein's General Theory of Relativity from

1915 that had the greatest impact and forced Grelling to reconsider the purpose of his thought and, eventually, to break with Nelson and his group. Increasingly, he aligned himself with Reichenbach and Neurath and a number of others who had started to call themselves philosophers of science. They would come to be known by other names – logical positivists in the case of the Vienna Circle, logical empiricists in Berlin – reflecting subtle differences in approach, though in reality the two main groups were closely aligned. A core belief they all shared was that much of earlier philosophy and entire branches of humanistic philosophical thought were redundant as ways to explain the world; that only science could do this, and the role of philosophy was to assist in this vital endeavour. In 1916, Grelling had questioned whether a scientific ethics was possible; increasingly, despite the danger that a vacuum would be left for others to fill, the positivists came to believe that it was not so much impossible as irrelevant.

The break with Nelson came about in 1922, but by then Grelling had already made clear his new thinking in a lecture given in August the previous year. Positioning himself with Reichenbach, who in 1920 had published a book called *The Theory of Relativity and A Priori Knowledge*, Grelling took aim at the assumptions of Nelson's group about what constituted *a priori* knowledge – things we know without needing to experience them. Years later, at a conference in Prague, during a discussion on the principle of induction, he laid out his settled view: that, 'we cannot conclude from the fact that a principle indispensable for science is neither logically nor empirically justifiable that it represents *a priori* knowledge'.[27] In other words, knowledge that couldn't be justified either by evidence or by logic was not real knowledge, the classic positivist posture.

This radical shift in his philosophical outlook seems to have coincided with changes in Grelling's personal life. In the early 1920s, having left behind his academic dreams, he returned to Berlin, his home city. He secured a post teaching physics, mathematics and philosophy at the Walther-Rathenau-Oberrealschule, a *Gymnasium* in the district of Neukölln. The relationship with his first wife Malvine was then in the process of breaking down. They had adopted a daughter, Eva Maria, who would later move to Switzerland, but there were no biological children from the marriage. In 1924, the couple divorced, leaving Grelling free to marry a much younger woman, a non-Jew called Margaretha Berger, in March the following year. Greta, as she was known, was working for a trade union when Kurt first began

Greta Grelling, 1928.
(© Kurt Grelling Archive)

to court her. Gerhard Weisser remembered her as *a very active and very aggressive, confirmed social democrat and unionist*,[28] a rather formidable picture corroborated to some extent by her children. Growing up, Klaus had seen her as the parent most responsible for discipline, the one who doled out the corporal punishment, with a rod when it was called for.

This paints her as somewhat cruel, but this kind of treatment of children was a routine aspect of parenting at the time. Perhaps Greta felt obliged to take on the role, but in any case, Kurt was mostly spared this task. His intellectual acuity was in direct contrast to his lack of competence with the everyday. His sister Else, who was not an intellectual herself, remembered him later as *an unworldly dreamer*,[29] but even close colleagues took a similar view. Paul Oppenheim's son Felix, who worked with him as a young researcher in Brussels in 1939, also remembered him as otherworldly and incredibly shy.[30] But perhaps a more significant opinion was his own. In a letter to Neurath dated 12 December 1934, referring to his inability to commit to a course of action, he compares himself unfavourably to Klaus, his 4-year-old son. *You can see I am such a schlemiel*,[31] *because I have so many scruples and so I can't do anything. That was always my misfortune. But that's how I will be used. Luckily, in the next generation, of whom you write so nicely, my four-year-old does not seem to have inherited this trait of temperament. He knows no scruple and walks straight ahead in approaching his goal, not always to the delight of his parents.*[32]

This self-image seems so at odds with the confident young man of 1908 or the author of *Anti-J'accuse* that perhaps it should not be taken entirely at face value. By late 1934, it was nearly two years since the Nazis had dismissed him from his job. At this point, the best he could hope for was to *be used*, as he puts it. Neurath was certainly giving him tasks that would occupy his time. In a letter of 28 November 1934, he asks Kurt to compile for the next international congress in Paris, a bibliography of relevant works by leading philosophers who were sympathetic to the goals of the Unity of Science movement. *You are thinking of the bibliography as a conference leader*, he writes. *The ambitious man will buy the bibliography and find out from that what he needs to know.*[33] The attempt to flatter him may well have felt subtly condescending, especially after Neurath had already asked for an extended summary – effectively, a form of recollected minutes – of a discussion of the problem of induction which had taken place at the recent meeting in Prague. Grelling had been present and perhaps had taken part, induction being a subject on which he had lectured and written influential papers himself. But others who were there were more important than he was, and according to Neurath, all of them – *Popper,*[34] *Carnap, Neurath and so on [...] have only washed-out memory pictures.*[35] Though these tasks were useful to the cause of what Grelling himself would later refer to as 'the logical ideal of the unity of science',[36] they also made little use of his talents. But, by now, his professional pride had been slowly eroded through month after month of near inactivity, as the natural dynamism of his 4-year-old son couldn't help but remind him.

So, perhaps everyone's memories were coloured by what became of him in the Nazi years, in a way that Gerhard Weisser's clearly were not. Either way, whether through temperament or a circumstantial loss of confidence, Kurt in middle age faced a future that could not be inferred from the past; confined to a present he could not escape, there is broad agreement that he was someone who needed looking after, and it was Greta who saw that as her role.

THE INVARIANT OF TRANSPOSITIONS

What would Kurt Grelling have thought about in July 1939 as he strolled along the seafront at Ostend in the company of his family? What should he have thought about, given developments in recent months? From the standpoint of history, of hindsight, perhaps the terrible likelihood of war. After the annexations of the previous few years, every nation that shared a border with Germany felt threatened. Addressing this feeling among his own people, on 23 June, a fortnight before the Grellings set off from Brussels for the coast, King Leopold III of Belgium had reaffirmed his country's determination to stay neutral in any coming conflict, despite the same policy having failed to protect it in 1914. But, after the fiasco of Munich the previous year, many also felt that, in spite of their promises to Poland, Britain and France would again back down if Hitler decided to take back its majority German-speaking regions.[1] If war was not inevitable, the Grellings should still have been worried by a possible invasion of Belgium. But perhaps they were also clinging on to hope, to a version of the future that resembled the past, a world in which taking a holiday with the family had been an expression of togetherness as natural as it now was necessary.

Grelling had begun travelling to Brussels in September 1937 to collaborate with Paul Oppenheim. That summer, the family had been forced to 'sell' the properties in Mitte to Himmler's *Kriminalpolizei*, without any compensation in return. The remaining income from his pension was insufficient to provide for his family, so Kurt was forced to look for new sources that could not be found in a country that prevented him from working. He had been planning to attend the 3rd International Congress for the Unity of Science in Paris, scheduled for September. He was supposed to give a lecture there, as he had done at the first official congress, in September 1935, which had also been held in Paris. But, as with the event in 1936, the Nazi authorities had again refused him a permit to travel. Instead, September 1937 marked the first of several trips he would make to Brussels over the course of the next year, each of several weeks at a time. The subject of his research, the application of formal logic to the rather vague definitions that underpinned the discipline of Gestalt psychology, was Oppenheim's conception; the working out of the arguments, the rigour of those arguments, was largely Grelling's achievement. The series of papers they produced over the next two years in the field of formal ontology – the conceptualising of reality in formal language – collectively represents his most original contribution to intellectual history.

Oppenheim was the son of the wealthy Frankfurt gem dealer Moritz Nathan Oppenheim and his wife Catherine. He had taken a doctorate in philosophy and chemistry and then worked in the chemical industry, at the firm of I.G. Farben, until the Nazis took power. By then Stephan, his younger son, was safely installed at a boarding school in the Swiss city of Basel. But Felix, his eldest, who was studying at the University of Frankfurt, was forced to emigrate after Jewish students were barred from higher education. He moved to the Belgian capital, to the home city of his Jewish-Belgian mother, Gabrielle Oppenheim Errera.

Her husband, Paul Oppenheim, was a German patriot to his bones. Felix saw his father as a throwback, a Prussian disciplinarian who regarded the liberal outlook of his wife and sons with suspicion; someone who would later describe his firstborn son as a *washed-out internationalist*.[2] When the Nazis came to power, Oppenheim at first could not believe the speed and extent of the changes taking place in his country. But, as a logical empiricist to his bones, he was also alive to the evidence of danger and where that might lead. In the spring of 1933, his wife was in Brussels when the first reports of Jews being persecuted began to emerge. According to Felix, she had phoned him in Frankfurt to let him know that, if he didn't leave Germany at once, she would throw herself under a train! He did as he was told but, evidently, had also been planning for such an outcome. His collection of Rembrandts and paintings by Impressionist masters had soon followed him to the Belgian capital.

Being forced to make the decision to leave was a trauma for everyone who made it; for all kinds of reasons, both emotional and practical, many Jewish Germans either could not or would not leave. Oppenheim's parents were pillars of Frankfurt society who had risen far above their roots. Moritz, his father, had endowed a chair in physics at the university, and his mother Catherine, who had studied the piano under no less a figure than Clara Schumann, had given a bust of the pianist and composer to one of the city's concert halls. But, as Felix later recalled in his memoir, *they evidently could not reconcile themselves to suddenly becoming pariahs, after a life of being respected and prominent citizens.*[3] The older you were, the harder it was to accept the new reality, the betrayal of decades of loyalty and service; not so much a stab in the back as a knife to the heart of every Jewish German.

The couple took their own lives, dying together the day after Paul had left. They were 84 years old.

Paul and Gabrielle's new life began in a rented house in a leafy suburb of the Belgian capital. A proud bourgeois, Paul was a believer in the capitalist system under which his family had thrived. Paul's grandson and namesake thinks his grandfather had been quietly preparing for the potential nightmare for some time, shifting assets abroad – to Belgium, Switzerland and elsewhere – and his parents' substantial art collection, as well as his own, to their new home in Brussels. This dual attitude – shock at events offset by their meticulous anticipation – would re-emerge when it was needed later on. But their social life also followed them overseas. A regular fixture in Frankfurt's cultural calendar had been the formal Saturday lunches that the Oppenheims held for the local and visiting intelligentsia, including figures from across the intellectual spectrum, such as the religious philosopher Paul Tillich and the Gestalt psychologist Max Wertheimer. Another, even more unlikely visitor was the young Theodor Adorno; along with the slightly older Max Horkheimer, he was a leading exponent of a new kind of social philosophy, known as critical theory, as practised by what came to be known as the Frankfurt School. These famous gatherings continued in Brussels, with many of the same figures, all fleeing Nazism – Wertheimer and Tillich in 1933, Adorno a year later – turning up in a city that was a natural stopover for those attempting to emigrate to Britain or America; Adorno himself went first to Britain, for further study at the University of Oxford, and then, in 1937, to the USA.

Adorno the lunch guest was apparently quite charmed by Oppenheim's vivacious wife, and quite charming himself. But his philosophical outlook was fiercely at odds with Oppenheim and the other logical positivists. The critical stance he adopted with Horkheimer saw in the positivists' supposedly uncritical faith in science and their dependence on mathematical, deductive logic a naïve, unthinking complicity with the Nazi regime. It's a judgement that seems both plausible, according to their own reasoning, and absurdly unfair. The letters that Grelling exchanged with Neurath and others show, quite clearly, how aware they were of the danger the Nazis posed; though, at the same time, some things were beyond their ability to imagine. Like Horkheimer and Adorno, who were Jewish themselves, Oppenheim and Grelling had also been driven out of Germany. Both Adorno and Horkheimer were from similar, affluent backgrounds to Grelling and Oppenheim. But they were highly sceptical of the supposed empirical certainties of science by which the positivists put such store. What they feared was not the vagueness of metaphysics that the positivists so railed against; rather, they attacked the scientistic certainties that made their own class, the bourgeoisie, so blind to the faults of the system by which they had profited, beholden to a model of exploitation and consumption that, in their eyes, served to alienate the greater mass of people from themselves, making them easy prey for those with ill intent. Above all, they saw positivism in the same way as the positivists did themselves – as a mere tool for science, and thus, for the critical theorists, a philosophical useful idiot for a capitalist system whose financial excesses and social abuses had tilled the ground for Nazism. Science and technology were the instruments by which an industrialist class with no interest in the spiritual well-being of those who bought their products could continue to maximise their profits. The moral failures of so many of the great German industrialists (those who weren't Jewish) who supported the Nazi regime, and profited by it, tend to bear out that judgement. As Horkheimer put it in his 1937 essay, 'The Latest Attack on Metaphysics', the positivists, 'these latter-day apologists for freedom from value judgments', glorified 'the fact that thought has a subordinate role, that it has fallen to the level of handmaiden to the prevailing objectives of industrial society with its extremely dubious future'.[4] A withering description, it was the template for others that would follow.

Above all, as powerless as they were in their role as Cassandras – as powerless as intellectuals nearly always are – the critical theorists felt that for the positivists to subordinate independent human reason, with its capacity for ethical judgement, to a system of thought that deemed ethics and most other 'unverifiable' areas of philosophy to be unempirical nonsense, was a fundamental abdication of the role that philosophical thinking had always played in human affairs, leaving a vacuum that malign actors were only too happy to fill. As Horkheimer put it in the same essay, 'When the thoughtless crowd is mad, thoughtless philosophy cannot be sane.'[5]

Naturally, the fiercely defended intellectual positions on both sides – for and against metaphysics, for and against pure empiricism – were of little interest to the Nazis, from whose perspective – antisemitic, anti-intellectual

– the differences between the critical theorists and the positivists would have seemed not just exaggerated but irrelevant – two sides of a divided, enfeebled opposition at war with itself, a spat between two radical, 'Jewish' visions of society, both of which had already been crushed.

In fact, whether positivist or negativist, as members of the Frankfurt School described themselves, the Nazis had captured the public imagination so completely – through a mixture of suggestion and fear – that any kind of rational appeal, whether philosophical or political, would have had little purchase on the popular mind even if it had not been suppressed. It was a measure of Nazism's lethal blend of atavistic and modern that both metaphysics and science and technology were integral to its appeal. The trains ran on time, factories produced new consumer goods and the economy seemed to be growing throughout the later 1930s (notwithstanding that this growth was increasingly sustained through a thoroughgoing larceny of Jewish assets). Life for the average non-Jewish citizen who did not oppose the regime looked so much better than it had done for many years. But, for Horkheimer and Adorno, to side unthinkingly with this kind of progress, even where Nazism was not part of the picture, was to be seduced by the amoral power of capital, which was willing to get behind any regime that did not prevent it from amassing ever more wealth. And science that was equally amoral – which refused to take a moral stance, staying faithful to the idea of objective truth, no matter what the uses it was put to – could be made to legitimise any activity that bore its stamp of approval.

Take the 'science' of race – science that seemed plausible but one that, long since, has been shown to be unempirical nonsense. Throughout the early decades of the twentieth century, this so-called science was used to justify a hierarchy that lay embedded in the stories of civilisation that America and the imperial powers of Europe and their settler colonies all told themselves. It was a doctrine so pervasive that even a humanist as enlightened as Bertrand Russell was not immune to thinking of this kind.[6] In Nazi Germany this assumption of racial supremacy plumbed new depths of perversity and sadism, placing so-called Aryan peoples at the top of an evolutionary tree and Jews, Slavs, Sinti, Roma, Lalleri and other groups at or near the base. At the same time, the Nazis' cultish ideology and exorbitant political language appealed directly to primitive emotions that drew from some mystical or indeed metaphysical realm ideas with the ability to inspire, even to inflame, that were seemingly beyond the reach of critical reason to analyse and debunk. Hence the positivists were concerned with the precise use of language to describe things. The problem they faced is that scientific, factual language of the kind with which they formulated logical propositions eschews rhetorical or narrative power and thus is inspiring only to those who already grasp the underlying concepts.

By the time Horkheimer's essay was published, both he and Adorno had been living in America for several years. But they were soon joined by many of the leading positivists, both Jews and non-Jews: among the Vienna Circle, in 1930, the young Jewish philosopher Herbert Feigl had been the first to leave, taking a position at the University of Iowa, long before the Nazis had got their hands on power; he was followed in 1935 by Rudolf Carnap, a non-Jew but a socialist who left the German University in Prague and took a post at the University of Chicago; then in 1938, Philipp Frank, Carnap's German-Jewish colleague in Prague and a founder member of the original Vienna Circle, was at Harvard as a visiting lecturer when Germany invaded Czechoslovakia, and he could not return; and in the same year the law scholar Felix Kaufmann, also Jewish, found a position at the New School for Social Research in New York City. Of the Berlin Group, the young mathematician Olaf Helmer, Jewish on his father's side, joined Carnap as a research assistant in 1937, while in 1938 Hans Reichenbach moved to UCLA in California, once his contract in Istanbul had run out.

By that point, both groups, in Vienna and Berlin, had experienced tragedies that profoundly shook the small world of academic philosophy. Even at the time, they may have seemed like portents of worse to come. In June 1936, Moritz Schlick had been shot dead on the stairs leading to the philosophy department of the University of Vienna by an ex-student who was mentally disturbed. That same year, Walter Dubislav, co-founder of the Berlin Group, had fled to Prague. He had suffered a mental breakdown in Germany after being arrested and imprisoned on remand for assault, before being released. Settling in the Czech capital, it was there, in September 1937, that he murdered his girlfriend before killing himself.

Grelling's efforts to find work abroad had begun in the summer of 1937, but the arrangement with Oppenheim at first was an ad-hoc, stopgap affair. At the same time, in his letters to Otto Neurath, he was always weighing up other options that Neurath, with his well-connected Mundaneum Institute in The Hague, put to him over the following months and years. But, as the work he was doing with Oppenheim bore fruit, Grelling felt that even taking on further writing assignments for Neurath, in this case a suggested bibliography of scientific logic, was out of the question. *It's not possible to serve two masters*, he writes on 12 September 1937, *and certainly not three or four. From my stay in Brussels, I am hoping to make it easier to make personal contact with notable personalities, but any writing work as a sideline, I'm afraid, will be impossible. That is certainly not a reproach of O., who would not even be unhappy if he knew of this; but as he has 'engaged' me and is financing my current stay in a very generous way, it is my moral duty in a case of conflict to put his interests first. So, please, do not be disappointed if my work for your institute is very little. I know that the work you have suggested is primarily for my benefit, but for now I have to take a step back.*[7]

This was Kurt to a tee, scrupulously loyal, ethical, in this case turning down a solid opportunity to moonlight when someone else in his place might have burned the midnight oil to fit it all in; notwithstanding that he might have thought a mere bibliography was somewhat beneath him. But no harm was done, as Neurath was not a man who took the small things personally; he always saw the bigger picture, and on 22 November he replied, still thinking about how Grelling might find himself a more secure long-term situation. He had just returned from the USA and was full of enthusiasm for what he had found. *They love us very much over there*, he writes, *at least in certain circles. That's why we are well-received when we go there. I spoke at the Human Relations Institute (1,000,000 dollars was spent on the building), Yale University – a nice talk, lots of professors, etc.*[8]

At the same time, for all his confidence in the future and his desire to help his friend, Neurath could see the risks of Grelling uprooting himself from what little security he could count on with Oppenheim. *Life there is so absorbing, particularly when you have only five weeks and have to go to Chicago. On the other hand, naturally, I was looking around for you, too. It's as I said: without going there you can't achieve anything. And then of course it's not that easy to get something quickly. It's a major difficulty that you would risk the safety net you have got at the moment.*[9]

With two young children and limited funds, Grelling wasn't able to think of going to America on any kind of speculative adventure, even if others were. In that regard, he was not the only researcher that Oppenheim was paying to work with him in Brussels. One of the rising stars of the empiricist group in Berlin was Carl Gustav Hempel, or Peter to his friends. Everyone who remembered him later spoke admiringly of both the philosopher and the man. A non-Jew, in a late reminiscence he recalled an incident in 1933 that shocked him into a clear recognition of what was coming. He was working in the State Library in Berlin one afternoon, not long after the Nazis had taken power, when a gang of stormtroopers marched in and ordered all Jews in the building to leave at once. Out of solidarity, he left with them. Hempel's wife Eva was Jewish, so, in 1934, as soon he had secured his PhD, the couple moved immediately to Brussels, when Oppenheim invited him to collaborate. It was a salaried position that was paid for from Oppenheim's own pocket.

The years in Brussels were productive, but Hempel knew it couldn't last. In any case, even if war didn't come, there were no opportunities for foreign academics living in Belgium. By 1937, he was committed to finding a post in America, though he realised it wouldn't be easy. He was in a similar position to Grelling, with a doctorate and papers published in leading journals, even a book co-authored with Oppenheim and published the previous year. But he had no university post to underline his solid credentials. Unlike Grelling, he did at least have youth on his side and, as yet, no dependents to worry about. Still, apparently with mixed feelings, in September 1937, not long after Grelling had first arrived in the Belgian capital, Hempel and his wife left to try their luck in America.

Neurath was never one to think small. His first visit to the USA, which had come that autumn, shortly after the Hempels had left, had filled him with a more expansive sense of what was possible. In a letter of 27 November 1937, Grelling raises the prospect of a visit to The Hague. Neurath is delighted at the thought of seeing Grelling again in person, more than two years since their last meeting in Paris. Riffing on his American experience, he writes, with even more generosity than usual, *I am really looking forward to your visit. The three-hour journey is nothing, as over there you think of distances like that as if you were going a little bit further in a tram. 'Come on over' is what one says there if one has to drive three hours! So, come on over!*[10]

He made it sound so easy, but restrictions on the freedoms that German Jews could exercise were tightening all the time. On 12 January 1938, Grelling writes again to Neurath, *What I feared might happen has happened. The Gestapo won't allow me to continue with my work here. I am allowed to pack my suitcases and as quickly as possible I have to return to my beloved fatherland, and it's probable that they will only let me out again for the purposes of emigrating. But if I now emigrate on empty air then I might as well go begging with my family. Well, sorry! For approximately another half a year I could live very modestly from the Sperrmarks*[11] *transferred from my assets.*

Oppenheim would possibly keep me on for a few years as a colleague depending on whether I had found a position in the United States. But you can imagine that it would not be an easy decision for me. And in any case, it looks like I will not be able to go to conferences or lectures in foreign countries.[12]

Grelling was clearly under no illusions. Reminded again by these new threats of how precarious his position was, he reiterates the need to guard against the danger that by now had loomed over him for almost five years. *If you write to me, please, preferably don't use institute stationery and not your name. I will work out from the context who has sent it to me, and I will work on the same principle for the letters I send to you, by changing names and addresses. I will reveal myself through appropriate allusions!*[13]

It was cloak and dagger because anything less cautious was a risk. Neurath's reply, by return of post, was typically generous in spirit. *I am deeply touched by what you write. How can one address such a wretched situation? I squeeze your hand wholeheartedly, and I would like you to know how much I would like to help in the future, whenever that may be.*[14]

Neurath had ideas of others within Germany who might be able to offer work to Grelling in his field. One man was the logician, mathematician and philosopher Heinrich Scholz.[15] A non-Jew, Scholz made accommodations with the Nazi regime – institutionalising his subject of mathematical logic at the University of Münster and publishing in Nazi journals – manoeuvres that today would seem to invite opprobrium. Such a judgement at the time was less clear-cut. In their letters neither Grelling nor Neurath are inclined to condemn him. Like many others in the Reich, Scholz's position was morally ambivalent. His status inside the Nazi regime brought benefits that would later enable him, in secret, to help Polish intellectuals to escape from Poland: whether Jews and their relations, such as the family of the philosopher Alfred Tarski, or non-Jews such as Jan Łukasiewicz and his family. He was now, apparently, eager to assist Grelling.

Neurath also suggests that it might be very useful to Grelling if he could publish a book. This certainly planted a seed in his mind, but aside from *Anti-J'accuse*, which he never mentions, Kurt had never written anything that long. Instead, as ordered, he seems to have gone back to Berlin in late January 1938. But then two months later, on 26 March, he writes again, having come back to Brussels on the spur of the moment for a further fourteen days. The 4th International Congress of the Unity of Science was due to take place in Cambridge, England, in September that year. But once again, Grelling suspected that he would not be allowed to attend. *Dr O. and I are trying to get a lecture together. Whether I can deliver my own paper as a*

Kurt Grelling at his desk, *c*.1936. (© Kurt Grelling Archive)

sideline is very doubtful. I'm still keeping the book in mind. Scholz was recently with me in Lichterfelde. He hasn't mentioned to me what he has written to you, but for me it is out of the question. 1) It's impossible for Scholz to employ a Jew in an official capacity. 2) There are lots of opportunities for scientific work in Germany, but I need some in foreign countries. The circumstances are becoming more unbearable. Hempel unfortunately can't seem to find anything in America.[16]

That last sentence was perhaps the most discouraging. If the brilliant Hempel, still in his thirties, was finding America a difficult nut to crack, what chance did Grelling have, with his strange CV and advancing age? The best he could do was to keep working on the problems that he and Oppenheim were engaged with. Over the course of the next year, this would lead to the four papers in which Grelling's gifts as a logician were fully deployed, as was finally appreciated by scholars when the four essays were published together, some for the first time, in 1988.

The concept of Gestalt had been a part of philosophical and psychological discourse for almost half a century, since the Austrian psychologist Christian von Ehrenfels had introduced it in 1890. So many sciences in the previous century, but especially biology and physics, had discovered underlying laws so fundamental as to unsettle not only that particular discipline but the broader view in society of the centrality of humans in the physical world. Psychology, no less than biology or physics, had undergone its own transformations. If there were vagaries that made the claims of psychology far harder to test than those of physics, Neurath, Oppenheim and Grelling were among those positivists committed to discovering the universal laws that they were sure must underpin all the various forms of science (including, presumably, sciences yet to be identified as such); Grelling and Oppenheim, in one of their joint papers, would describe this goal as 'the logical ideal of the unity of science'.[17] Instinctively sympathetic to any discipline that called itself a science, the positivists were minded to find the empirical proof that would bring it into logical congruity with its sibling disciplines. Oppenheim was a leading proponent of this idea of a unity, someone whose life project as a philosopher was to establish a relational order among the sciences, a term that for him included not only physical and social sciences but even disciplines such as history, which is usually thought of as one of the humanities. Such a tolerant view, so typical of a man who took pleasure in bringing a catholic range of thinkers together at his dining table, gives a sense that for Oppenheim the word *Wissenschaft*, science, meant something more like *Wissen*, knowledge. It was in this generous and curious spirit that he seems to have suggested to Grelling that they make a study of Gestalt psychology, using logical analysis to examine the validity of its claims.

As with his recent collaborations with Hempel, Oppenheim seems to have sketched the broad outline of the study, its basic hypotheses, leaving Grelling to work out the details through the rigorous application of formal logic, the discipline in which he excelled. Though nearly 50 years old, in the opinion of Grelling and Oppenheim in the first of the papers they wrote on the subject, Gestalt as a psychological concept was still poorly understood, having never been clearly defined. The authors identify two distinct usages with meanings that needed to be clarified. The title of the essay, 'The Concept of Gestalt in the Light of Modern Logic', makes clear their intention. It is less clear why Oppenheim was interested in the subject, though one of its basic questions – the relationship of wholes to the parts of which they are comprised; in fact, a subdiscipline in philosophy known as mereology – has a long history in philosophy going back to Plato. For his part, Grelling had delivered a paper proposing a new theory of perception at the 1st International Congress of the Unity of Science in Paris in 1935, so this was clearly a philosophical problem he had recently addressed. But perhaps personal acquaintance might also have had something to do with it. Gestalt psychology was a young discipline developed in the German-speaking world, and in their generation two of its leading practitioners — Max Wertheimer and Wolfgang Köhler — had taught in Berlin during the Weimar period and were closely associated with the Berlin Group. Wertheimer was Jewish, Köhler not, but both had emigrated to America during the early years of Nazi rule.

The logical empiricists, the group to which Grelling and Oppenheim belonged, believed that any science seeking to explain facts about the world or, in this case, our experience of the world could only be valid if its propositions were able to be demonstrated empirically in logically consistent language. So, the scientific aspirations of psychology and the other social sciences were fertile territory for logicians seeking to verify these claims, to confirm their status as positive knowledge; it was philosophy as intellectual quality control. But what is a Gestalt?

In his original paper of 1890, Ehrenfels makes clear that what he is defining as a Gestalt (the German word for 'shape') is an object of perception made up of distinct parts but apprehended as a whole. Ehrenfels insists that when we listen to a melody, for example, we are aware not only of the note being sounded at any given moment but of those that preceded it and (though Ehrenfels doesn't spell it out), assuming that we're familiar with the melody, those that are yet to come. Even to think of the melody, by evoking it in memory without hearing it, we perceive it whole and entire as a thing in itself that is different from the succession of tones (and other musical qualities such as rhythm) of which it is comprised, and different, too, from the aggregate of that succession. The melody, perceived as a whole, has a quality distinct from its parts, an identity that survives even when on another occasion, or even in our minds, the melody is transposed — when it is played in a different key.

After clarifying various terms and relationships, Grelling and Oppenheim's precise definition of Ehrenfels's original idea is that the Gestalt is the *invariant of transpositions*, the indelible quality or shape or form by which it retains or preserves its core identity, no matter how dramatic the change in circumstances. Where they differ from Ehrenfels is in widening the range of factors by which the Gestalt is articulated. As an example, Grelling and Oppenheim choose a melody, *The Blue Danube* by Johann Strauss, which anyone would have known. It's a melody that, for Ehrenfels, would surely have embodied the stable world of Habsburg Vienna in which he had written his paper; for Oppenheim and Grelling, some fifty years later, it may well have been something of a nostalgic choice, an appeal to simpler, more peaceful times. For Grelling and Oppenheim, transposing *The Blue Danube* means transposition not only to another key, but to another register, higher or lower, a different timbre when played on a different instrument, a different tempo, either faster or slower, a different dynamic range, either louder or softer, and so on. But no matter what the nature of the transposition, what defines the Gestalt is the original melody – the rhythmic and tonal relationships in time – whose basic character does not change. Like a man moving between countries, or between circumstances more or less difficult, the Gestalt remains identifiably itself.

Then comes what some scholars regard as the paper's most original turn, when Grelling and Oppenheim address the age-old question of the relationship between the whole and the parts that comprise it, specifically, whether the whole is somehow more than the sum of those parts. This proposition had also been a feature in Ehrenfels's original paper. But Grelling and Oppenheim suggest a new way of thinking about these relationships, that of a determinational system, based on concepts developed by Rudolf Carnap, one of the leading members of the Vienna Circle. Such a system can be found wherever a complex set of components determines the nature of the system not only by what they are in themselves but in the way they interact and the effects of those interactions. The original example of a melody would still apply. It is only the specific order of tones (including their relative durations) that comprises the Gestalt of *The Blue Danube*. Its irreducible identity is more than the sum of its parts. Any other order of the same set of tones and durations and, for Grelling and Oppenheim, it would cease to be that tune.

Other examples of determinational systems the authors cite are atomic nuclei, atoms, molecules, cells, organisms – examples from the hard sciences of physics and biology – as well as economies, an example from the social sciences, to which we might add various social groups – societies, communities, religious groups and, of course, families of whatever size and character – whose identity is determined by the interdependence of their members.[18] Not to mention numerous, self-limiting groups who gather for a specific purpose that can only be achieved through collective, constructive effort: the cast of a performance of Hauptmann's *The Weavers*, for example, or a colloquium of academic researchers discussing the meaning of a term that they are trying to define, or an orchestra collectively playing *The Blue Danube*; though it could also denote more defensive or protective groups, such as the members of a national polity defined in opposition to those who do not belong, or those of a persecuted minority for whom mutual aid is the only kind that they can count on. All of these, according to Grelling and Oppenheim's definition, might be candidate examples of a Gestalt.

At the same time as he was working on this paper in Brussels, Grelling was still looking around for new forms of income or escape. Neurath, as ever, was a consistent source of ideas and encouragement, apparently unworried about his own future in the Netherlands, whose declared neutrality was no less fragile than that of its neighbour. He even suggested that Grelling could take over from Carnap (now in America) and Reichenbach (soon to arrive there) the editorship of *Erkenntnis*, the journal most closely associated with the logical positivists and the Unity of Science movement. Grelling had contributed many articles to the journal, especially in recent years after other avenues for his talents had been blocked. He wanted assurances that if the badly paid position was offered, it wouldn't then be taken away from him later. He writes that he would only accept it as a springboard to further opportunities. So, having hardly jumped at the chance, eventually, in May 1938, he agreed to send his CV for approval by the editorial board, *and also a menu of all the things I can do*, as he puts it;[19] but he is also unable to stop himself from adding, *I will try hard not to give in to my natural instinct to minimize my achievements.*[20]

Self-promotion was not in his nature, so a lot was riding on the success of the efforts of others. If Hempel managed to find a position in America, then his own place with Oppenheim would be more secure and the editorship of *Erkenntnis* would be something that he could happily turn down. So far, Hempel had drawn a blank and in June would be returning to Belgium after a nine-month absence. But at least their colleague from the Berlin Group, the mathematician and logician Olaf Helmer, had found a post assisting Carnap at the University of Chicago. So, all kinds of future were still possible, and any feeling he might have had about what they might be could turn out to be wrong. It was a question of those who could afford it, such as Oppenheim, giving assistance and opportunities to those who needed their help.

At the beginning of June, Grelling was again obliged to return to Berlin; he spent the next few months trying to get back to Belgium. Another, undated letter that seems to have been sent in the summer of 1938, reiterated Grelling's feeling that the Brussels plan was his best bet. He writes that *for me it would be the cheapest. I hope you will understand that and won't hold it against me.*[21] He then responds to a question that Neurath must have put to him in a letter that doesn't survive, *For the same reasons, I don't want to answer the question of whether I would want to go to a negro college.*[22] He concludes with one reason why any American offer was already so difficult to carry through from the position he was in, weeks or months before Kristallnacht made it almost impossible. *At this time, the American consulate is totally overrun. New registrations will not be considered until 1940. Would you advise me to register in any case, or is there another way to get the American immigration visa, if applicable?*[23]

Grelling clearly wasn't ready for yet more upheaval. At this point, Lotte and Hans Sachs were still in Heidelberg, trying to work out the best way to get to England with at least some of their assets intact. His niece Marion, young and single, was in Switzerland, planning for a new life in America but still months away from setting sail. But, with Kurt stuck in Berlin with Greta and the children, in the house whose top floor was occupied by his sister Else, perhaps the thought of being even further away from his family than Belgium seemed too much of a wrench from a situation that was difficult but not deadly. In any case, the addendum that Grelling included with the undated letter made it clear he had other, long-term reservations in considering the potential offer of a job at a black college in the southern United States. *In principle I am also prepared to teach at a negro college*, he writes. *In that respect, I have absolutely no prejudice whatsoever. But I would like to know whether a position like that, in such a college, would be linked with a downgrading of social status, which would make a potential later transfer to a white college impossible.*[24]

The frankness of his caveat is striking, and maybe a year later he might have jumped at the chance, if a real chance it actually was. But Grelling knew that the American system was one of race-based class, of which Hitler himself was a known admirer; and he also knew, from five years of living under Nazi rule, exactly what that felt like, the stigma of being seen as unequal in humanity to others with less distinction, and, far worse, of having to accept that judgement, for fear of what would happen if he didn't. As a Jew in Germany, in the past five years he had been not only racialised but consistently persecuted on account of his 'race', his social status downgraded to the level of subject, when, until the coming of the

Nazis, he may not have had too much overt cause to think that he was different, perhaps never to imagine that he might not be properly white. Whiteness was the gold standard, after all. Race science said so, and what science had proved wielded natural authority that could only be countered by a weight of evidence to the contrary. To belong meant to be truly equal with all, no matter how white they were – to presume such equality *a priori*, not just to pass as equal. Grelling may never have held a lecturing position in a German university, but, as the questionnaire answer of 1920 and the autobiographical profile from 1940 would both insist, he was sure that if circumstances had been different, he would and should have done so. Seeing so many Jewish friends and colleagues being offered prestigious appointments to elite universities in America – the white colleges he refers to – would have made him unwilling to accept a lesser status for himself, on terms dictated by the racial structure of American society.

According to Neurath, the private black college in question was Talladega College in Talladega, Alabama. Hermann Kranold was an old friend of Grelling's from the days of the Nelson circle, a political writer and economist who, along with Neurath, had been involved in the failed Bavarian Revolution of 1918. He had been professor of economy at the college for several years since fleeing Nazism in 1933. He had since done work on the economic condition of African Americans that earned the interest of the great black historian and philosopher W.E.B. Du Bois.[25] Neurath writes that the principal of the college has concerned himself wholeheartedly with Grelling's case, and in the following months Kranold personally wrote a *nice and comprehensive letter*[26] to his old friend from those days in Göttingen. Whatever the contents of that letter, which has not come to light, Grelling writes candidly to Neurath on 28 January 1939 that what Kranold has said *about the situation of whites in a negro college is anything but enticing,*[27] though he doesn't elaborate on what he means by that. But in any case, he insists that *the prospects there (just as elsewhere) seem to me to be very minimal, so perhaps at the moment I don't need to worry too much about this.*[28]

Of course, had this potential opening resulted in a concrete offer, there would still have been many hurdles to overcome, not least what would happen to his family. Since November, the work he'd been doing with Oppenheim was under contract between them, on terms far better than anyone in his situation had a right to expect. If he had not had that level of security, perhaps his hand would have been forced. But he did have it, so the prospect of an offer from Talladega College was not yet enough to persuade him to give it up, and the situation in Europe outside Germany was not so desperate that he felt obliged to take any old offer that came along, whether the editorship of *Erkenntnis* or a teaching position in rural Alabama. Perhaps it never would be desperate. War was likely but not certain. But, as he also knew, things were difficult everywhere for people like him. As he had written in a letter to Neurath on 30 October 1938, even before Kristallnacht, *the other ('democratic') countries are closing more and more doors to Jews, the more unbearable the circumstances become in the Nazi hell.*[29]

That was also true of England, though it is striking that the idea is never raised that he might go there, where by late 1938 both his niece and nephew were already settled, soon to be joined briefly by their parents, Hans and Lotte Sachs. But only a small number of German-Jewish academics found permanent positions in Britain during that period of deepening crisis and, of course, Kurt would have known of his brother-in-law's struggles in that regard. So, America may have seemed to be the only place that could offer him a viable future, as he admits in the same October letter. *As you are concerned with my fate in such a heartfelt way,* he writes, *I want to say the following. My position here with Oppenheim cannot be looked on as a permanent arrangement. Of course, I know that something like this, for people like me, doesn't exist anymore. So, I still see it as my duty to continue with my efforts to get to the USA and therefore I ask you not to stop your efforts because you think I'm taken care of.*[30]

What was needed was a leap of faith that to Grelling still felt like a leap in the dark. But the potential danger was this: that if he didn't make the leap, he would be pushed.

EVERYTHING IS A RISK

In July 1939, as the Grellings spent time together at the Belgian coast, Kurt was feeling more settled than he had done in months. He spells out exactly what that meant in a letter of the 19th to Otto Neurath, in which a series of three simple sentences – bare, positivist statements of fact – sets up the emotional punchline of the fourth. *I've been here with my family for a week. We can stay together for 4 weeks. The Oppenheims are also very close. You can imagine that I'm happy.*[1]

With so much stacked against them, these weeks must have been especially precious to Kurt and Greta and the children, no matter what they were doing, whether wandering the streets or eating ice creams or sitting in the sand dunes that fortify different parts of the Belgian coastal strip. There was no longer any question of children living separately from the adults, when being together was so important. Things seemed to be looking up, with the children now safely installed in the boarding school on Lake Geneva, and the work he was doing with Oppenheim surpassing anything that Grelling had done before. The past year had been among his most productive, restoring his intellectual confidence, and now the visit of his family brought with it a different kind of fulfilment that was no less necessary.

Happily, he was not the only one to feel that things were working out. At the end of January, the Hempels had left again for America. Grelling had been sad to see them go; like everyone, he recognised the human qualities of Hempel and his wife, and counted them as friends. But every individual departure was also a sign of communal hope. As he had written to Neurath on 28 January, *Yesterday the Hempels left. Very painful for me. We were together almost every day. We exchanged our personal worries and our scientific thoughts, and often we 'messed around', as Hempel puts it so beautifully. All of that I will miss very much. Those two are such magnificent people in every way, as you so seldom find. Hopefully, this time Hempel will find a position there. In this there is for both of us (him and me) a harmony of interests that happens so rarely.*[2]

Kurt Grelling with bicycle, Brussels, 1938–39. (Courtesy of Paul Oppenheim)

Grelling's optimism was soon to be justified. After working as an assistant to Rudolf Carnap in Chicago since arriving in America in January, by early summer Hempel had received an offer to teach on a year's contract at City College in New York. This meant that he and Eva would not be returning to Europe and would no longer need Oppenheim's financial support. The news meant security for Grelling of a kind that few in his position could hope for.

Hempel's health was suffering as it often did during these years. In this case it was boils, no doubt the result of overwork, the common fate of most early-career academics. His wife Eva Ahrends-Hempel's job helping refugees was also exhausting, but, on the whole, life in the new land was positive for them both. Hempel's main worry had been Eva's father, in desperate need of a place of refuge, like every other German Jew. But this, too, had come good, in part because of Grelling. As Oppenheim explained to Hempel in a letter of 25 May, *In the next few days,* [Grelling] *will be sending money to your father-in-law and writing to him. Mr Ahrends has consulted me in this matter.*[3] Ahrends had received an Australian visa, but had had to rely on the good offices of others to secure it. Oppenheim quotes Ahrends's letter of thanks, in which he wrote that such a visa was *'extremely difficult to get and I don't know which angel helped. In January I wrote to them*[4] *in my stupidity and without any support, and already after only 4 months I received their decision.*[5]

In 1939, four months was indeed very little time to wait. But, despite strings having clearly been pulled on his behalf, the visa still came with the usual financial hurdle that had to be cleared, in this case a 'landing fee' of £200. Oppenheim quotes further from Ahrends's letter: *'I already have half a commitment from the International Hebrew Alliance, who will give me 100 pounds, and if I could, the rest from another committee. Maybe you know another place I could ask. Because I am baptised, the German-Jewish Aid Committee is out of the question. It would be awful if my emigration were to founder on this matter.'*[6]

Luckily, it wouldn't. As Hempel wrote to Oppenheim in a letter of 1 June, Grelling, acting as intermediary for the Hempels, would pay the sum for Ahrends that the couple had transferred to him for this purpose; once this was done, the approved emigration could go ahead. So, as this commitment and his letter to Neurath in June about Luise Rothstein show, Grelling's confidence, a renewed sense of being plugged into life, had grown since the turn of the year. Not only the contract with Oppenheim, with a salary, a thirty-hour week and a month's paid holiday per annum, but the offer of a lecture tour of Scandinavia – at the universities of Copenhagen, Stockholm, Uppsala, Gothenburg and Lund; with Oppenheim's blessing, this took place in the second half of March. Even now, unimpeded travel around Europe for Jews was still possible outside the Nazi zone of interest, as also was meaningful dialogue with fellow academics on the problems that Grelling was trying to address. As he writes to Neurath on 4 April, shortly after arriving back in Brussels from his Scandinavian journey, *Almost everywhere I could find a great respect for the precision work of mathematical logic. That is already a lot.*[7]

Neurath's reply, by return of post, is eager to know more about Grelling's recent tour, in part to learn of any problems with the visa that he might encounter when he goes there himself, but also to understand how fertile the ground might be for the positivist–empiricist programme. Neurath was a proponent of the doctrine of physicalism, a term that he and Carnap had introduced to philosophy. Simply described, the doctrine asserts that everything that exists is physical, that there is nothing which is not subject to physical laws, a statement that clearly rules out the existence of the metaphysical. In the letter Neurath is keen to assert his own priorities, a bias towards one side of the logical–empirical diode anchored in the experience of physical reality. *Respect for mathematical logic is important*, he writes, *but for empiricism is more so. Mathematical logic doesn't protect against metaphysics.*[8]

If this last remark was a rebuke of sorts, Grelling would not have taken it as any kind of slight. He was buoyed by his travels and being so well received wherever he had been. He was still thinking about the USA, both the upcoming International Unity of Science Congress at Harvard in September and now, asking whether Neurath has heard from Hermann Kranold, the more long-term prospect of a teaching post at Talladega College. In the extant sequence of letters that the two of them exchanged, this comes as something of a surprise, given his earlier hesitation. But the earlier letter was sent when he was stuck in Berlin, and in this one, written in the far more liberal environment of Brussels more than six months later, his confidence and optimism were high. In the same spirit, once again he proposes a visit to his old friend in The Hague. Neurath himself had recently returned from a second trip to America. He had managed to persuade the University of Chicago Press, which already published the growing monograph series of the Library of the Unity of Science, to take on the full range of the movement's publications, including *Erkenntnis*.

In America Neurath had also been looking out for any opportunities that Grelling might take up, in particular with Richard Courant, another Jewish refugee. Courant was a social democrat who had left Germany in 1933 after being sacked from his post at the University of Göttingen. He had ended up as professor of mathematics at New York University. On the recent visit Neurath had suggested that Grelling would be an excellent choice as a visiting lecturer. Courant had seemed open to the idea. As Neurath frames it, *I spoke with Courant about you, and he was in a friendly mood, so I started to mention that it would be easier for you to get to the congress if you could lecture there, and that would in any case be good, etc., etc. And then he told me more warmly than before: tell Grelling that he should write to me and lay out everything, etc.*[9]

Neurath then coaches him on exactly how any letter should be couched. *It makes sense to me that you should write to him saying that I have told you that, in his letters to me about you, he has sympathetically taken up your cause, or something like that.*

Then mention that I have told you that I have spoken with him, and the possibility of lectures has been raised. That would make the journey to the congress so much easier.

And then you continue: 'As you know, because of the situation, I had to give up my lecturing position.' You have to use the terms 'lecturing' and 'professor' and whatever is fitting, because 'teaching' can't count on support, and moreover, for people who have lectured, entry is possible outside of the quota.

And then you briefly outline your situation, tell him about the lecture tour in Scandinavia and other nice things you know about yourself. Mention again the introduction from Russell, which Courant has a copy of and finds very valuable. Tell him how important it would be if you could speak in connection with the congress. Tell him subjects associated with a certain area, so that they can honour you as a mathematician, logician and also possibly as a philosopher. But be careful with the last one, because that's the most likely to be seen as controversial, in a way that mathematics and logic are not.[10]

It is clear from this last point that the US authorities were on the lookout for anyone who might be deemed a political risk, and philosophy's habits of speculative thought were enough to raise a red flag in such a worsening climate of suspicion. Neurath continues that he is writing *all of the following in detail because I find it very difficult to explain to you in a letter how the USA is. Everyone is overworked – and Courant, too* [...] – [...] *so the time needed for each intervention is a huge sacrifice for them.* [...] *Please don't talk about the lectures too intensely, so that Courant doesn't get the impression that you are counting on it.* [...] *But please write immediately, because now is job-hunting* [season] [...] *I have to write to Courant anyway, and I will fleetingly refer to you again. Let's hope that, as a first attempt, this will be a success.*[11]

It was clearly a delicate business, one that was second nature to Neurath, the ebullient sociologist, an inveterate networker with the kind of confidence that could carry any situation. But for Grelling, who by this point in his life was diffident and self-effacing, it was certainly a challenge, whether or not he needed such solicitous instruction.

At the end of the month, Grelling paid a visit to Neurath in The Hague. There he met the mathematician Martin Strauss, also German-Jewish, who was on his way to Cambridge in England, having just received a six-month visa for himself and his wife. In advance of the visit, Grelling had been asked by the Dutch police to register his arrival, even for an overnight stay; in a letter of the 25th he asks Neurath for a verified invitation to this effect. Neurath replies on the 27th. *Yesterday our Dutch employee went to the police to personally ask for a stamp on your invitation. It was rejected because the regulations* [now] *are significantly stricter. The official was quite accommodating and regretted that he was not allowed to make a different decision. You can file a complaint with the Ministry of Justice, etc. If it were vital for you, I would of course try all possible avenues (as we did with Strauss), but you will understand that we have to reserve the demands from our Dutch friends for the most urgent cases.*[12]

Restrictions were tightening all the time, and Neurath ends his letter with a sentiment that shows just how much the sickness had spread, threatening his own safety and that of so many colleagues and friends. *A horrible world*, he declares. *And how come in the 'free' countries we ask, 'Jewish parents?' etc. It's not enough anymore to say what religion you are – and so it keeps on growing.*[13]

As Neurath suggests, racialised thinking now afflicted even those directly affected by it. The Nazis had shifted the window of what it was acceptable to discuss and what could not be ignored. Throughout their correspondence, Grelling and Neurath are often vexed by the so-called Jewish question – that is, the question of what it meant to be Jewish that the antisemites had obliged them to think about. Grelling returns to it several times, with the sense of a man who is struggling to find some kind of dignified refuge in an identity he had once worn so lightly. In a letter of 4 May, after praising Strauss's all-round qualities, Grelling is given to observe, *what a disproportionately high number of Jews of all languages (and of course those of mixed race!) are involved in modern mathematics. Have you ever made any statistics about this?* he asks. *What percentage of the world's white population are employees of mathematical journals, and how many are Jews?*[14]

Several weeks later, in a reply dated 15 June, Neurath the empiricist puts his measured response in the proper context, that of statistical analysis, yet another area in which he was a recognised expert. *The statistics of Jews*, he writes, *is a tricky subject. Since they are not allowed to do many things, they are of course in science in a higher percentage than normal.*[15]

That was certainly true, and with all those Jewish scientists and mathematicians moving abroad, Kurt was hoping that he would follow. In the meantime, the official stamp for the Dutch visit wasn't needed, and Grelling spent a restorative twenty-four hours at the end of April with his old friend Neurath, and new acquaintance Martin Strauss, before returning again to Brussels. On 1 May, Oppenheim wrote to Hempel that Grelling had come back safe and sound from his trip, and the two of them were working on the papers on Gestalt that they were due to present at the Harvard congress in September. But there was some doubt over whether they could obtain the visas they would need, and by 25 May, writing again to Hempel, Oppenheim admits that, on the grounds of cost, he won't be able to make it to America. *As you know, the pastoral care of refugees has taken up more and more of my time*, he writes, *and I can't really justify this to my family [...]: this year I have spent so much money on helping refugees that I have to get my budget back on an even keel.*[16]

This financial commitment is not surprising, given Oppenheim's standing in the Jewish community in Belgium but also the sheer level of demand. Grelling was lucky in having regular status and paid employment. In late May, he was still thinking that he would travel to America for the congress; Oppenheim had decided to stay in Europe, though even his situation was far from secure. The Oppenheims had been facing the need to find somewhere else to live, as the owner of the well-appointed house at 21 avenue Victoria, which they had rented for the previous six years, now wanted it back. Then, on 20 June, Oppenheim wrote that they had been granted a reprieve until the end of January and thus, for the time being, the threat of eviction had been lifted. But, given the general turbulence of events, this did little to restore a sense of equilibrium, as Oppenheim admits to Hempel in so many words in a letter of 3 July. *We live in a time where it's very difficult to make plans more than a few days in advance. You ask what I think about the political situation. To answer this question, I hesitate twice: first of all, I feel that whatever I say is just empty talk when it doesn't have the necessary basis in fact. Second, I could well have disavowed any opinion I offer by the time you get this letter. My feeling is that there will be no war, and more likely England and France will secretly pressurise Poland, finding a compromise formula in regard to Danzig, and both parties can then say to their own people that they are right.*[17]

From the vantage point of years or even months later, this seems like an extraordinary assessment, informed by a sense, or at least a wish, that, deep down, Hitler was a reasonable man who would stop, having achieved his avowed aim of reuniting all fellow German speakers under a single flag. But Oppenheim was far from alone in that wish. It was something like the one which had governed the actions of Chamberlain and French prime minister Édouard Daladier at Munich the previous year, in a deal that Hitler had broken within months. But at the same time, Oppenheim knew personally from the great westward movement of people, including himself, which had already happened, not to mention the despair of those who had stayed behind, that any hope for peace was not to be heeded too closely. He would have seen the results in the official refugee camps in Belgium, in Merksplas and Marneffe, set up to house those with no independent means of subsistence. In the letter he had written to Hempel, he adds that *the care of refugees shows no sign of stopping.*[18] In fact, it had kept on growing after the Netherlands had closed the border to refugees from Greater Germany at the end of May 1938, and even more so after Kristallnacht. By July 1939, the number of Jewish refugees in receipt of direct financial aid from the charitable organisations that Oppenheim supported was approaching the peak of 15,000 it would reach in March the following year.

In early June, Neurath received news that his son Paul had been released from Buchenwald concentration camp on 27 May under an agreement that allowed political prisoners – as Paul was, in addition to being Jewish – to go into exile wherever they could find it. Paul Neurath had friends in Sweden and, by the time his father wrote to Grelling on the 15th, had secured a visa and made the journey to safety.

In his reply on the 24th, Grelling mentions the case of Luise Rothstein, in which he wanted help from Bertrand Russell, before updating Neurath on his own situation. *I don't have a tourist visa for the USA yet. To secure this, my certificat d'étranger[19] must first be extended, and in this matter the local Sureté[20] takes its time. There are always the same bureaucratic obstacles, and one is happy if they are only of a bureaucratic nature. However, it is questionable whether I will still get a place on the ship.*

The affordable ships in question from Compagnie Maritime Belge were sold out 4 weeks ago. I have provisionally booked a place on an English liner, but I can only [confirm it] once I have the visa. Recently, however, I have become doubtful as to whether the very expensive trip is even worth it for me. Going on Hempel's experience, my chances in the USA are practically zero. First of all, I would need to live over there for about a year without work and income before maybe I could find something. But it would be at least 2 years before I get the visa (the immigration visa): by then I'll be over 55. It's almost impossible that I'll find a position then. What's the point of making plans so far in advance these days? At a big congress like the one at Harvard promises to be, the individual vanishes if he isn't a big gun. And outside of the congress I wouldn't be able to visit many people because 1) it's still the holidays and 2) I can't travel all over the continent, but have to limit myself to a few cities around New York. Of course, I would love to come to America one day, but given the position I'm in, that can't be the deciding factor.[21]

This was a realistic assessment of his prospects, but there is also the sense that he was talking himself out of whatever limited chance of success there may have been. It didn't help that, as Oppenheim discloses to Hempel in a letter of the 20th, in submitting his request to the Sureté, *instead of writing the number of the identity card, he has sent the original!*[22] Given the distracted state of mind that anyone in Kurt's predicament might have suffered, this kind of mistake is not surprising. But the subtext of Oppenheim's comment is surely that this is exactly the kind of error that Kurt's typical unworldliness might have led him to make. On the other hand, in the same letter Oppenheim also insists that *Grelling is determined to go there in August and is already looking for a visa and a place on the ship.*[23] But it's also clear from

Grelling's own letter to Neurath just four days later that he was already caught in two minds, as the accidental submission of his identity card seems to bear out.

On 2 July, the indefatigable Neurath wrote to him again, urging him not to give up. *It's very difficult to advise you about Harvard. Everything is a risk. It's just like that: if you don't play roulette, you can't win. I don't mean that you will stand out at Harvard because of your presentation – who stands out if they don't start off as someone who is going to stand out? – but I do mean that you will speak to a lot of people personally. And with the Anglo-Saxons it's the personal that matters. It's possible that you will establish a good contact with one of those present, and that person will take you on; that is possible – but of course that's not something you can prepare for. Hempel is probably less like your case than Helmer, since you could try to find a place as a mathematician. Maybe write to Russell and see if he wants you around. It's conceivable that he needs someone like you. You could write to him, saying how happy you would be to help him, if necessary, in addition to [giving] courses, academic work, etc., though I don't know how he'll respond to something like that. It's hard to guess, especially in the area of gambling. As experience shows, with the exception of typically unadaptable people, of whom you are not one, gradually everyone finds accommodation.*[24]

As usual, Neurath was doing his utmost to help, but by the time that Grelling responded a week later, on 9 July, he had clearly made up his mind, coming down in favour of a longer-term plan. *I have now given up on my trip to the USA*, he writes. *Maybe this decision is wrong; but that can hardly ever be ascertained. It's unfortunate, but can hardly be changed, that one is limited to such a low level of rationality when making important decisions about one's personal fate. The fact that Hempel is now fortunately settled has made my situation here a little safer. Nevertheless, I now want to register for the immigration visa and at least take advantage of this opportunity. You once wrote to me or said that in your opinion it would not be difficult for me to obtain an affidavit. Do you still maintain this? If yes, I would be grateful for any advice on how I should go about obtaining it. I don't have any blood relatives over there who would be able to do that [for me], but I don't have a sufficiently wealthy friend either.*[25]

So, for a myriad of reasons that weighed in favour of staying, for now Grelling put aside any thoughts of going to America. One reason he doesn't mention was the imminent arrival of his family, who of course he would have to leave behind, unable to do anything to help them, even as he tried everything he could to help himself. The choice was invidious, and even Peter Hempel, who knew how hard it would be in America, was supportive. As he wrote to Oppenheim on 29 July, he and Eva thought that *Grelling made the right decision to give up his travel plans.*

*It was very reasonable under the circumstances, as much as we would have loved to see him here.*²⁶

The Hempels were now in New York City, and Peter was thoroughly enjoying the courses he was teaching at City College. The couple were an obvious point of contact for anyone from their circle arriving from Europe. In the first instance, that meant the Oppenheims' youngest son, Stephan, who had just completed his degree in Belgium and was emigrating to America, to begin a PhD at Harvard or Columbia. Eva Ahrends-Hempel wrote to him on 28 July, to congratulate him on his graduation and to explore the possibilities for graduate study in the USA. She and Hempel were excited that he was coming to America, she says, though they wouldn't be able to meet him at the pier. To escape the humid heat of the city, they had decided to spend part of the summer in Vermont with the American philosopher Ernest Nagel and his wife. In his own letter to Oppenheim the following day, Hempel writes that he has heard from Grelling that Oppenheim would not be coming to the congress at Harvard in September, though he also thinks that perhaps *Stephan's presence here will have a more attractive effect on you than the congress does now. Besides, not only a pull but also a pressure will be exerted on you, because your wife won't have the heart to leave your youngest alone in a foreign country for so long!*²⁷

Hempel's letter and the one that Oppenheim sent on the 30th would have crossed in mid-ocean. Oppenheim's confirmed that Stephan was leaving Europe on 19 August on SS *Pennland*.²⁸ But the relief that he was going would be tempered by the anxiety of separation, as he can't help but reveal when asking Hempel and his wife to keep an eye on his youngest son. For once, he is quite unable to button up his worries, admitting that, *despite the almost unlimited trust that we have in his character, I think of the danger of bad company or of the fact that, as a subjectively understandable reaction to the all-too-long stay in his parents' home, in his youthful desire for freedom he lets off steam through dangerous adventures. New York is particularly questionable ground! Hopefully more in jest, he talked about repeated tours of the Bowery, the Chinese Quarter, etc. I would be very happy if you would point out to him in a very conspicuous way, again and again, the great dangers which, as I know from personal experience, the visitor will find in such quarters, such that he should only go there once and under the guidance of a reliable expert. But this is just one example of many! I hope for your friendly help in this matter not only with regard to warnings and clarifications,* but also *confidential reports to us insofar as these warnings and clarifications are not sufficiently taken into account.*²⁹

At the time of this rather anxious letter, preoccupied with the dangers of freedom, Oppenheim was alone in Brussels, working in the library, while Grelling had remained at the coast with his family. So, he was clearly expecting the two of them to resume their work, once Greta and the children had left. His eldest son, Felix, had taken Belgian citizenship shortly after moving to the country. Felix had hated growing up in the volatile environment of Weimar Germany, where his schoolteachers were often angry nationalists bitter at the military defeat and the punishment terms of the Treaty of Versailles. Very soon after settling in Belgium, in a move that his father acknowledged was necessary but was still dismayed to have to witness, Felix gleefully embraced his new identity as a Belgian, feeling at home for the first time in his life. With war seeming increasingly inevitable, he had eagerly joined the army and was now preparing to defend his motherland against his fatherland, should events take that turn. At the same moment, Gabrielle was with Stephan in the South of France. According to Felix in his later recollections, his mother often went on trips with one or both of her sons, most often to Italy, and especially Florence, where her mother was from. Her husband, who did not like travelling, stayed at home. If Paul could ever be persuaded to go anywhere, it was always to the Engadin valley in the German-speaking part of Switzerland, and, even then, the first thing he packed was his letter scale, to enable him to weigh his letters.

Stephan confirmed his whereabouts in a letter to Eva Ahrends-Hempel of 4 August, handwritten from the city of Toulouse in the midst of what he calls *a farewell tour of Europe.*³⁰ He was anxious about making sure of his place at Columbia University by the time of his departure, but the clipper with his letter of acceptance had broken down in the Azores and the copy he had sent by ship would take a little longer. Eva replied reassuringly on the 8th that she had checked with Columbia, who had now received the letter he had sent by clipper. And on the same day, she wrote to Oppenheim that while they were due to go to the Nagels for a week, they had to see a specialist beforehand about Hempel's health problems. The doctor thought a staphylococcus infection was the cause. If the diagnosis was confirmed, and the doctor advised that they should not leave the city, they would go and meet Stephan from the ship. She also reminded Oppenheim, gently but firmly, that Stephan did not need the level of supervision his father would like them to offer; that *we are honoured by your trust, and will be really happy to look after Stephan as much as we can and as much* as he likes. *So as far as his physical well-being is concerned, I think we'll be able to report to you more often; and we'll definitely take care of him if he does get sick! However, we would rather not take responsibility for the rest, though we think that you don't need to worry about this either; Stephan is already an adult, and probably more adult when he's alone here than he appears to be at home: plus, in our opinion, the likelihood that he will end up in bad company at Columbia is very small. And I believe that the Bowery and Chinatown, which the police have now made safe for visitors, will soon lose their great appeal!*[31]

If this was less of a commitment than Oppenheim had hoped for, it was something that, apparently, he could live with. He wasn't going to America, as Grelling confirmed in a letter to Neurath on 12 August, the day after Greta and the children had gone back to Berlin. The plan was for Hempel to read out Grelling and Oppenheim's joint paper at the congress, a less-than-optimal solution but one that would at least associate their names with the subject of the paper. For now, Grelling was wrestling with a more immediate problem. *We are hesitating over my wife's emigration precisely because of the general uncertainty, because we don't know whether she could return with the children if necessary, and it's easier for a single person to get by than a family of four. It is [...] very difficult to weigh up the pros and cons.*[32]

Then at the end of the month a card dated 25 August arrived at the Hempels' address, in response to Grelling's belated attempt to arrange a lecture tour in the United States. Just three days earlier, the unnamed writer had received a request on Grelling's behalf from the Emergency Association of German Scientists Abroad, based in New York City, and they could only apologise, said the writer, that it was now too late to arrange anything for the coming season. At the same time, toward the end of August, Neurath was setting off for America from Rotterdam on board the RMS *Aquitania*. The congress he had organised was due to begin on 3 September.

And then, quite suddenly, without warning, Oppenheim and his wife were gone. They are likely to have left from Antwerp on the same route that Stephan had taken just two weeks earlier. The change of mind must have come at the very last minute, the result of the kind of pressure from Gabrielle that Hempel had foreseen. After all, it was she who'd insisted that Oppenheim should leave Germany back in 1933. She seems to have had an instinct for trouble that wasn't complicated by the balance of probabilities her husband felt obliged to weigh up, and not a bit by a need that he could never quite abandon to see the land of his birth in the best possible light. But perhaps he had also been planning for the worst, just like in 1933, though at this stage, so late in the day, the obligatory visa, not to mention the berths on a ship, could only have come at considerable cost.

The day before they left, Germany invaded Poland. Two days later, as the ship that bore the Oppenheims steamed across the North Atlantic, and on the same day as the congress began, Britain and France declared war on the Nazi state. It would have cast a pall on proceedings that even the most optimistic positivist would have struggled to dispel.

LETTERS FROM AMERICA

Oppenheim would not have left without first having spoken to Grelling. It must have been a difficult conversation and may well have been a brief one. But whatever its content, Grelling's first letter to Oppenheim, dated 5 September, is frank about the predicament he now faced, which Oppenheim's departure had suddenly exposed. *Personally, my health is good; but I can't deny that I'm a little depressed. The news from my wife isn't bad. She hasn't travelled to Switzerland yet because there were no trains. But she doesn't know whether she should even bring the children there during the war. [...] The pros and cons are very difficult to weigh up. Of course, I would rather have the children in currently neutral Switzerland than in Germany. But if they don't get any money from Berlin, I would have to send the money from here, because I can't claim any charity as long as I still have my own resources. On the other hand, I need to save what little I do have here as a nest egg, if possible. This is all very difficult to decide. Of course, the ideal solution would be to have the whole family here, and if the war lasts longer, I will try everything I can to achieve that.*[1]

The contract with Oppenheim would continue for now, but it was not a long-term solution. Searching for an alternative, Grelling wrote to the ministry of education in Brussels, though more in hope than expectation; there had been no openings for Jewish refugees even before war was declared. With a bracing awareness of how vulnerable he had suddenly become, Kurt had also applied to the *Foyer Israélite de Bruxelles* (Brussels Jewish Welfare Agency), where different lists had been drawn up for German nationals and other refugees; such was the level of demand from German Jews.

Grelling and Oppenheim numbered all the separate items in their correspondence of the next months and years, lending it a businesslike air that often belies its content. Kurt was fortunate that Oppenheim would continue to pay him a salary, now even more of a lifeline. But the anger and the sense of abandonment he felt cannot help but seep out in more or less obvious ways. In item 9 of this letter of 5 September, he can hardly contain himself: *I believe I am doing you a service when I write about what I have encountered regarding you in the past few days. I spoke to 3 people, 2 emigrants and a Belgian, about your departure (I'm asked about it everywhere). All three have expressed disapproval in various forms and degrees. Of course, I portrayed your trip as long-planned and calculated for a short period of time. I didn't have the impression that this changed the judgement of these people very much. That's probably because people don't expect to hear anything else from me. I assume that this interests you and that you don't blame the messenger for the message.*[2]

Grelling makes an unconvincing go-between when it's obvious that the critical remarks of others act as proxies for his own. Some of the critics he refers to were almost certainly among those whose names crop up in the letters of the next few months – friends and acquaintances, fellow German-Jewish intellectual refugees, a snapshot of the many hundreds, and possibly thousands, who lived in Brussels alone. Most appear to have been at least middle-aged, transplanted from comfortable affluence in their native lands – Germany and Austria – to a life of genteel poverty in the Belgian capital. Among those he mentions are the Grossmans, the Sackses and the Hirsches, couples that he and Oppenheim both know well. Professor Grossman had recently had an operation and was still convalescing, having just been discharged from hospital. It was no doubt for this reason, according to Grelling in his letter of 15 September, that Grossman had yet to realise that war had been declared. Felix Oppenheim, on the other hand, was all too aware: he was a serving NCO with the Belgian artillery whose barracks were a fifteen-minute bike ride from his parents' rented house, where now only he was living. When on leave, he worked at the house with Grelling, who, in addition to his own work with Oppenheim, was helping Felix with the logical analysis of the philosophy of law at the heart of his PhD thesis.

Felix's unit was stationed near the border with the Netherlands, as part of a notional defensive line on the western side of the Albert Canal. In his later unpublished memoir, he paints a picture of an undisciplined Belgian Army, unprepared for the ruthless brutality of the Nazi war machine. His parents had paid him a visit at this forward position at the end of August, in the days before their departure. As Felix later recalled, *I could see in their eyes how awful they felt to have to leave me behind.*[3]

But leave they did, on SS *Westernland*, on 2 September, the day after German troops had marched into Poland. It had certainly been a close-run thing. Oppenheim had not received his US visa until 28 August, where Gabrielle's had been issued back on 2 January, at the start of the year. Oppenheim had not been thinking that he would go, having written as much to Hempel just weeks earlier. But, just as Hempel had foreseen, it was almost certainly under pressure from his wife that he did.

On the 15th, Grelling writes again, somewhat forlornly – *Tomorrow it will be 14 days since you left*[4] – as if he still couldn't quite believe it. The contentment of July and August had vanished, replaced by more worry than ever for his wife and children, who were still in Berlin. *I try to console myself with the fact that there doesn't seem to be any immediate danger to the family*, he writes. *However, the food must be quite scarce; of course, my wife can't write anything about that.*[5]

Three weeks later, on 12 October, they were still waiting for the Swiss visas and getting by on whatever small means Greta had at her disposal. It seems that the Nazis controlled her access to the money that Kurt had inherited from his mother, so it may have been that his small teacher's pension was all she had available to feed three people. With the house at Wilhelmstrasse 13 having been sold, they were living in temporary quarters that Kurt describes as being of very poor standard. He was sending regular shipments of butter and coffee, but otherwise was powerless to help.

The house at 33 avenue Legrand, Brussels, where Kurt Grelling rented rooms in 1939–40. (© Julian Beecroft)

In Belgium, the community of exiles made it easier to get by when there were setbacks. Professor Grossman, who had seemed to be on the mend, deteriorated suddenly and died. Dr Goldfinger, another friend of Grelling and Oppenheim, had organised a fund to raise money for Grossman's widow. Grelling thought that she would try to stay afloat by renting out rooms, and that most likely he would move in with her, though in the event he remained in the rooms he was already renting at 33 avenue Legrand in the Ixelles district in the south of Brussels.

After two months of silence, a letter arrived from Neurath, dated 23 October, not from America but from The Hague. *I returned home from the USA after a very long journey*, he writes. *There were shots fired at German pilots by a nearby warship, floating mines, which as you know are very dangerous, a bomb thrower* [Bombenwerfer][6] *that circled our Dutch ship, an investigation by the English, who were very nice and polite – checking that the lifeboats were always 'clear', also the lifebelts on board, etc.*[7]

Such upbeat reporting was typical of Neurath. Why he came back he doesn't say. But he had always relished the heat of battle, so a risky Atlantic voyage would not have put him off. The congress had been successful, a particular feat of organisation given the circumstances, with some surprising guests. *Met our friend Paul and his wife in New York, at the congress, which was attended by about 200 people (including about a dozen from Europe). I saw many acquaintances who asked me to pass on their greetings to you. I would have to lie if I claimed I could remember who they were. Frank, von Mises*[8] *are at Harvard, Kelsen*[9] *went back to Switzerland, Rougier*[10] *hadn't left yet when I left, as far as I know. Tarski, Wundheiler,*[11] *etc. remain over there.*[12]

How Paul and Gabrielle had got there so quickly is something of a mystery, though it may be that Neurath is misremembering events: the congress took place at Harvard, and most likely Neurath had seen the Oppenheims in New York soon after it had finished, as he waited to come back on the ship. But in any case, for Grelling the news of colleagues was heartening. He had been worried for some time about the Polish-Jewish logician Alfred Tarski, the leading positivist in Poland.[13] So, to hear that he had managed to get out of the country before the invasion of 1 September, and was now stuck in America, having left his family behind,[14] would have stirred up feelings that for Kurt were decidedly mixed. Grelling's own family was still in Berlin, awaiting their Swiss visas, when he replied to Neurath on the 25th, by return of post. Stuck in his Brussels limbo, perhaps he was wondering if America might have been better after all, given that any distance now seemed unbridgeable. *They don't let anyone out. As you can imagine, the situation is pretty depressing for all of us, and the fact that many people have it much worse is little consolation. Luckily, I'm starting to become numb to these things. I seek refuge in science, and it always provides it.*[15]

Such are the consolations of academic research, the pursuit of knowledge that will always reward the effort made to obtain it – the reward being in the effort – but in this case was of little practical use. Then a PS at the end of the letter to say that Greta had phoned, the visas had arrived and the three of them would be leaving on the 30th for Switzerland, where Greta would stay on for a few days.

Sometime in October, the letter that Oppenheim had written from the ship finally arrived in Brussels. The carbon its author retained is practically illegible; Oppenheim's handwriting is challenging to read, to say the least. But the first of his typed letters, dated 6 November and sent from the Shelton Hotel in New York City, gives evidence that, as usual, he'd been working for the benefit of others since finding sanctuary for himself in America. For one thing, he'd been trying to arrange a lecture tour for Grelling, to begin the following autumn, though whether Kurt could make enough money from such a venture even to cover his costs was doubtful. But, after the recent good experience in Scandinavia, it had to be worth considering.

Oppenheim had been trying to send food parcels to Greta in Berlin, but this was increasingly difficult to do from the USA. But he had also spoken to Max Horkheimer, editor of the *Journal for Social Research* and critical–theoretical opponent of positivists or empiricists such as Grelling and Oppenheim; someone who in his own recent writings had taken a hatchet to what he saw as the naiveté of the positivist programme. As ever with academics, the intellectual conflict was both deadly serious and, as they could all clearly see, utterly trivial when set beside the persecution that Jews and intellectuals like themselves were actually facing. Ideas, whether right or wrong, could be lethal in the wrong hands and powerless in the right ones. Horkheimer was offering Grelling paid work for a forthcoming issue of the journal, '*a collective discussion of around four short printed pages about interesting literature on pragmatism*'. Oppenheim was quoting from Horkheimer's conciliatory letter, which further stressed '*the commonality of the philosophical point of view*' and was also at pains to point out '*the fact that we have repeatedly asked declared opponents to collaborate and, among other things, have published an article by Neurath'.*[16]

In a time of crisis, Horkheimer was trying to do the right thing, and Grelling was known for the breadth of his knowledge. In the event, Oppenheim, perhaps imagining the difficulty Grelling might find in getting hold of the recent literature of American pragmatism in war-threatened Belgium, had suggested an alternative assignment: a review of a new book or a suite of books on positivism that Grelling would be better qualified to assess. Horkheimer had agreed. If the hatchet wasn't exactly buried, the urgency of what they all faced had at least alerted the opposing sides to what they had in common, threatened as they were by those who would shut down any kind of argument with deadly force.

One man who never lost sight of that common purpose was Einstein, of whom Oppenheim had personal news. The great physicist had been associated since 1933 with the Institute for Advanced Study at Princeton University, and it would not be long before the Oppenheims found a house in the city themselves. Paul had known Einstein for almost thirty years. They had met in Brussels in November 1911 at a reception given by Gabrielle's father Paul Errera, the noted Belgian lawyer, at the conclusion of the first Solvay Conference on physics. With other invited luminaries including Marie Curie, Ernest Rutherford and Max Planck, Einstein, already a global figure, was by far the youngest member of the gathering. At the reception held at the Errera home at 14 rue Royale, Paul and Gabrielle, who had only recently married, were charged with handing out the canapés. According to Oppenheim family legend, Errera had pointed out to his daughter and son-in-law the man who had come up with the Special Theory of Relativity: *'"You see that man?"* he said. *"He's very famous. Make sure he gets an extra piece!"'*[17]

The young Oppenheim went up and introduced himself, and the two men hit it off immediately. They remained such good friends that once the Oppenheims had themselves settled in Princeton in late 1939, the pair would meet every Sunday for a walk. In this latest letter to Grelling, Oppenheim writes of Einstein's praise for a book by Bertrand Russell, which he may have been reading in translation: *Perhaps you will be pleased to hear that, as my sister-in-law, who also lives in Princeton, tells me, Einstein is downright enthusiastic about Russell's book, which you translated and which you kindly dedicated to me.*[18]

Oppenheim's brother-in-law, the physicochemist Jacques Errera, had sent his wife Jacqueline and their son Paul to live in Princeton, while at the age of 43 he joined the Belgian army as an officer and was now preparing to defend his country against a likely German invasion. Jacques was also a close friend of Einstein, through the same connection as Oppenheim; a generation later, in 1933, he had participated in the seventh Solvay Conference himself. Of the four works by Russell that Grelling translated during the late 1920s, the book that Oppenheim is most likely referring to was *ABC of Relativity*. It was a small sliver of praise, but Einstein was so revered by everyone that it would certainly have given Grelling something of a boost, which was clearly Oppenheim's intent.

Oppenheim's own relationship with Einstein seems to have been a conversation between equals in which Oppenheim could scarcely believe it was his privilege to take part. On 12 December, he writes to Kurt of another *unforgettable conversation* with Einstein, *based on the letter I sent you on the 24th of last month. Of course, it's difficult to describe the content in just a few words, but I would have liked to have had you there!*[19] And he then does describe in some detail Einstein's opinions on the relationship between terminology and experience, and the nature of quantum mechanics, including what Einstein viewed as Russell's mistaken idea of the subject in contrast to the clarity of Schrödinger. Finally, ever aware of his good fortune in being the confidant of one of the greatest minds in history, and the dangers of misreporting the thoughts of someone whose every word the press was eager to print, Oppenheim ends that section of his letter with a caveat. *It is hardly necessary to add that — simply because of the possibility of inadequate reproduction on my part — E's comments are not intended to be passed on.*[20]

Einstein's delight in Grelling's translation of Russell's book was a nice affirmation of his skill as an interpreter of complex ideas, and Kurt is full of praise for both men. On 14 December, Grelling writes of being *pleased that I have contributed something to making the intellectual relationships between E. and Russell more symmetrical. The fact that R. is a great admirer of E. is well known to him. R. somewhere called E. 'the greatest Jew since Jesus'; unfortunately, I don't remember where that is.*[21]

In truth, for all their reverence, Einstein went to places, intellectually, where neither Grelling nor Oppenheim could follow. One of these was the great man's sympathy for metaphysics (and his scepticism about the positivists' fear of it). Referencing Einstein's support for the pantheistic God — the God in everything — of the seventeenth-century Dutch philosopher Spinoza, Grelling describes this to Oppenheim, diplomatically, as *quite bold; because in my opinion it is the philosophical language that matters.*[22] Given his pedigree as a philosopher, we wouldn't expect him to say anything else. In any case, he disagrees with Einstein's criticism of Russell and suggests a discussion between the two revolutionary heroes of theoretical physics and analytic philosophy had to happen; it just needed someone to set it up.

It was easy for Grelling and his correspondents to become absorbed in their world within a world; it was the normal life that each of us inhabits. But events in the outer world could not be ignored. Writing on 11 November, Grelling was clearly worried by the pressure that was starting to build. *At the moment*, he writes, *the political–military situation here is viewed as very serious. There is great anticipation of Hitler's invasion of Holland and a subsequent attack on Belgium. Long before this letter is in your hands, you will know for sure what has become of it. But, in any case, you can make even fewer decisions at present than in recent times.*[23]

Under the circumstances, it's not surprising that Grelling's health was beginning to suffer. The illness that afflicted him at this juncture involved the kind of perceptual distortions beloved of modernist writers, as metaphors for existential distress. But the symptoms he experienced in fact seem like a normal physical reaction to the kind of assault on the person which, as a Jew, he had had to endure for years. *Attacks of dizziness have started again, like I had for a while last year*, he writes. *Dr Hirsch, the person treating me, calls it 'Menier's symptom complex'*[24] *(I don't know if I'm spelling that correctly). It also appears that its treatment has been successful; but as a result, recently, my ability to work has been quite a bit reduced.*[25]

Greta was still in Switzerland, convalescing after catching the flu when returning the children to their boarding school at the end of October. There seemed no way that she would be able to visit him in Belgium now that war had broken out, notwithstanding that any war in the west was in abeyance and Belgium was still insisting it was neutral. But the frustrations were legion, and in the same letter Grelling is unable to stop himself from venting them again at his benefactor. *What I wrote 2 months ago has now only been confirmed. In addition to you, as you probably don't know, a number of other rich fellow race members have travelled from here to the USA. They are sometimes envied by those who remain here, and sometimes morally condemned, more or less violently depending on their level of personal honesty and tolerance. I have heard very little about the views of Belgian Christians on this matter. Maria M. can certainly provide better information about that. In this context, you may be interested to know that Louis shed tears when you left, and that – if his statements are to be believed – he feels nothing but pity towards you both. I'm no expert on human nature; but I have the impression that L., despite all his business skills, is a loyal soul.*[26]

It was all too raw. Louis is just a first name, referred to in the letters a handful of times, with few other qualities attributed to him beyond his skills in business and the utility of his apparent reaction to Oppenheim's departure in conveying something of the anger that Grelling couldn't bring himself to personally express. The deployment of the word *loyal* seems especially loaded with hurt. Maria M. was Maria Mussafia, who may have moved to Brussels from Vienna (Mussafia is a Viennese Jewish surname). She later became a nun, though it is anyone's guess as to why. She seems to have been a central figure in the German-speaking Jewish circle in Brussels to which Oppenheim and Grelling belonged. Kurt knew her well enough to talk on the phone. His account of one exchange they had gives a glimpse of the handsome Young Turk that he may once have felt himself to be, someone who was enlivened by female company, perhaps with a fair amount of charm himself. *Maria*, he writes, *with whom I just had a telephone conversation, sends you a heartfelt kiss (unfortunately she didn't give it to me herself to pass on).*[27] It is certainly surprising that for someone as shy as Felix Oppenheim believed he was, Kurt had rather a lot of friends.

Oppenheim had ignored Kurt's earlier barbed remarks, but in the next extant letter, dated 12 December, he feels obliged to defend himself against the critical judgements in Grelling's of the previous month. *In the absence of evidence to the contrary*, he writes, *I suspect that each of the critics would have travelled to the USA under similar circumstances. But I don't assume that anyone, for reasons of conscience, would have wavered before the trip and then constantly tormented themselves like I did after arriving.*[28]

It's a rare moment of personal revelation for a man who was normally so reserved. It was clearly intolerable to be looked on with scorn for a decision that almost anyone would have made, given the chance, and most with fewer misgivings than he had. But there was no way to avoid the guilt he felt at the fortune that enabled him to leave. His *fellow race members* were in the same mortal danger that he had escaped and for reasons of race that could not be denied, whether or not they were grounded in science. So, Oppenheim's response to Grelling's reference to *fellow race members* is to broach the subject of race science, which had been forced to the forefront of the minds of secular Jewish scientists and intellectuals like themselves. After suggesting, pointedly, that Grelling may find it easier than he does to divide people into races, Oppenheim writes that he has been speaking to Franz Weidenreich, a German-Jewish anatomist and a leading authority in the field of evolutionary theory. Weidenreich had recently arrived in America from China, having fled Nazism in 1935 to take a position in the Chinese capital, then known as Peking. He was now at the Museum of Natural History in New York City.[29] Oppenheim had asked Weidenreich about the anthropologist Heinrich Poll, whose opinion was *that a correlation can be found between belonging to Judaism and certain characteristics of fingerprints.*

Oppenheim recounts that *W. strongly denies that such a correlation exists and accuses Poll of methodological errors.*[30]

Heinrich Poll was a leading German-Jewish advocate of eugenics during the Weimar years, and in that soon-to-be-uncomfortable combination of scientific expertise and ethnic background he was not unique in Germany. Poll had been a founder member of the national Committee for Racial Hygiene; another member, Richard Goldschmidt, was also Jewish. The committee was set up in 1920, at the start of the Weimar period, to examine the effects of the losses of the war on the demographic make-up of the German population, along with other aspects of what they regarded as racial public health. These discussions, which included the potential sterilisation of people diagnosed with hereditary diseases or psychiatric conditions, formed the background to the later development of Nazi social policy. So, the scientific codification of race-based ideas of human value had roots in attitudes and practices that long pre-dated the Nazi era and were widespread across the advanced Western world, including America and the United Kingdom. In Weimar Germany, there were different factions within the field, with the more socially progressive – those who felt the discipline could be used to improve society, no matter how misguided those ideas now seem – being represented by the likes of Poll and the Committee for Racial Hygiene. The other faction, explicitly racist, was closely connected with the rising National Socialist movement, whose political success would see the darkest interpretation of scientific facts, which even then were doubtful, become official government policy.

By the end of the decade, a poisonous stream of Nazi propaganda bearing the imprimatur of science had polluted even some of the strongest minds. In a letter of 1 January 1940 Grelling responded to Oppenheim's observation with a dark hypothesis that speaks to the self-conscious burden that he, like every Jew, was having to carry. *On the racial problem: What you report from Weidenreich is certainly very interesting. Of course, I cannot assess the scientific reliability of Poll's investigations. But I would like to suggest to you a thought experiment in this context: You have a gathering of 1,000 residents of Frankfurt in front of you. Among them are 100 Jews as defined by the Nuremburg Laws. Now select the 100 from the 1,000 who, according to your impression, look the most 'Jewish' (to an experienced observer). On the other hand, let 100 be chosen by lot. In the last group there will probably be 10 Jews. How many do you think there will be in the first 100? I estimate at least 90. If for you the outcome is as certain as it is for me, you have to admit that within the German population the Jews are statistically distinguished by certain anatomical features. That doesn't change even if Poll's claim about a special such feature turns out to be insufficiently justified. I certainly do not claim that Jews form a pure race, nor that there are biological characteristics that every Jew and no non-Jew possesses; but only that between the characteristic 'Jew in the sense of the Nuremberg Laws' and certain physiognomic, anatomical, characterological features that are difficult to define but are well known to both of us, there is what is called a positive correlation in statistics, etc., [...]. I would be interested to know whether Mr Weidenreich disputes this.*[31]

This dogged pursuit of a topic, with its distressing fantasy of racial selection, is typical of Grelling's insistent mind, determined to apply logic dispassionately to such evidence as there was, regardless of the motives of those who had gathered it. It was perhaps an old habit of many generations, to try to adjust even to the most hostile conditions; though there was always the fear that it would not be enough, as the chilling prophecy of his imagined gathering seems to portend. But to reject the entire model of the science of race without empirical evidence that it was bogus would have meant the cutting of a Gordian knot, an act of intellectual dishonesty, an unthinkably brutal action for someone as scrupulous as Grelling. After all, it was inconceivable that something calling itself a science could be so fundamentally wrong. So, with no tools to fight back, and no alternative strategy, Grelling seems here to embrace precisely those superficial and debatable aspects of Jewishness with which the Nazis had made Jews the figures of general contempt; to assimilate himself by the means he knew best, logic and science, to these supposedly indicative measures of Jewish particularity; to accept what were meant by the Nazis as markers of shame not even as badges of pride but as matters of fact.

Though they don't remark on it, by the time that Oppenheim and Grelling took to discussing his ideas, Heinrich Poll was dead. Originally from Berlin, in 1922 he had been appointed the first Professor for Human Heredity at Berlin University, before being called a mere two years later to the Chair in Anatomy at the University of Hamburg. But in September 1933, after months of mounting attacks within the university by newly emboldened Nazi-supporting students, and in the absence of a defence from anyone in the faculty, Poll was dismissed from his post by virtue of the very science whose pedigree he had helped to establish. Now retired with a pension that was barely enough to get by on, Poll and his wife Clara, a non-Jew, moved back to Berlin. There, for several years, he lived the same existence of private research and growing despondency as Grelling and Hans Sachs and so many other brilliant Jewish thinkers who'd been forced from their jobs. In 1939, he decided to emigrate to Sweden, gaining permission for that purpose from the Nazi authorities, under certain strict conditions. At the beginning of June, he finally got the go-ahead to leave. But an administrative error, which may not have been entirely accidental, meant that Clara would have to wait behind until her own papers had been issued correctly. So, Poll went alone to Sweden, settling in the city of Lund, awaiting his wife's arrival. The heart attack that killed him, quite suddenly, happened just days later, in the apartment he had rented for the two of them. On hearing the news, Clara was granted special permission to attend his funeral in Sweden, before having to go back to Germany. Once the original paperwork had finally been cleared, at the start of August she travelled again to Sweden, with permission to emigrate to the country. Having made it to a meaningless security, it was there on the 5th that, on the evening of what would have been her husband's 62nd birthday, she brought her own life to an end.

Presumably, news of what had happened to Poll and his wife had not yet reached either Grelling or Oppenheim by the end of the year. It was a small tragedy among so many larger ones, not all of them connected with the Nazi threat. Less than a week after Oppenheim's letter, the Soviet Union invaded Finland. Neurath and Grelling had worried in the run-up to the start of the Winter War about their Finnish colleagues Uuno Saarnio and Eino Kaila, the leading proponents in Finland of both logical empiricism and Gestalt psychology. Now, the invasion was yet further evidence that the world in which to differing degrees they had all prospered, a world where connections between colleagues in so many countries had been easy and fruitful, was falling apart. As Grelling put it in a letter to Neurath dated 1 December, the day after the Soviet invasion, *In Europe one cultural centre after another is collapsing.*[32]

The journey across eastern Finland that Else and Marion, as Jewish Germans, had made so freely just ten years earlier had now become impossible for anyone.

MANY PEOPLE ARE DISAPPEARING FROM BRUSSELS

As Christmas approached, Grelling was in the mood for another visit to The Hague. To that end he and Neurath took steps to meet new rules of entry that were even more onerous than before. As Neurath framed it in his letter of 12 December 1939, they had to find a plausible reason connected with the professional activity of the Mundaneum Institute for any permit to have a chance of being granted, even for a three-day trip. *Maybe you can write to me formally that you want to come to our business meetings about publications, lectures, etc. I will then immediately try to get permission for you to visit; please let me know that you have the right to return, etc. Yes, now everything is understandably very difficult. A horrible time.*[1]

In his reply of the 15th, Grelling confirmed that he had the so-called white card, a residency permit, valid in his case until 10 February 1940, which allowed him to travel to and from Belgium. He also had a valid German passport and, in a second letter of the same date, with which the first was included, he is defiant about the obstacles he now faced. *Enclosed is the requested formal letter*, he writes. *I didn't explicitly mention that I have a 'J' in my passport. If asked, you can say that I do have that 'mark of intelligence'.*[2]

This awareness of the reason for the new restrictions was never far from their minds. But life in Brussels was lonelier than ever, so the physical fellowship of a colleague and friend was something to grab with both hands, no matter the challenges it brought. Far more difficult was keeping contact with his family. On 4 December, he wrote to Oppenheim that Greta had applied for a Belgian visa for fourteen days, *on the grounds that she had urgent financial matters to discuss with me. It seems that someone gave her this tip. Economic interests are apparently considered preferable to 'sentimental' ones by all authorities.*[3]

But, as he outlines in the next letter, from the 14th, it would never be quite that simple. *My wife was summoned again to the Gestapo [...]; the earlier advice they had given her to divorce me was obviously repeated in a very urgent form. It seems that, this time, nothing can be done about it. Attorney Külz, whom she consulted, apparently couldn't tell her a way out either. My wife's wish to speak to me is understandably all the stronger under these circumstances. Unfortunately, there seems to be no possibility that it will be fulfilled. Miss Blitz, who received me last week and was very kind, tells me today that the Sureté has rejected her attempt to intervene. She was told that at the moment no visas would be issued at all. Under these circumstances I currently see no possibility of achieving our goal. The divorce itself scares neither of us all that much, as it can't change our relationship. But one doesn't know what other bad consequences could result from this. I am particularly concerned about the fate of my children. I met for advice with Dr Herrmann, who gave me information in a very nice manner. But, of course, he can't offer me any way out. I only received the message from Miss Blitz an hour ago. It won't surprise you that it doesn't have a particularly positive effect on my well-being, which has been very good for the past fortnight.*[4]

With Christmas almost upon them, it was clear that Grelling would not be together with Greta and the children. He was spending time instead with Oppenheim's eldest son, Felix, helping him with his PhD thesis whenever the young artillery officer was home on leave. In the same letter, he thanks Oppenheim for the unexpected gift from Felix of three neckties, one each for *Nikolaustag*, Christmas and New Year. These staples of the German calendar were important to remember, and the community of exiles in Brussels also did their best to support each other through the holiday period. In his letter of 12 December, Oppenheim responded to the kiss from Maria Mussafia that Grelling had written about in an earlier letter. Lamenting that, *for technical reasons*, he was not able to give Kurt a kiss that he could then return directly, he hoped that Grelling would act on his behalf in this regard. In the event, Kurt seems to have needed no encouragement in rising to the challenge. As he writes on New Year's Day 1940, *I have now conveyed the kiss for Maria M. orally. (I always like to carry out such orders myself.) I hope that I have served everyone involved well, last but not least myself. I was at the Mussafias on Christmas Day with the Roufards, the Waldecks, a sister of Mrs Roufard and another young girl. Even though you two and my family were missing, it was still a lovely Christmas Eve. Maria had once again made a great and successful effort to delight us, among other things with a truly Viennese meal.*

Kurt in tank top and tie smiling, Berlin, 1936. (© Kurt Grelling Archive)

For my part, I tried not to let your two friends feel your absence too much. They will have to tell you whether these efforts were successful. (What can I put into my expense account for this?) On the 26th I was invited to Goldschmidt's, where I also had a very good time. Both of your ears must have been burning on those days. We spoke about you a lot. Mr. G. was very interested in our work together (or at least acted as if he was). I tried to give him an idea by explaining to him the topic of our Gestalt essay. He seems to understand it quite well.[5]

In the same letter, Grelling thanked Oppenheim for sending Greta *the gift of life*, as he puts it – a parcel of food that had made it to Berlin just days before Christmas. Grelling's form of words is a clear indication of how bad things were, but it also shows how much his wife was willing to endure so as not to succumb to the pressure to make her own life easier by divorcing him. It was pressure that came from the Gestapo and also, as later became clear, from members of the Berger family, her own family, who lived in the city. But, in other respects, things were looking brighter. *My wife's affairs have not developed unfavourably in the meantime*, he goes on. *On the one hand, a Gestapo officer came on 18 December to tell her that* the Gestapo was not insisting on a divorce. Perhaps this is due to an intervention by Attorney Külz, whom she had consulted. As Mr Engel, who recommended him to me, told me, K. ought to have good relations with the Gestapo. Nevertheless, I continue to push for my wife's entry into Belgium so as to have my family with me during this time – because you never know whether the Gestapo will again think of something worse.[6]

At the same time, Felix was exploiting his father's connections at the upper echelons of the Belgian government, helping Grelling to push the merits of his wife's case. A Monsieur Vermeylen[7] sent a memorandum to the minister of justice and also arranged for an interview to take place with Robert de Foy, the director of the Sureté; this was scheduled for 3 January. Grelling believed that it would represent a crucial opportunity to get Greta into the country. But two days later, in a long postscript dated the 3rd, his hopes were being thwarted by the closed mind of the Belgian state. *M. de Foy did not receive me personally*, he writes, *but had me checked in by another official. [This man] wrote everything down and promised me that I would receive a message, but my hopes are not very high after this. When I responded to the usual comment (that there were already so many foreigners here) that I couldn't see how anyone in Belgium could be harmed by the presence of my family ('except you, of course'), the gentleman said: yes, but when the children grow up, they will want to work here! I simply replied that after the war everything would probably be different anyway, and as a result there was no need to worry about it for too long. But, in reality, I found the gentleman's objection grotesque. If you take the stupid position that everyone who wants to work is an annoying competitor, then you have to take into account that my children would be consumers for at least 8 or 10 years before they could work here. As long as people keep sticking to this stupid protectionist attitude, the world cannot be made healthy.*[8]

The exchange has an all-too-familiar ring to it, but in the event, the outcome was better than Kurt had feared. On 12 January, he wrote to Oppenheim with surprising news: *M. Vermeylen has just called to inform me that the Belgian embassy in Berlin has been instructed to issue my wife a three-month visa,* pour établissement provisoire,[9] *after completing certain formalities. So, this goal has been achieved with the help of Felix and M. Vermeylen. Now it's important that the Gestapo lets my wife out. That is by no means certain.*[10]

And then, on 6 February, with as much trepidation as joy, Grelling declares: *My wife has been here since 1/2. She received – quite improbably – an exit visa from the German police, valid until 20th February. Due to the Belgian authorisation,* l'établissement provisoire, *she has been entered on the list here and will receive her white card in the coming days. We are not yet entirely sure what will happen next. If she returned on the 20th, she could theoretically emigrate*

Kurt and Greta in Brussels, March 1940.
(© Kurt Grelling Archive)

legally from G., taking at least her personal clothes with her (this time naturally she could bring only a little with her). But no one in Berlin could say whether this possibility would actually become a reality. She could also stay in G., but then she would have to divorce me, because I would be expatriated and my wife would lose her assets and pension. In the event of a divorce, it is to be expected that she would be completely cut off from me, and either her from the children or I from them, for the remainder of the war. 3rd option: My wife stays here and we let the children come here too. All three procedures are fraught with dangers and difficulties, and you can easily imagine how hard it is for us to choose between them. The fact that my situation is very uncertain also plays a big role. Since you have terminated our contract, I cannot foresee today what my circumstances will be after 25 August. My wife is in very poor physical and mental health. It's no wonder given the hardships and excitement she is subjected to. Fortunately, she has already recovered here somewhat.[11]

The contract termination, when it came, was not unexpected. It was carried out, with a six-month notice period, by Oppenheim's attorney, a Mr Peffer. At the same time, on 1 February, Oppenheim confirmed the ending of the contract in a letter of great warmth that extolled their work and friendship. *I feel compelled to take this opportunity to tell you again what happiness it brings me in these unfortunate circumstances to have found in you a colleague with whom I get on so well, both personally and objectively. The non-contractual situation that we are approaching with this termination, and which existed and still exists between Hempel and me, is basically better suited to the harmony that exists between us.*[12]

It can't have been an easy decision for Oppenheim to make. Perhaps surprisingly, given the financial security he stood to lose, Grelling took the news on the chin, though with understandable concerns about what their working relationship would be from then on, as he wrote in the letter of the 6th. *According to information from Mr Peffer, I have to expect that you will maintain your notice of termination, which cannot take effect until 25th February at the earliest. Nevertheless, based on your statements so far, I assume that you desire to continue working with me after 25th August, if conditions allow. If this assumption of mine is correct, I would ask you now to say something about the conditions under which you envisage this further cooperation. Of course, I am aware that events may occur between now and then which throw all such agreements out of the window. But apparently it is primarily me who is in danger of being prevented from either doing academic work at all or from writing to you. In such a case, you are already covered by our existing contract. If I can work scientifically at all, I think I will be able to continue working on our book for quite a long time, even without corresponding with you. But there is no need for me to justify how extremely valuable it would be to know soon whether and under what conditions you want to continue working with me.*[13]

Any kind of certainty would have done, but even Oppenheim couldn't offer that. At the same time, Neurath was trying to complete the paperwork for Grelling to come again to The Hague. *I went to the immigration police today. For a long time, there have been regulations that, in a case like yours (I was immediately asked whether you were an emigrant), a visa must be requested from the consul in Brussels. They then ask again here. So, I'm enclosing a letter of invitation to you and I hope that everything works out, even if it's difficult. I was immediately asked about the 'urgency'. They would have preferred it if, for example, someone had died or something like that – I would hope that a birth or a wedding would be good and not just something sad.*[14]

Later in the same letter, in referring to his own state of mind, Neurath reiterates his crisis theory of cultural production. *I'm doing relatively very well. Reading, writing, thinking, listening to music, playing chess – whatever cultural opium one has at one's disposal. If I were Dante, I would write poetry and have* all the people who annoy me roasted in hell for future generations. Let us imagine that Dante had not been banished. He would be an intelligent Florentine official with poetic inclinations.[15]

This was clearly a view, and a situation, that further encouraged this highly motivated man. But men like Dante or Neurath are always rare, and Grelling had more immediate concerns. As he wrote to Oppenheim in the letter of 6 February, *On your and others' advice, I reported to the American consulate general. I'm now on a list there. Normally my turn wouldn't come until several years hence. But, in the event, I think it is possible that I could get a non-quota visa if I can prove that I have a secure academic position. Maybe now that you are there, together with Hempel, you can achieve something for me in this regard.*[16]

It was both a challenge and a plea to his friends in America, with almost nothing he could do from Brussels. In the meantime, Greta had made up her mind that she would not be returning to Germany. As Grelling wrote to Oppenheim on 2 March: *After carefully considering the pros and cons, my wife stayed here. [...] We are trying to get back as many of her personal belongings and our furnishings as quickly as possible. But at the moment we don't know anything in this regard. My wife, who has been here for 4 weeks now, has already recovered well. Yesterday I received permission for the children to enter the country. Now we need a French transit visa for them. We hope to have them here by the beginning of April. We will probably stay in the rooms we are renting until the end of March. Then we want to get an apartment.*[17]

In that regard, a sudden death had changed their immediate prospects. *The good Mrs Grossman unexpectedly followed her husband in death on 27th February. She had the flu for 10 days, accompanied by pneumonia. Unfortunately, we only found out about her illness when she was already dead. She had just had a secretarial position for a few weeks with a Dutch-Jewish scholar living here (Dr Prins), which seemed to satisfy her. [...] On 29th February we buried her in the cemetery of Uccle, near her husband. [...] Especially since G.'s death, we had seen each other often and were actually even closer friends. Because my wife arrived and Mrs. G. was very busy with Dr Prins, I no longer looked after her as much as before and, of course, I'm particularly sorry about that now. She was always ready to help others, but she apparently took only inadequate care of herself. In any case, she did not suffer from any shortage, because almost a third of the money collected by Dr Goldfinger was still left.*

It is possible that this very sad event will help to ease our current situation, the Grelling family. In fact, we'll probably rent the Grossmans' furniture until we get our own. With a few additions, perhaps from Hempel's holdings which are still for sale here, we will probably get by. That way we can choose a suitable apartment from the large number of empty ones. Furnished ones are rare and not very cheap.[18]

Oppenheim's next letter, from the 13th, is full of praise for Grelling's spirit. *Of course, we are all extremely excited to hear the decision you have come to and understand how incredibly difficult it is to weigh up the alternatives, some of which are so incommensurable. Perhaps it is reassuring for everyone involved to remember how large the chance component is in every decision, no matter how well thought out. There is a very great temptation to discuss the pros and cons of the various options. On the other hand, this is a very big responsibility. The fact that your decision will have long been made by the time these lines arrive relieves me of this dilemma. In any case, I hope that you both got through the excitement that inevitably comes with such considerations. As far as you are concerned, you undoubtedly have excellent resilience; because it is astonishing how 'witty' and 'astute' the scientific explanations are that you have sent again this time, which, as I have often done, I will first address together with H. at the end of this letter.*[19]

Oppenheim was working hard to be encouraging, knowing that keeping up his friend's morale was a gift as valuable as money. But he also offered a realistic assessment of Grelling's prospects in America, based on Hempel's personal experience. *He sees no prospect of you getting an academic position of the aforementioned kind as long as you are not in the USA. But even if this were a prospect, as far as we know it would not help you to get a non-quota visa, because you cannot provide evidence of at least 2 years of teaching at a university. But perhaps it is worth the effort to inquire in Antwerp to see if you might be [eligible], on the grounds that you can receive a non-quota visa for your activity at the* Gymnasium, *if you teach the same subjects at a local college. By the way, it could be that a quota visa can be obtained much faster than 'in several years'. I just remind you of the surprising speed with which Ernst Goldschmidt and his wife, from Brussels, received their visas, apparently because they were moved up into vacant quota numbers. And I hear of many such cases. In any case, please keep me promptly informed about your plans for America, and in particular whether an affidavit is required and, if so, for how long and in what number. If you have the feeling that you cannot achieve your goal at the American consulate general in any other way, please ask Felix if he can ask my brother-in-law to recommend an introduction for you to the American consul general in Antwerp [...]. It might also be worth considering that we can get you letters from here for the consul general, showing the cultural gain it would be for the USA if you immigrated.*[20]

Oppenheim was going out of his way to demonstrate that he would not abandon his friend and colleague; in a supplement he details exhaustively the ways in which a commitment to Kurt and his family could continue for as long as he can afford it. But he also raises the prospect that the value of his financial resources that remained in Belgium could decline rapidly, to the extent that help for Grelling would no longer be possible, especially when Felix still needed them. As Oppenheim puts it in the same addendum, dated 12 March, *one can't make provisions for every possibility, especially in these times. And I have to say that when we made our current agreement, we thought about possibilities that seemed quite remote to us at the time, which nevertheless came about almost exactly as we did foresee in principle – even if not the specific form* [they took]*: you will remember that we had provided for an exceptionally long period of time within which the agreement could be terminated in order to cover a case like the current one.*[21]

It was no consolation that they had foreseen the outbreak of war. What now seems inevitable would have been a plausible hypothesis at the end of 1938, when the contract was drawn up, despite the Munich agreement supposedly having drawn a line under Hitler's territorial claims. But hypothesis was all it had been. In any case, the prospect of another war would have been too distressing to examine directly for men who knew from experience what a war of that magnitude would mean and whose philosophical outlook was in some ways a refusal of that prospect.

By the beginning of April 1940, any optimism was getting harder to maintain. Kurt spells out the difficulties that now faced anyone in a position like his: *Non-quota visa: In my letter to the consulate general in Antwerp, in which I sent in the form I filled out, I also pointed to the fact that I worked as a 'college professor'*[22] *in Germany until 1933. I further quoted Russell's letter of recommendation and wrote: 'If necessary, I could easily get similar recommendations from several university professors in the USA. So, I am pretty sure that once there I will soon become a professor of some college or university.'*[23] *(I hardly need point out that I see this as a gross exaggeration.) I wrote all of this to justify the sentence: 'Perhaps I could get non-quota status.'*[24] *The only answer I received was the pre-printed letter in which I was informed that I had been placed on the German quota waiting list on 24th January 1940 and would have to wait several years. The letter is signed by the consul, L'Heureux. Based on this result and reports from friends, I very much doubt whether there is anything I can do with non-quota. If at all, it is probably only on the basis of personal recommendations and also letters like the ones you mention in the penultimate sentence. One without the other would probably be pointless.*

By the way, I don't know how to think that if my previous teaching activity plays a role at all, it is essential that I teach precisely the subjects I taught in German schools. I don't care much about that, although of course I wouldn't refuse if such an activity were offered to me. The fact that unfortunately the 'cultural gain' sometimes does not cause the American immigration authorities to interpret their laws broadly is shown by the case of the Viennese Dr Loewy, a world-famous hydraulic engineer, so I am told, who has the best recommendations from American experts and associations, and who still had to wait here for 1 year in very straitened circumstances for his number to come up. Now he has finally left with his family. One cannot conclude from this that the same would happen to me. But this and other similar cases are a warning against optimism in this regard.[25]

Grelling's account of the case of Dr Loewy may have been hearsay; he suggests as much himself. There were indeed two Jewish brothers called Loewy, Ludwig and Erwin, both renowned hydraulic engineers. But they were Czech, and Ludwig, having emigrated to the UK in 1936, by 1940 was heavily involved in the war effort against Nazism; Erwin had gone to France and, then, at the last minute in June 1940, escaped overseas, most likely to England or Ireland, before emigrating in November to the USA.[26] Neither of the brothers seems to have gone through Belgium, but in any case, even if the Loewys had not been among those who succeeded via the Belgian route, there were others whose numbers did come up, though not everyone was thrilled at their luck. Their fortunes suddenly transformed by the stroke of a diplomat's pen, for some the thought of being uprooted again was too much to take in. *You write that the Ernst Goldschmidt family unexpectedly received their visa. Maybe that's the reason I haven't heard from him since mid-January, when I met him at a concert. Many people are disappearing from Brussels. When I recently called Dr Herrmann, I found out that he had left for Palestine with the whole family a few days earlier. Dr Caro [and family], from whom I am supposed to send you greetings, also have their visa, but have not yet been able to decide to leave Brussels. You can now hear from many people that they feel so comfortable here, they don't want to move again to an uncertain foreign country.*[27]

What Kurt and now Greta were holding on to wasn't comfort, but some kind of faith in the future, though sources of hope were thin on the ground. In the same letter of 2 April, he is almost defenceless about the extent to which they now looked to Oppenheim for help. *We, my wife and I, have absolute confidence that you will not let us down. However, this does not mean that I expect you to provide for me or possibly my family until the end of our lives. Rather, I have confidence that you will give me the opportunity to work with you in the same way as before, for as long as circumstances allow and I depend on it. It goes without saying that, on the other hand, only with your consent would I take up an activity that would prevent me from continuing to work with you.*[28]

At the same time, on the basis that they wouldn't be going anywhere soon, he was thinking about the future in Brussels. *I intend to ask Alfred Errera to arrange for me to be given a course on the fundamentals of mathematics* (or similar) next year at the Institut des Hautes Études. I can probably assume that you have no objections.²⁹ Alfred Errera was a mathematician, a professor at the Free University of Brussels, so Kurt was clearly planning to be there with Greta for some time to come. It was out of the question that either one of them would ever dream of going back to Germany, a reality that a week later, on 9 April, the German invasion of Denmark and Norway would have only confirmed. A week after that, in a letter to Oppenheim dated 16 April, he treats the threat that they would soon have their citizenship removed with a grim sense of humour for which his own line of work supplied the jokes. *Dr Hirsch found out a few days ago about his own expatriation,* he writes. *No one has yet been able to discover a law that would determine the order of expatriations. Maybe von Mises can calculate the probability of this happening to me in the next two months. It appears to work by quantum leaps. Maybe in the specific office of the department in Berlin they are drawing lots. Be that as it may, removing our citizenship would affect us in a very unpleasant way. But even in this situation, we cannot do anything but wait.*³⁰

By the middle of March, it had become clear that a visit to Neurath in The Hague was now impossible. In a letter of the 22nd, Neurath had expressed his own disappointment. But his natural optimism was not only undimmed, it was fortified by the hardship they faced. It was enough for Neurath to be aware of the world around him. From that basic condition a new beginning would always be possible, as he could see just by looking out of the window. *It's spring here,* he writes; *there are flowers (and sales of these have increased a lot since the start of the war — one reads, a lot!) and sunshine. Beautiful music is independent of the weather and world affairs, as is the behaviour of Dutch friends.*³¹

When he wrote again a month later, on 20 April, Neurath was even more bullish in the face of what was coming. *We have just been put under curfew across the entire country, after a really very reassuring speech by the prime minister. Think how peaceful and quiet it is to work here. When the Inquisition ruled in Spain and wars were waged, Cervantes, Lope de Vega, Calderón de la Barca, etc. were still at work. When they weren't working as slaves in North Africa, or waging war, or too busy with their priestly profession, they were busy writing. [...] And around the corner, Jews and heretics and the like were being condemned or 'interrogated' using the harsher Socratic method. And even that we can endure if we survive it.*³²

Neurath was certainly a great survivor, and perhaps for this reason his view of history, informed by wide reading and his own remarkable life, seems quite cavalier. He imagined that the current persecutions, and those to come, would resemble the trials that Jews had always suffered. Even to him, the great visionary with no illusions about human nature, some things were inconceivable. And what you could conceive of, you could always fight. Hearing about the review that Grelling had been commissioned to write for Horkheimer's journal – he'd been given just four pages and felt he needed more – was enough to get Neurath's blood up, conflating the critical theorist's attacks on positivism and unified science with the dire political situation in the world outside. Given the circumstances, he needed someone he could aim at, a reason to assert his creed. *We work through CONSTRUCTION*, he insists, *by showing what we can do*.[33] It was a practical mantra that distinguished the positivist project, as he conceived it, from what he saw as the attempts of the negativists to cast their opponents as holy fools beside the forces that were trying to destroy them. *Whether you write a lot or a little will not change the attitude of the Horkheimerites*, he goes on, *which is not only critical but also makes all kinds of insinuations, with the help of half-hidden statements. Oh, you know the melody – the lyrics change. Sometimes they are more theologically oriented people, this time they are [...] into dialectics – I just don't know exactly which one. [...] Fortunately, this has little influence on our work.*[34]

But Neurath could see as clearly as the critical theorists exactly where things were heading, and there was nothing he could do to change it. *World situation is depressing. Everything like in a game of poker. What to do? If the sky falls, we will all get blue night caps – but if not, we will continue to discuss protocol theorems, physicalism, unified science.*[35]

It was a waiting game for soldier and civilian alike. At this point, Felix Oppenheim had been serving with his artillery unit for more than a year, shuttling between his barracks, the Caserne Major Géruzet[36] in the Etterbeek district of Brussels, and, until 1 January 1940, when the lease expired, his parents' rented house at 21 avenue Victoria. In his unpublished memoir, written half a century later, he describes the outdated thinking of the instructors who oversaw his basic training. They were still wedded to the static battlefronts of the last war when it was already common knowledge, even among the recruits, that the Germans had highly mobile tank divisions that would soon make mincemeat of the Belgian defensive plans. By early May, the Belgian artillery had moved north to within a few miles of the supposedly impregnable Albert Canal, running south of the Dutch border. The French Army, some 2 million strong, was right behind them, strung out along the border with France; to their right the Maginot Line, while overhead flew squadrons of RAF Hurricanes, ready to defend them all. Despite the inadequate planning of the Belgian high command, sheer numbers alone gave good reasons to be confident. Then, in the early hours of 10 May, the German divisions, which had massed along the border to the west, struck suddenly. Parachutists dropping from the sky had quickly snuffed out the Belgian plan to blow up the bridges spanning the Albert Canal. The poorly armed Belgian troops of the artillery brigade in which Felix was serving were quickly overwhelmed and taken prisoner.

On the day of the invasion, 10 May, officers of the Belgian police came to the guesthouse at 33 avenue Legrand, where the Grellings were renting rooms. All the citizens of Hitler's Greater Germany who'd found refuge in the country were now enemy aliens. Grelling was arrested without time to gather up any clothes or belongings or even to say goodbye to his wife. Most likely, he was taken to the same barracks where, so recently, Felix had done his basic training, and where hundreds of men with a German passport, most of them Jewish, had now been interned.

FRANCE

THE CAMP ON THE BEACH

The defeat of Belgium and the Netherlands in May 1940 was followed a month later by the fall of France. Western Europe was plunged into chaos, as millions fled the German onslaught. Otto Neurath and his partner escaped, with immense good fortune, on the last boat that left The Hague on the night of 14 May, after neighbouring Rotterdam had been destroyed by bombing and Dutch surrender seemed inevitable.

At the same moment Kurt Grelling was already in France. The round-ups of the 10th and the following few days had taken place all over Belgium. To extend their stay beyond fourteen days, every foreigner entering the country over the previous few years had had to register for a permit of residence within forty-eight hours of arriving. In January 1940, when the Belgian authorities learned of Hitler's intention to invade, they drew up plans for the mass arrest of all those Greater German nationals – Germans, Austrians and, most recently, Czechs, mostly of Jewish background – whose status when this happened would change instantly to that of enemy aliens. It didn't matter that almost every one of them had had to flee the regime with which they were now suspected of colluding.

Working from lists of names and addresses gleaned from a census conducted the previous autumn, the police carried out arrests with a speed and efficiency that the Belgian Army could have learned from. Within hours, thousands had been detained. In Antwerp and in Brussels, they were helped in this task by the foreigners, and especially the foreign Jews, having gathered in certain areas of the city. It's clear from the letters of Grelling and his colleagues that, in the absence of other kinds of aid, such close proximity made it easier to support each other. Those who weren't picked up at home were plucked off the streets – men, women and children – and interned in the nearest barracks, sleeping on any surface they could find. They wouldn't be there for long, though in many cases that was long enough for the Belgian police to strip them of the documents they would later need to have any chance of escape: residence permits, passports, precious visas for travel to countries like the USA. The women and children were soon released, but, beginning on 12 May, the men were loaded onto lorries and taken to the Gare du Midi. From there, the first of as many as ten long trains of cattle trucks, at least fifteen per train, began heading south. Grelling could not have known where the convoys were going because the Belgian reservists, or *gardes mobiles*, who went with them would not have known it themselves. An agreement had been drawn up between the Belgian and French governments – it may well have involved some financial exchange – that, in the event of a German invasion, Belgium's enemy aliens would be sent into France to be interned. The arrangement was so secret that there is almost no evidence of its existence.[1] But one document does make clear that this mass movement of people by train had been authorised in advance at a very high level. It was allowed to go ahead even then, taking up space in the schedule of departures and arrivals when half the population of northern France was fleeing in the same direction by any mode of transport they could find.

Despite the German panzer divisions advancing rapidly just a few dozen miles to the north, the convoys all seem to have stopped at least one night in the city of Tournai in the south of Belgium, where the prisoners were herded into another barracks. The following morning, they crossed the border into France, locked in their trucks in the stifling heat of late spring, crammed together without food or water and just a single bucket for the pissing and shitting of as many as forty men. The prisoners on board were casually abused by the *gardes mobiles*. Some were shot without reason while others died on account of the terrible conditions they endured. Often, let out of the wagons and coming into contact with Frenchmen distraught at the prospect of imminent defeat, the prisoners were attacked by angry mobs who took them for spies. In some cases, entire wagons were looted by the *gardes mobiles* who, often drunk, stole whatever they could grab from rich and poor alike. At transit camps where they stopped along the route, the prisoners were still at the mercy of the *gardes*, but also ordinary officers of the French police and regular soldiers, including commissioned officers, any of whom might decide to confiscate without receipt whatever the prisoners possessed: personal items, watches, rings, pens, money. The policemen or soldiers might promise that these belongings would eventually be returned to their owners, but often they would never be seen again.

The Belgian trains were heading towards a single destination but took several different routes in reaching it. Grelling's train would have travelled through Orléans toward southern France. He was briefly interned at the camps at Le Fauga and Mazères, both of them south of Toulouse. It isn't clear how long he spent in either one, but at the beginning of June he arrived in the town of Elne, a few miles south of Perpignan. From there Grelling and the other prisoners were loaded onto trucks and driven to the nearby fishing village of Saint-Cyprien.

The sight that greeted them as they got down from the trucks would surely have confirmed their fears. Today a sleepy retirement town and tourist resort with a beach that goes on for miles, in 1940 Saint-Cyprien was one of a number of smaller settlements lining the Roussillon coast from the Spanish frontier to the salt marshes south of Narbonne. Not long before, the region had been overwhelmed by a flood of refugees from another European conflict, the Spanish Civil War. Some 450,000 Republicans – men, women and children – and their thousands of farm animals had streamed across the border after the fall of Barcelona in January 1939. They fled to camps that grew up in different regions in the shadow of the Pyrenees, from the Mediterranean to the Atlantic,

The beach at Saint-Cyprien, France, with the Pyrenees in the background.
(© Julian Beecroft)

to accommodate fellow Catalans and Basques from the other side of the mountains. By far the largest of these places of refuge was the strip along the coast. A series of linear camps of flimsy wooden barracks, stretching for 20 miles from Argèles-sur-Mer to Le Barcarès, had been hastily erected to meet a massive humanitarian crisis. But with so many people to house, conditions were never more than primitive. The individual barracks had no floor, so people had to sleep on the sand or on thin mattresses made of straw, while the walls of the huts leant over at alarming angles. It was to these premises in the camp at Saint-Cyprien that Grelling was delivered in early June 1940. Thankfully by then, the Spanish refugees, some 90,000 at the height of the crisis, had either gone home or had settled elsewhere in France.

Saint-Cyprien was in one part of a newly divided country. The capitulation of the French Army was followed by the armistice of 22 June, whose terms of surrender included German annexation of Alsace-Lorraine, the last remaining region that Germany had yet to take back from the settlement of the Treaty of Versailles; its French inhabitants were expelled. The new French territory was now split into two unequal parts, with Paris, the industrial heartlands of the north, and the Channel and Atlantic coasts formally occupied and run by the Nazi regime. The strategically less important South, including the large cities of Lyon, Marseille and Toulouse, was allowed to remain unoccupied, a client country with a new capital in the spa town of Vichy. From here, a government strongly aligned with the ideology of its Nazi overlords could pretend it was still in charge of a viable French state. Saint-Cyprien and most of the other camps to which enemy aliens and other so-called undesirables were deported were in this rump state in the South.

It isn't hard to imagine the condition that Kurt Grelling was in when he arrived at Saint-Cyprien, after a weeks-long journey of unremitting squalor. Conditions in the camp were hardly any better, though at least he could rest on the sand in the early summer sunshine and swim in the sea. But the camp was plagued by mosquitoes, lice and rats, and prisoners were ravaged by disease, with malaria as well as outbreaks of typhus and dysentery an ongoing hazard. In fact, in spite of his age Kurt seems to have borne the journey far better than some. Before long, he had set about finding paper or a postcard and some form of writing implement with which to let people know where he was.

By the time he'd succeeded, Lotte and Hans in Dublin had received a letter dated 14 June, from their niece, Karin Grelling.

Today I have to tell you something very nice and that is that we know where mum is. She wrote to us today that she is still in Brussels and that she is doing well.

Apparently, someone from Belgium took her letter with them; because the envelope is in my mother's handwriting and the stamp is a Swiss stamp.

Now I'll write you the address. Bruxelles-Uccle, iii avenue Bel-air.

Mum is still writing to Dad while he is away. Please excuse my spelling, but I'm very crazy today, because I just received the letter. By the way, Mum wrote the letter in French.

I'm going to stop writing now because I still have a lot of people to write to.

P.S. The letter from mum is dated 4th June.[2]

It is hard to gauge the truth of Karin's claim that Greta was writing to Kurt. It is possible, though unlikely, that in early June she could have known where he was. But there is no chance that any letter from him would have reached her by the 4th unless he had written from Le Fauga or Mazères. It does seem likely that the first person that Kurt would have written to from the camp, whether Saint-Cyprien, Le Fauga or Mazères, would have been Greta. But there is no way of knowing, as no letters between husband and wife have survived.

Grelling's first letter to Oppenheim, dated 17 July, is in French; it's also in pencil and has faded so much over time that large parts are impossible to read. Kurt may have realised that for various reasons his message might not get through, as he wrote again on 4 August, this time in pen in his native tongue; the contents are broadly similar to the gist of that earlier letter.

About a fortnight ago, I wrote you a clipper letter to the Shelton Hotel. Since I don't know whether it reached you, I will repeat the most important thing: I was arrested on 10th May without being able to say goodbye to my wife. We were transported to southern France. Since the beginning of June, I have been here on the Mediterranean near the Spanish border. I have nothing with me but what was on my body. Luckily, I had 1,000 B.frs in my pocket, which was taken away from me but given back after about 3 weeks, so that I could at least buy some urgent things to make up for the poor nutrition. My wife has stayed in Brussels, as I recently found out, and I keep in touch with my children by letter. In contrast to the situation a fortnight ago, the chances of being released here in France are almost = 0; even people with overseas visas that are about to expire cannot be quickly released. As a result, after careful consideration, I've decided to have myself taken to the demarcation line and from there to go to Brussels with the permission of the German authorities. I am of course aware of the great risk that I am taking; but living here voluntarily also involves great risks. In any case, I have made a decision and will probably leave here tomorrow or the day after with about 1,000 other Jews. If you have sent me money in the meantime, I only hope that it can be forwarded to Brussels. Postal traffic between Brussels and the USA will probably be quite complicated but hopefully possible. I assume that Peffer stayed in Brussels and will of course contact him straight away. It is also best to send to P any mail addressed to me; my wife's address: 111 rue Bel-Air, Uccle, with Mr Adolf Levi (from Frankfurt). If conditions permit, I would of course like to start working with you again soon.[3]

The letter continues with a recognition that his was a collective fate, a perspective he never loses sight of from now on. *I'm doing well healthwise. I swim in the Mediterranean every day and am very tanned. I grew a full beard. Those in the know consider August to be very unhealthy. Another reason for my decision. I am (or was) here in the camp with Pringsheim (who will shortly be free), K. Mayer (similar), and Dr Caro, whose visa has unfortunately expired and from whom I should send you greetings. He suffers greatly from his fate. He recently found out that his family has stayed in Brussels, but has had no news from them. I am also together with our friend Dr Waldeck and the former Frankfurt lawyer Dr Franz Fraenkel. He hopes to be able to leave for New York in a few weeks. I recommend him to you. One of the brothers Eltzbacher (the painter) is also here. The other, the diabetic, died during the transport. I am worried about Felix, but I hope to find out something about his fate in Brussels.*[4]

No one yet knew what had become of Felix when the Belgian forces surrendered, though his parents would surely have feared the worst. But at least he was young, an advantage that wasn't shared by the others that Grelling mentions in his letter. One of the challenges in deciphering the letters has been to identify the people that Kurt and his correspondents refer to. Sometimes, this hasn't been possible, though mostly there is enough to go on to make an educated guess. In the case of this letter, almost all the names can be attributed to people who can at least be identified. In fact, though it is clear from the long list of names compiled by Marcel Bervoets in his book *La liste de Saint-Cyprien* that those deported from Belgium included men of all ages, from the young to the very old, in this instance all of the men Kurt mentions seem to have been from his own generation. They were people of professional accomplishment, even great distinction, until the Nazis came to power. Pringsheim was Dr Peter Pringsheim, Professor of Physics at Berlin University, whose sister Katia was married to the novelist Thomas Mann. It was largely as a result of Mann's efforts in America, and those of physicist and Nobel laureate James Franck, another German exile since 1933, that a position for Pringsheim had been found at Berkeley, University of California, on a salary, half of which would be paid by Mann.⁵ K. Mayer could be one of three men called Karl Mayer listed among the deportees who spent time at Saint-Cyprien; the oldest was born in 1888, the youngest in 1904. Of the three, two were sent to the Drancy transit camp in Paris, and from there to Auschwitz to be murdered: the eldest on 17 August 1942 and the one next to him in age, born in 1894, three days earlier. Only the youngest of the men on the list who bore this name survived; two out of three did not.⁶

Waldeck was the Mannheim lawyer Dr Florian Waldeck, born in 1886, the same year as Kurt, who had lived in Brussels since fleeing there with his wife in February 1939; this Dr Waldeck may have been the same man with whom, among others, Grelling had spent a pleasant Christmas Eve at the end of the year just gone. Somehow, he seems to have made it back to Belgium later in the war, where he lived in hiding until the country was liberated in September 1944.⁷ Franz Fränkel, born in 1890, is also on the list of those who were present in the camp and seems also to have survived the war. So, too, is Hans Eltzbacher, a former lawyer from Cologne who'd become a painter after being banned from working as a lawyer in 1933; his brother Arthur, the diabetic, had died on the transport from Belgium. In time, Hans's lawyer would manage to obtain his client's release from the camp, which enabled a move to Switzerland, where again he saw out the war.⁸ Poor Dr Caro was Friedrich Wilhelm Caro, who along with his wife and two daughters had resided in the rue Veydt in Ixelles, the district in the Belgian capital where so many Jewish exiles lived. His ordeal at Saint-Cyprien was made worse by knowing that the choice they had made to stay in Brussels, when he and his family might have left, had turned out to be the wrong one.⁹

These were just a few of the men in his barracks, barrack 5, among the many barracks in his *îlot* or block, block 6, among the many more blocks in the camp, thirteen in total, each comprised of twenty-eight barracks. Between 6,000 and 8,000 men had been deported from Belgium in 150 cattle trucks; most, though not all, were Jews. That summer, the camps were combed by a Nazi commission, the Kundt Commission, looking for German citizens to take back to the Reich; that is, those non-Jews deported along with their Jewish compatriots, who were no longer citizens themselves. Less than a thousand non-Jews were identified and removed. Even now, in the second half of 1940, it was still official Nazi policy that Jews – at least, those in western Europe – should emigrate from the territory under Nazi control. The presence of so many German Jews on soil that still theoretically was French suited the Nazis very well; any attempts by the French to send these prisoners back to where they had come from were firmly rebuffed. No one wanted them. As he always had been, the stateless Wandering Jew of antisemitic legend was the troublesome creation of the democratic governments of Christendom; his condition a sign of his guilt, an invitation to all to treat him with contempt. As the fiasco of the Évian conference had shown a year earlier, these governments would all have denied that this was their intention. A few years before that, they would have flatly refuted that such a situation could ever occur.

Perhaps more surprising in the light of the future which had yet to arrive, is that Grelling and the thousand other Jews he writes of were intent on returning to the dragon's lair of Nazi-occupied territory. Kurt himself can see the absurdity of that decision, which seemed to defy all logic. But the future was unknowable, and anything was surely better than life in the camp, where living conditions were as bad as in many of the camps under Nazi control in which Jews were being held at the time.

A month later, on 4 September, Kurt wrote again to Oppenheim, telling him that their plan had failed. He describes what has happened in the meantime as *one of the saddest and most shameful episodes of my odyssey. To keep it short*, he writes, *the Germans did not allow the transport of around 1,000 Jews to get back into Belgium but sent it back to the unoccupied part of France, where we are again interned in the 'hell of St-Cyprien', which is currently infected with typhus. And this despite a German officer repeatedly telling us that we were free and that under no circumstances would we be interned again. Those who still had some money were able to flee from Bordeaux to Belgium, where according to reports received here, the same people live unmolested, like those emigrants who were able to stay in Belgium from the start. It's a shame that I didn't have enough money in Bordeaux to attach myself to those who made a quick getaway. Our fate is still completely unclear. If the 4 to 5,000 Jews still in this camp have to spend the autumn and winter here, not many will survive.*[10]

It is no surprise that, in his grim forecast for the winter, Kurt switches to the third person, as if the Jews he writes about do not include himself. And for now, at least, his immediate prospects had been improved by a cheque that arrived, apparently from Jacques Errera, who was acting on Oppenheim's behalf; how Errera had avoided being captured by the victorious German Army as Belgium was overrun isn't clear. But in any case, Grelling was grateful for the gift. *Now I am in a position to replace my shredded clothing and underwear*, he writes, *and also to buy myself some little things essential to being a civilised human.*[11]

Kurt still knew what it meant to be civilised. He was civilised to his core. Not only those traits or qualities that were typical of a man of

Drawing of Kurt Grelling made on 10 June 1940 by an unknown fellow inmate while both were interned at Saint-Cyprien, France. (© Kurt Grelling Archive)

learning and culture: his measured sentences, his erudition, his scrupulous commitment to logic, to empirical knowledge, to truth, his passion for disseminating what he had learned – not only those but other qualities, his human qualities: his reticence, his modesty, his devotion to his wife and children, his evident gift for friendship, his courtesy and compassion for fellow inmates in the camp – qualities which in life may well have held him back. Whatever were the true markers of his level of civilisation, they were all intact, despite everything he'd been through. But he had not changed his clothes in months, or had access to personal hygiene of any meaningful kind. Over many years since 1933, his status and living standards had suffered both sudden and gradual declines. Each new measure, each erosion of fortune and of rights, he had hoped would be the last. A few years, even a few months earlier, he could not have imagined that he would end up in the position in which he found himself, though now at least he could clearly see the state that they would all be in, a few months hence, if they stayed where they were.

There was still the hope of getting back to Brussels, despite the setback at the demarcation line. Greta had moved again, and was now living with Dr Hirsch, another of those with whom Kurt had spent the previous Christmas Eve (and who had treated him for Menière's disease), at a house in the rue Dautzenberg in Ixelles, close to their old address. Her health wasn't good, and the Gestapo were pressing her yet again to divorce him. She was not able to send letters to the children, but Kurt had heard directly from Karin that they were staying with a Swiss family during the holidays. Neither Kurt nor Greta had any idea who was paying for this arrangement, but clearly someone had stepped up to the mark.

The typhus epidemic which had run through the camp meant that Grelling, who had not been vaccinated, was forced to live separately from his friends. Otherwise, he was trying to occupy his mind by giving lectures about the birth of the worldview of modern science or, for a smaller audience, the fundamentals of maths and logic. Anyone could turn up and listen, but there were also a few specialists in the camp, including some old pupils of Moritz Schlick, with one of whom he was having what he calls *a stimulating exchange of views*.[12]

What really kept him busy was his emigration plan. In that regard, a letter in English from Peter Hempel, dated 28 September, was a new source of hope. *This is the situation*, he writes. *One or two of the scholars to whom I wrote on your behalf after the arrival of your first news brought your case to the attention of A.S. Johnson, the Director of the New School for Social Research, 66 W.12th Street, New York City. (That's the so-called University in Exile, where at present among other people Felix Kaufmann, Max Wertheimer, Kurt Riezler*[13] *are teaching.) Dr Johnson has taken action to make it possible for the New School to invite a certain number of eminent representatives of philosophy and social science who lost their positions in Europe. A few days ago, I received a letter from Johnson, asking me to give him information about your curriculum vitae, your publications, and a list of scholars in this country who would give information about your scientific standing. At the same time, however, he added that the funds he had available for the purpose were so limited in comparison with the number of recommendations of eminent scientists he had on file that he did not see how he could extend an invitation to you unless it were possible to raise funds towards your salary. I informed O. about this situation, and immediately he declared his willingness to make such a contribution. Thereupon we succeeded in getting an interview with Dr. Johnson in which we discussed the question.*[14]

Hempel could see three main conditions that needed to be satisfied: the raising of funds for Kurt's salary; obtaining strong recommendations from scholars of high standing already in the USA; and overcoming the fact that he had not held an academic post in Europe, an obstacle to obtaining a non-quota visa. The salary itself would afford Kurt and his family what Hempel describes as *a reasonably modest standard of living*. He goes on that *O. has agreed to pay to the New School 40 per cent of your salary for two years if it extends an invitation to you. Thus, Johnson would have to raise only the balance of 60 per cent*. He seemed reasonably hopeful that this might be done, and he expressed his conviction that *O.'s offer was an important help in the matter*.[15]

As for the references, while there were a number of European scholars at US universities who would vouch for him – Hempel had mentioned the names of Russell, Carnap, Tarski, Reichenbach and Kaufmann – Dr Johnson felt that Kurt needed other endorsements from American scholars to fully justify his claim. Finally, against his lack of experience teaching at university level could be set his association with noted academics such as Reichenbach and Dubislav through the activities of the Berlin Group, his lectures in Scandinavia, and the fact that the courses in philosophy he taught at the Berlin *Gymnasium* were of a difficulty equivalent to the lower grades of US university courses. Ultimately, the person with the power to decide whether this would be sufficient to warrant a non-quota visa would be the American consul in Marseille.

It was clear that there were many people they would need to persuade before Grelling's passage to America could be secured. It was a complex undertaking that would call upon the help of Oppenheim, Hempel and many others, including members of his own family. In a letter written to Oppenheim on 4 October, Hempel makes clear that they were trying to get in touch with Otto Neurath in connection with Grelling, possibly to secure an affidavit, but they didn't know his address. They clearly hadn't heard that Neurath was no longer in The Hague; that, having stepped onto British soil, he and his partner and collaborator, Marie Reidemeister, were promptly arrested as enemy aliens and interned on the Isle of Man.

Eva Hempel was now heavily involved helping Jewish refugees through an organisation called the Selfhelp, an American NGO. She'd been tasked with sending him the parcels of food, clothing and books that Grelling had asked for, though Peter Hempel thinks that books, as printed matter, will take a long time to get through. At the end of July, Kurt had written a postcard to Lotte and Hans and Else in Dublin, telling them his whereabouts and circumstances. But it clearly hadn't reached them by the time that Lotte wrote to Oppenheim on 27 August, asking for news of her brother and expressing the state of near-bewilderment in which so many Jewish refugees were living, even those who apparently were safe. But at least Hans's contract had been renewed for a further two years, removing the theoretical risk that they, too, might be deported.

By the time that Hempel wrote to Grelling a month later, Kurt's card would have finally made it to Dublin; it seems something of a miracle that, even when connections of every kind were breaking down, the post was still, largely, reaching its intended recipients, even if it took a long time to get there. Privately, in a letter to Oppenheim of 7 October, Hempel was frank about the challenges they faced in securing the cooperation of everyone they needed to help them. Johnson wanted to see the personal affidavit that Bertrand Russell had written at Kurt's request just two years earlier, but no one had a copy. Luckily, Russell was already in America, in rural Pennsylvania. Hempel thought it would not be a problem to obtain a new affidavit, but it was one more request to have to make, to add to all the others. It was a delicate business; the New School was now more or less their only hope.

By the time that Kurt wrote again to Oppenheim, on 22 October, the summer had come to a sudden, very brutal end. A few days earlier, on the 16th, the worst storm in almost 200 years had descended on the eastern Pyrenees. So much rain streamed down from the mountains that the brackish lagoon which lies behind a stretch of the beach of Saint-Cyprien overflowed its banks, flooding that part of the camp. Some of the inmates woke to find their makeshift beds were almost underwater, though Kurt himself doesn't mention it and may not have been directly affected. But perhaps he had also grown so used to this level of calamity that he was choosing to count his blessings; he was certainly buoyed by the efforts on his behalf that Oppenheim and Hempel were making, and above all by Oppenheim's offer of financial support, if also realistic about his prospects of success. *I have to use the opportunity to express to you directly my deep gratitude for the generous help you have given me, which has contributed so much to the calling I have received from the USA. My wife is right when she says, 'O. is our good angel.' I hope one day to be given the chance to repay you. Should the plan come to fruition, I will be at the service of your scientific plans. The teaching post that is being proposed will not be too taxing. But I am not overoptimistic that it will happen. I don't think there is much chance that I will be able to leave France before the end of* the war. *As far as I know, nobody has been able to gather all the papers together to get the necessary visa.*[16]

In that regard, he had heard from Peter Pringsheim, who still hadn't left, that the State Department would only issue a non-quota visa if the person was about to be expelled, and that *Mr Johnson would have to apply to the State Dept to instruct the consul in Marseille to issue me a visa. This has the advantage that the State Dept can better explain the reasons for granting an exception than I could myself.*[17]

Everyone in the camp was in the same boat, petitioning anyone who might help them. But Grelling did at least have a means of refuge and absorption, intellectual habits which in that environment were a great source of comfort to himself and others. *I am glad that I can work with my head*, he writes. *I have gathered a small circle around me, to whom I'm explaining the foundations of neo-positivism. With a young writer, I am writing a collection of essays and aphorisms, working together to explain philosophical ideas to the forum.*[18]

Work was the best defence against despair. Culture of any kind, the exercise of mental life, had never been more important to any of them. But the flooding had made physical life at Saint-Cyprien unsustainable, even by the very low standards that the French had set. In the same letter, Grelling writes that, in a few days, they would all be sent to a different camp *with a tougher climate high in the western foothills of the Pyrenees.*[19] The camp on the beach would be closed.

THE NEW SCHOOL

Like Saint-Cyprien, the Camp de Gurs, where the internees were all being sent, had been built to accommodate Spanish refugees at the start of the previous year. By the summer of 1939, the Spanish had mostly gone home. They were soon replaced by so-called undesirables – German and mostly Jewish exiles living in France (in this case also female), who, being redefined as enemy aliens, were sent there in October, the month after war was declared. A small number who were young enough, including the philosopher Hannah Arendt, had managed to escape during the chaos that followed the capitulation of the French Army in June 1940, the disaster of swift and crushing defeat that soon became known as the Debacle. But most were still present when Kurt Grelling and nearly 4,000 male inmates from Saint-Cyprien arrived at Gurs at the end of October. Just days earlier, the local gauleiters of the German regions of Baden, the Palatinate and the Saar, which all shared a border with France, had been ordered to deport their Jewish populations. More than 6,500 German Jews from Baden had been sent to Gurs, arriving there on 24 and 25 October. Other Jewish populations were also in danger. Since July, the Vichy government had passed several pieces of anti-Jewish legislation, culminating in the *statut des Juifs* of 3 October. This mirrored the Nazi laws in both defining the 'Jewish race' and restricting the range of occupations in which Jews in France were allowed to work. A day later, another statute was passed, the Law Regarding Foreign Nationals of the Jewish Race, which authorised the internment of all foreign Jews still living in the country. Very quickly the camps across the South were filled to bursting.

With the closure of Saint-Cyprien, Camp de Gurs became indisputably the largest of the French camps. With the Pyrenees brooding in the distance, its thirteen blocks, each containing an average of twenty-eight barracks, was a match for the beach camp in size. From one end of the camp to the other was a distance of almost 2km. After the cities of Pau and

Bayonne, it was the largest agglomeration in the eastern Pyrenees. Today the memorial site is a mature woodland, but in 1939, when the camp was constructed, it was a treeless expanse of open ground, exposed to the wind and the lashing winter rain. The barracks at Gurs had been better built than those at the coast, with wooden floors and asphalt-covered roofs. But by the autumn of 1940, with the weather having taken a turn for the worse, they were clearly in a poor state of repair. Of the 13,000 prisoners who lived there from the end of October, many, especially among those who had just been deported from Germany, were old and infirm and, above all, in a state of shock. It wasn't long before conditions in the camp were atrocious. Worst of all was the quagmire it turned into as the winter progressed; soon so bad that, stepping out of the barracks to go to the toilet or the canteen, the inmate would sink to their ankles, and sometimes up to their knees, in mud.

Kurt's first letter to Oppenheim from Gurs, dated 8 November, is frank about the shortcomings of his new home. *A week ago, we arrived at a new camp, which in many respects is a lot worse than Saint-Cyprien. Above all, the food is extremely poor and you can hardly buy anything here. On the other hand, what little there is, is exorbitantly expensive. In St-C we could come and go from neighbouring parts of the camp, as if on holiday; here you can't visit the other îlots, so I'm cut off from my friends, such as Caro, Pringsheim, Waldeck. The barracks do have electric lighting and are also better protected from the weather than in St-Cyprien; but they are so crowded[1] that it's almost impossible to work mentally. We have also not been able to resume our lecturing work due to the worsening circumstances.*[2]

Grelling rather skates over the full squalor of the conditions in which they were living. For one thing, he doesn't mention the obligatory hunt for mice and rats in the barracks, which had to be prosecuted every night before the lights went out. But there was little to be gained from dwelling on such trials. Any news from Greta came only through the children, so they must have known everything she told him. As usual, the news wasn't good. With the Gestapo pressing her once more to divorce him, she had told them again that she would never agree. So, they warned her, he writes, that *she must 'bear the consequences', though what these consist of, of course she doesn't say.*[3] Grelling adds that the process of stripping him of citizenship was well under way and might even have been completed. He may have been surprised it had taken so long, though records in the Berlin archives show that actually he was jumping the gun: his and Greta's citizenship was formally revoked only in November the following year. This is hardly a great surprise: with such a huge backlog of expatriations of Jews to be carried out, even the Nazi bureaucracy, for all its cruel efficiency, would have struggled to cope.

In any case, Grelling was thinking only of America and the New School, though he didn't underestimate how difficult the process would be. His half-sister Eva – married to a man named Felix Oppenheim – had written to him from Portugal that it was easy now to get an emergency visa for the USA. If only that were true! But Kurt had also had news of the other Felix Oppenheim, Paul Oppenheim's son, after Greta had met him in Brussels. It isn't clear what the young man had told her; perhaps not a lot, given the position he was in. Soon afterwards, Felix left Belgium and was on his way to Portugal, trying to get to America like so many thousands of others. As his later memoir makes clear, when his unit surrendered on the day of the invasion, he had thought that his number was up. He survived because he understood that the issue of race, of identity as defined by it, about which the Nazis were so obsessed, was a game he had to win. Taken prisoner, the first thing he did was to tear up his military ID. Knowing what the Nazis would assume from the name Oppenheim, among the most common German-Jewish surnames, he became Felix Orban, persuading all the members of his unit, his fellow prisoners, not to call him by any other name. None of them had known that he was Jewish, but to a man no one betrayed him.

The next day the prisoners were sent across the border to a prison camp in Germany, a country Felix had not set foot in for seven years. He was held with the Flemish speakers, whom the Nazis had targeted with propaganda, trying to turn them against their Francophone compatriots. Then, in August, he was given the option of moving to the French side, which ought to have suited him better. But he also knew that any offer the Nazis made would turn out to be false, so he declined. It was the right choice: while the French remained captive until the end of the war, a few days later the Flemish troops were sent back to Belgium, to be interned in a warehouse in Antwerp.

Felix escaped without papers, made his way back to Brussels and was taken in by the family of a friend. Retrieving his passport, he obtained the one visa he could get, at extortionate cost, to the unlikely destination of the Dominican Republic; it would later prove to be invalid. Then, in early October, he hitched a lift into France with a distant cousin, an Italian on his mother's side who was heading that way. At the border late at night, as Felix sat motionless in the passenger seat, the German guards failed to spot him in the dark; once again, he had managed to avoid an inspection of his papers. In Paris, he took a train to Bayonne on the far south-west coast. He was still there at the end of October, waiting to cross into Spain, when the inmates of Saint-Cyprien were deposited at the Camp de Gurs, a few dozen miles inland.

The camp was surrounded by a double row of barbed wire, beyond which lay miles of open country with few settlements of any significant size. Only the young could think of escaping, with the risk they could be shot in trying by the armed guards at the camp. But Grelling wasn't young, and after the August fiasco, turned back with a thousand other Jews at the demarcation line, he knew that for now his only option was survival. A month after his letter to Oppenheim, on 8 December Kurt wrote at some length to Lotte and Hans Sachs and his sister Else. *Apart from a very persistent cold, fortunately I'm healthy. My main concern now is that I stay that way until liberation, which will happen one day. Unfortunately, it is not certain whether I will be able to do this if I have to spend the winter in this camp. In any case, the conditions are extremely bad. As I already wrote to Eva,*[4] *the food is completely inadequate. Thanks to a money transfer from P.O. that I received in September, at*

Interior of a modern reproduction of an original barracks at the Camp de Gurs, near Oloron-Sainte-Marie, France. (© Julian Beecroft)

the moment I can supplement it. I have enough so that, to some extent, I can feed myself. Hopefully, P.O. will continue to support me. Eva sent me 3 packages of food that were very valuable to me and has told me today that more is coming. P.O. also sent a food parcel, but who knows when it will arrive?

I've been able to provide myself with the bare necessities of clothing. But you can hardly protect yourself from the cold when you have to live in a barrack that is completely unheated for 19 hours a day and only poorly heated the rest of the time. I'm writing now wrapped in blankets in my 'bed'. It's 9 o'clock.[5] We're almost in darkness as the electric light is switched off at 8.30 and only weak daylight comes through the few little windows. It's been raining heavily for four days. The clay soil of the camp is in such a condition that one doesn't go out if it isn't absolutely necessary.[6]

He adds a list of things that he desperately needs – *toiletries, soap and the like* – but can also see that others are worse off than he is. *I would like to direct your attention to my neighbour Friedrich Spiro, a nephew of Eugen Sp., who is completely penniless and has no one to help him from outside. Could Grete Grünfeld do something for him? His address is the same as mine.*[7] Spiro was a couple of years younger than Kurt Grelling. Kurt's great nephew, John Cooke, thinks he may have been related to Herbert and Ernst Spiro, who later worked for the Grünfelds' company in London; hence perhaps Kurt's suggestion. But whatever help Spiro may have later received, it wouldn't be enough. In the summer of 1942, the Friedrich Spiro on the list compiled by Marcel Bervoets was transferred to the transit camp at Drancy and, on 9 September, from there to Auschwitz to be murdered.[8]

Grelling was well aware that he was luckier than most of his fellow inmates and that, even if his ideal solution came to nothing, he had well-connected advocates in America. He reprised the details for his sister and brother-in-law. *I've been recommended for a lectureship at the New School for Social Research in NY. P.O. has agreed to pay 40% of my salary and the Rockefeller Foundation will pay the rest. But, unfortunately, no decision had been made by 2nd November. If this fails, P.O. and our friend and colleague Hempel will try the so-called 'danger visa'. Of course, O. would either pay the crossing for us, the family and me, or would guarantee it in advance. If I didn't have this really generous friend, my situation would be completely desperate.*[9]

Grelling was correct that, by early November, the decision had not yet come from the New School. But, though he didn't yet know it, on the 15th, the director, Dr Alvin Johnson, had written to Oppenheim in

English with news that wasn't good: *I am very sorry to tell you that the foundation has declined to make an additional grant for Dr. Kurt Grelling. I do not know of any other sources from which additional funds might be secured. Therefore, I am unfortunately not able to invite Dr. Grelling to join our Faculty.*[10]

Oppenheim responded to Johnson in a letter of 11 December, almost four weeks later. The letter has not survived, but we do get a clear sense of its contents from Johnson's immediate reply. *I think you will find the case of Dr. Grelling more understandable if you consider the plan of bringing over scholars on which I have been working covers the entire range of the sciences and the arts, and that the distribution is fairly fixed; the social sciences and the humanities being listed for twenty-five each.*

Under the humanities are listed literature, music, art, education, psychology, philosophy; and this means at the most three or four philosophers can be brought over under the plan.

In the judgment of the foundation, which seems to me reasonable, while Grelling is a good man there are a number that are better.[11]

The verdict feels all the more damning for being so measured. Oppenheim may not have shared its exact form of words with Grelling. The New School itself and the Emergency Committee in Aid of Displaced Foreign Scholars, the board that oversaw the exercise of its mission, would help more than 300 thinkers across all fields during the dark decade in which it was needed. Johnson's own role was instrumental. Some scholars were offered places at the New School for Social Research, while others found positions elsewhere. Among the programme's notable beneficiaries were the philosopher Martin Buber and the novelist Thomas Mann. But with people of this level of renown needing help, the scheme could never be much more than an intellectual lifeboat for a few of the fittest minds. Anyone who didn't get on it would need to find another means of passage, sink or swim.

By the middle of December, Grelling probably knew what the committee had decided from a letter that Oppenheim sent him which also has not survived; Hempel's letter, dated the 14th, assumes that he has heard. But he also makes an effort to reassure him that *people are working very hard to find a solution that works for everyone currently in unoccupied France. You must be patient,* he urges, *and I know this is easy for me to say, but we are trying every avenue we can to get you out. For now, the New School will not be possible, as their means are too limited, and they can only invite two to three philosophers, which includes Polish philosophers. [...] O. is going to try to find ways of paying the necessary sum (i.e. the salary to be offered to you by the New School minus the sum promised by O.), as we still have the faint hope that the New School will invite you if they can get the remaining money from somewhere else. Oh, and we're looking at options. Since probably it will hardly be possible to raise the full remaining amount as a foundation, we have already thought about what you would think if some of your friends here contributed to the 'Grelling remaining sum fund' on a loan basis. The result would be that only you (modestly!) and not your family would be able to live here from the residual sum. Please write to us what you would think of such an arrangement; but please, don't talk about it to anyone, because the whole idea is in no way ready for discussion and, moreover, is not applicable to the cases of any of your camp comrades; if one of them found out about it, it could only destroy the slim chances that the idea might offer you.*[12]

Hempel also writes that this idea of the fund was one they could try if all else failed, but in the meantime, Oppenheim was being *tenacious and surprisingly energetic* in pursuing the main plan. In a letter written two weeks later, three days before the end of the year, Oppenheim spells out exactly whose would be the main commitment to the fund. *Only after the Hempels' letter of 14th December was sent did I have the opportunity to discuss it with them. If I had seen the letter beforehand, I would have requested significant changes. Changes are necessary because the Hempels, which was understandable for this couple, were too tactful: they did not prejudge what I might achieve. In reality, I have already agreed in principle to accept obligations that are equivalent to an affidavit (one I can't issue to the outside world because I am only a temporary visitor). Furthermore, I am generally prepared to contribute a higher amount to the New School than I had originally agreed to. At the time of that commitment, the New School stated that it believed my involvement was sufficient. It later became clear that, contrary to their expectations, they were unable to raise the remaining money. It was this latter statement that prompted the Hempels to write in their letter of 14th December, 'unfortunately, nothing has happened with the New School for the time being'. On the other hand, I had written you a letter shortly beforehand in which I was not so pessimistic about the New School, because I was thinking about the aforementioned increase in my participation if all else fails. An immediate commitment of the entire amount required for 2 years is not possible for me for the following reason: all of my accounts are blocked; I can only use a certain amount each month. So, my contribution to the New School must be diverted from these monthly amounts, and I need to start saving before you arrive. In this respect, too, it is important to me to make additional comments on Hempel's letter; because without what I just said about my blocked accounts, it might look like I'm not doing everything I can.*

The same applies to your release against the provision of a monthly sum.

Without prejudice to the above, I ask you to comment on Hempel's question as to whether you agree with the 'Grelling Residual Fund' plan. With the realisation of such a plan, the most important concern that I have in this context would be greatly alleviated: it is impossible to foresee what restrictions will be imposed on me by further legal measures and generally by the military complications; so, it could be that, despite my best intentions, it is not possible for me to guarantee you a reasonable level of subsistence. These concerns become even more serious when I am not looking at the next two years, but rather the more distant future. I have therefore considered with the Hempels how it is possible to find a community, similar to the 'Grelling Residual Sum Fund', which, to a certain extent, supports me and, to a certain extent, steps in at those times when I am unable to help.[13]

By the time he wrote the letter, Oppenheim had already put out feelers for anyone willing to contribute to the fund, principally through Leo Forchheimer, an old colleague from his days in industry. Forchheimer knew Werner Sachs, Kurt's nephew, through his subsequent employment with GfE; he was now in America but, by the turn of the year, had managed to enlist what appeared to be the help of the Grünfeld family in London. As he announced in a letter of 3 January, this amounted to £150 per year (about $600 at the exchange rate of the time). In fact, the true benefactors, as Hans Sachs later confirmed to Oppenheim in a letter of 6 April, were Sachs and his wife, Kurt's sister Lotte, together with their two children in England, Ilse and Werner. Either way, it was a very good start. But as Herbert Grünfeld, head of the London firm, made clear in his reply to Forchheimer's request, the transfer was currently impossible: strict foreign exchange controls had been in place since the start of the war.

With these new financial arrangements taking shape, Oppenheim and Hempel petitioned numerous European and American scholars with positions at US universities to write testimonials in support of Grelling's renewed application. So, to those of Rudolf Carnap, W.V.O. Quine[14] and Alfred Tarski, already received in September and October, were added several more endorsements by philosophers of very high calibre: Hans Reichenbach, Herbert Feigl, Felix Kaufmann, Ernest Nagel, Sidney Hook and Bertrand Russell, with a second reference to follow the one he had written in 1938. On 15 January 1941, Oppenheim wrote again to Alvin Johnson, confirming that, with the help of generous friends, he was now in a position to guarantee the full amount of Grelling's salary at the New School. Taken together, these measures would have represented a notable elevation of Grelling's stature in the eyes of the emergency committee with the power to decide his fate.

On the same day, Greta Grelling wrote to Oppenheim herself from Brussels, her first extant letter. *A few weeks ago, I received your address from Kurt. This letter should actually have been written a long time ago, but I've always had inhibitions. Above all, I would like to wish you and your dear family a very good 1941, even if it is very late. […]*

Now I would like to tell you a little about myself. I have lived here with friends for months. But since I couldn't have my own room, this situation was unbearable in the long run. When Madame Gedeuvert[15] *heard that I had to move again, she asked me to move back here. I now pay two-fifths of what Kurt paid for the same room. Of course, I clean my room myself and knit clothes and costumes for Madame and her friends free of charge. Through this work I earn my keep, because the little I pay in cash cannot even cover my food at the moment. As you can see, I was once again lucky in my bad luck. They have such love, attention and respect for me that I have often been moved to tears. I've been seeing Maria Mus. more often lately. I should like to greet all four of you* [from her] *very warmly. When we are together, we talk a lot about the wonderful times in the past. My health is currently quite good. In the summer I was quite miserable because of all the excitements. Kurt wrote to me saying that you, dear doctor, and Dr H. are trying very hard to help us. This greatly strengthened my confidence, my faith, but above all my inner resilience. Thank you very much for everything you do for us. I will be very happy when I can finally see Kurt and the children again. My situation here is quite uncomfortable because I have almost no clothes. Unfortunately, I can't wear Kurt's things. Until recently it seemed that I could at least get my personal clothing.* […] *I ask all my friends for socks and sturdy shoes. The few socks I brought with me have all gone the way of everything earthly and my light shoes are completely inappropriate for the weather here. Unfortunately, none of my friends can help me because no one has an abundance of shoes and socks. These things can no longer be obtained with money either. Maybe I'll decide to wear Kurt's shoes and socks after all. Since I don't have to do so much housework anymore – of course, I did all of my friends' housework – I'll save the few clothes I have. This is also a great blessing in my current situation.*

My biggest concern is Kurt and the children. It's terrible for me to know that Kurt is cold and the clothes are lying here and I can't give them to him. The children always write me very sweet letters. Karin always comforts me in a way that is truly touching. We all have only one wish, to be finally reunited as a family.[16]

Greta was making the best of her difficult life. Helped by her friends in Brussels, the hope she felt that her family could be reunited was in fact in the process of being justified as she sat down to write her letter. On the same day, the 15th, Oppenheim wrote to Alvin Johnson that he was now in a position to guarantee Grelling's entire salary for two years. Two days later, with that condition fulfilled and no doubt greatly persuaded by the long list of affidavits he had now received, Johnson wrote to Oppenheim to offer Grelling the position he had sought. So, a major hurdle had been overcome, but there were others still to be cleared. Grelling would need to secure the non-quota visas for himself and his family. He would also need some $600 for himself alone, payable in US currency, to fund his voyage to America. As Johnson points out at the end of his letter, *It would be rather inhuman to offer Dr. Grelling this chance of liberty if he is left without the means to pay his passage.*[17]

Oppenheim and the Hempels were alive to the problem, as the cost of the voyage is an issue that Hempel raises in his letter to Grelling, dated 28 January, in which he confirms the offer from the New School and, in this regard, the help they have had from the family in England. A letter from Johnson and a contract from the New School was on its way to Gurs; copies had also been sent to the US consul in Marseille and by cable to the commandant at the camp. Hempel had also sent certified copies of various official documents relating to Grelling's appointment. The Rockefeller Foundation had a middleman in Lisbon who would look after him once he got there. Oppenheim would arrange the money for the ticket, potentially from another source, which Kurt should purchase on arrival in the Portuguese capital. In theory, it was all in hand. But it was also clear that bringing his family with him would be a problem. Hempel was sorry to have to say it, but, as he puts it in that letter, *we have to advise you to come alone for the time being. From everything we hear, it would be more difficult and time-consuming for your wife to come here, if it's even possible at the moment, and it would delay your own departure if you wanted to wait for that. As I'm sure you understand, it is extremely important that you do not delay your own departure for one day longer than is absolutely necessary. On the other hand, your relatives are not in direct danger; and in these times that is the first thing to consider. In any case, we can't see any possibility at present of getting the money together for one further person, let alone three. It's also the case that if you emigrate through a non-quota visa, you will be able to obtain the same visa for your family, and maybe it would be easier to get the money together quickly if you are already here.*[18]

There was clearly a lot for Kurt to think about, but for now, having received Hempel's letter, and before that a cable from Oppenheim confirming the basic facts of his appointment, he allowed himself a small celebration. In a letter of 8 February, in reply to a letter of Oppenheim's that has not survived, he writes, *You can imagine the joy that cable brought me. It is the promise to free me from my current situation and the fulfilment of my life's dream: a lectureship at a university.* But, again, he seems caught in two minds, in this case about his family. Having not yet received Hempel's most recent letter, he writes that, *unfortunately, it will still be a long time before my wife has obtained the necessary documents from Germany.*[19] But then, later in the same letter, he seems to anticipate Hempel's advice while at the same time distancing himself from the pain of a choice that only he could make. *I'll leave it up to you to decide whether I should take my family with me or not. I do not have to emphasize how difficult it is that we are separated.*[20]

Many of the same anxieties are rehearsed in a letter he wrote a week later, on 15 February, to Lotte and Hans and Else in Dublin, in which he thanks them personally for the money they have agreed to pay to support his position at the New School. He had also recently received 4,000 francs each from Oppenheim and from Eva, his half-sister. This, along with the approach of spring and the good news from America, had made life at Gurs a lot easier to bear. It also encouraged his belief, motivated by genuine worries about their welfare, that he might yet be able to take his family with him on the ship. *It has also got warmer here,* he writes, *at times spring-like, so I don't have to suffer cold or hunger now. I can wait for my freedom and my departure in peace and without danger to my life or health. If at all possible, I want to take Greta and the children with me. The food situation in Belgium is catastrophic and Greta has no means to live there in the long term. I also can't burden the school with my children for any longer than is absolutely necessary. But given I would have to send money to support them and Greta from America (which gets more and more difficult), we might just as easily live together over there and would be reunited at last after such a long separation. Of course, the final decision rests with P.O., and I have to wait for the fine details of my employment contract. In any case, I hope to get out of this camp soon and to be able to have Greta come to the South of France.*[21]

For the first time in this letter of 15 February, he mentions his half-siblings from his father's second marriage, Hans Richard in Zurich and Annemarie in Florence, whose help he was also hoping to receive. Annemarie, who had married an Italian called Gentile, had just got out of bed, two weeks after having her second child; Hans had been generous in giving Christmas presents to Kurt and Greta's children, although he had only once replied to the letters that Kurt had sent him; or it may have been that only one of Hans's letters had reached the camp. In his previous letter, from 8 December 1940, Kurt had also mentioned the thousands of Jews deported from the German border region of Baden who were with him at

Gurs, including, he thinks, people that Hans and Lotte Sachs would know from Heidelberg, whose fate they had managed to escape. In this letter, he mentions one of them, a man he calls *Director Leser*, whose surname was one that John Cooke recognised from the stories his grandmother had told him. The 'director' in question was Walter Leser, a judge from Mannheim, who survived the camps and returned to Germany once the war was over. Grelling writes that Walter is particularly worried about his brother, Guido Leser, who like him had been a judge in Mannheim and had once been a neighbour of the Sachses in Heidelberg. But, unlike them, after being removed from his position soon after the Nazis took power, Guido and his wife Irmingard felt that antisemitism in a small city like Heidelberg, where he was born and had always lived, would be worse than a bigger place, where there were more Jews. So, in 1936 they moved to Berlin. Like Marion Samter, their son Conrad had emigrated, in his case in 1934, to study in Switzerland and then in 1939 to England, where Lotte Sachs would later make contact with him. But, in common with so many Jews of middle age or older, his parents couldn't face the prospect of further upheaval when even their move to Berlin, cut off from their friends and with no professional ties to give them a sense of community or purpose, had left them isolated and increasingly depressed. So, they remained there for many years, where at least the language and the culture were familiar and, until the imposition of the yellow star in September 1941, it was easier to move anonymously among the crowds. But a year later, in October 1942, informed that they would soon be deported to the camp at Theresienstadt near Prague, they chose instead to end their lives.

For the many other Jews deported to Gurs from Baden along with Walter Leser, many of them elderly, the Pyrenean winter of 1940–41, the worst in living memory, was often lethal. By 1 January, more than 11,000 people were living in squalid conditions that sheer numbers alone would have given rise to, even without the cold and the driving rain. More than 1,000 died in just a few months and were buried in the cemetery at the camp. Their headstones bear the names of people – Adler, Bodenheimer, Kaufmann, Knapp – and the places in which they were born – Mannheim, Trier, Steinbach, Bühl – that could hardly be more German, but how much is known of who they were or how they had lived? Even the names that Kurt mentions of people he has met in the camps, such as Friedrich Spiro or Walter Leser, are like human flotsam, fragments of lives that had once been substantial, not only in themselves and their intimate relations but as members of professions in which they had risen to notable heights – a standing in society that Kurt Grelling had never quite attained but which, with his prospects in America, seemed suddenly, belatedly, within reach.

With the offer from the New School confirmed, Kurt was told that he would soon be transferred to another camp, one specifically reserved for those with a realistic prospect of emigration. It was a sign of progress that he had already moved there when Hempel wrote to him, on 18 March, that obtaining a visa would not be a problem but, at the moment, getting a place on a ship appeared to be more difficult. Add to this that they could only get the money for Grelling himself, and that Kurt would need to turn to other sources – his relatives or charitable organisations – to secure funds for his family, and it was clear that the offer from the New School created problems that he had not had to think about before. Having discussed with the Oppenheims whether or not Grelling should bring his family with him, Hempel literally underlines his earlier advice: *Do everything in your power to bring your family with you now. But do not delay your own departure if the paperwork for the rest of your family takes longer than for you.*[22]

Knowing what we do now about what was coming, the choice seems simple. But the prospect of rescue was snagged on the horns of a quandary that few people will ever have to face. How could he think of saving himself and leaving his family behind, even if they weren't in imminent danger? How could he abandon his wife, who had given up so much to be with him when she might easily have saved herself? What civilised man could do that and how would it affect him if he did?

A BOOK OF ESSAYS

The cemetery at the Camp de Gurs. (© Julian Beecroft)

That the camp authorities let people live in the appalling conditions at Gurs, doing nothing to improve them, says a lot about the values of the Vichy regime. It says something else that they set aside land in which the interned could bury, in orderly rows, those who had died on account of this indifference and neglect. That the walled cemetery is so large that almost half the plot was never filled says something further, and more disturbing, about what they thought would happen. Life in the camp was intolerably hard, but, as at Saint-Cyprien, the inmates enjoyed certain freedoms that were simply unavailable in the camps in Germany or in any part of Nazi-occupied Europe. At Gurs, as with the other camps in the Unoccupied Zone, culture of every kind took on an outsized importance.

Artists recorded their experiences in stark images that bring home the debasing reality of daily life. Theatre performances were staged to offer respite from that reality. All kinds of intellectual pursuits flourished in spite of the hardships. As Kurt Grelling records in one of his letters, those who could work with their minds were fortunate that this was possible, no matter how bad the conditions became, and there were many students hungry for a way of seeing the world that transcended the squalor. One of these was a young Austrian writer who had also been deported from Belgium, whom Kurt had first come across at Saint-Cyprien and who was also sent to Gurs in late October. In the last letter to Oppenheim from the beach camp, Grelling mentions the young man that he had asked to help him write a book of essays in an accessible style; he hoped to take it with him to America, as an example of what he could do. By early January, after they had found each other again amid the sprawling mudbath of Gurs, one of these essays was finished. Kurt had identified the writer as Hanns Mayer,[1] a fairly common Austrian name, but said nothing more about him. As such, this would almost certainly have offered yet another fleeting glimpse of one of the many men that Grelling mentions in his letters, had Mayer not written of their friendship himself, many years later, in a book called *Unmeisterliche Wanderjahre*[2] ('Unmasterful Journeyman Years') under the French name of Jean Améry.

An anagram of Mayer, which he adopted after the war had ended, just as Jean is the French equivalent of Hanns, Améry is known above all in the English-speaking world as the author of *At the Mind's Limits*, a book of essays based on his own experiences of torture and imprisonment at the hands of the Nazis,[3] including the period of more than a year he endured in Monowitz-Auschwitz until just before it was liberated in January 1945.[4] First published in 1966 as *Jenseits von Schuld und Sühne*,[5] it was widely praised for its unflinching moral honesty and courage. *Unmeisterliche Wanderjahre*, which appeared some five years later and has yet to be translated into English, is a kind of intellectual and spiritual autobiography. Its reflections on logical positivism, on the author's experiences in the Camp de Gurs and his friendship with Kurt Grelling make a strong case that the problems of philosophy with which Grelling and his colleagues, but also their opponents, were wrestling have implications for democracy, for the place of reason in political life, and for how we think of history and its victims, which have never gone away. For Améry, after what he had suffered, they never could.

The book's second chapter, '*Die Scheinbaren Scheinfragen*', or 'The Apparent Pseudo-questions', reflects upon the author's time as a very young writer in Vienna in the 1930s. It was there that he was drawn to the logical positivists, who were shaking up the discipline of philosophy, challenging the political outlook of anyone, like Mayer, who could see what positivism implicitly rejected: the world of forests and folklore and irrational belief in which he had been raised in rural Austria, whose appeal was being twisted by the Nazis into the warped ideal of an exclusionary Utopia for those who belonged. Mayer was half-Jewish through his father, who had died in the First World War, and was raised as a Catholic by his mother. Without any living connection to Jewish culture or belief, he had grown up imagining he was as Austrian as Johann Strauss.[6] But when the rise of Nazi Germany began to threaten the integrity of its neighbour, he was shocked to realise that he did not and could never belong; that 'the Nurembergers had alienated me from myself by imposing the law that I was that and only that, nothing else'.[7]

He threw in his lot with the Vienna Circle and their logical, empirical view of the world. He also made common cause with other exiled writers, 'comrades' a generation older and much better known than he was – men like Bertolt Brecht, Lion Feuchtwanger,[8] Walter Hasenclever,[9] Hermann Kesten[10] and Stefan Zweig[11] – whose only common outlook was their fierce opposition to the Nazi regime. It was no coincidence that most of them were Jewish, but what mattered for Améry was their shared conviction that 'the positive was the truth [...] and the truth excluded the political lie'.[12]

Clearly, Kurt Grelling had found an ideal collaborator, though at the time the young Hanns Mayer did not have much experience of the essay form. Thirty years later, when Jean Améry sat down to write *Unmeisterliche Wanderjahre*, he was an acknowledged master, looking back with fondness on his youthful enthusiasm for the positivist programme, admiring its pellucid optimism and the nobility of the men who led it; above all, Moritz Schlick, a man of 'princely manners', 'tall and good'.[13] In the mid-1930s, Mayer was not a member of the Vienna Circle, but an ambitious young writer, schooled in the new philosophy through part-time study at the University of Vienna, where until his murder in 1936 Schlick was professor. It was during this period of instruction that Mayer had first begun to understand 'the logical construction of the world', as Rudolf Carnap had deemed it in 1928. Rejecting the dogmatic Marxism of the Stalinists, Mayer embraced the moderate leftism of the positivists – socialists or social democrats whose rational outlook sought to illuminate everything that was real in the belief that everything else would be seen as the illusion it must be. But every illumination also casts a shadow, and, as Améry was later well aware, it was these shadows that the opponents of positivism, Horkheimer and Adorno, had insisted could not be ignored.

Throughout the essay, Améry wrestles with his youthful beliefs and the doubts he now has about them, the long shadows which had never stopped growing as a result of the experiences he had later survived. As he does so, he is perhaps surprised, perhaps relieved that something of this early belief in a rational view of the world and its logical structure has also survived, and that this belief in rationality was what the exiled writers he calls 'comrades' were all defending, a goal they shared with the Vienna Circle, even if they all had nothing else in common. For both groups, he thinks, 'even if the rational was by no means the real for either of them, it was still the moral for both';[14] and whether morality is based on reason or its opposite is of critical importance.

The essays Améry was writing with Kurt Grelling in the Camp de Gurs have not survived. But, given what we know of their likely contents, and despite its recourse to an ethics the positivists would have disavowed, perhaps faint echoes can be heard in this affirmation of positivist values written thirty years later, the weak belief he still maintained 'that reason and morality are partially congruent, that unreason causes anti-morality, that truth [...] is one of the basic conditions of morality and that untruth, as a lie, but also as an error, is pregnant with atrocity'.[15] For Améry, the 'congruence of truth and morality'[16] were not inevitable, but were 'given as an opportunity, while untruth [...] has immoral consequences'.[17] Those immoral consequences had come to pass in Nazi-occupied Europe because of what he calls 'the unreason of everything historical, which also includes the contradictory belief that apparent unreason is reasonable because it forms itself as reality'.[18]

Améry's dispute with the unreason of history stemmed from his outrage at being its plaything, to the extent that, at times, he seems to set himself the impossible goals of someone who finds no solace in his beliefs, which offer the flimsiest defence against the facts of both his own history and what history as a condition of existence that he cannot escape has done to him. 'I will no longer allow anti-morality to be justified by the morality of history,'[19] he writes, by which he surely means that he will not let history's winners define what is true. He insists that only those who care about the truth should be allowed to define the past; and also on the vain hope that 'only those who exist morally have the right to exist and act historically'.[20]

But Améry the moralist finds Améry the man and his youthful alter ego, Hanns Mayer, profoundly wanting. He accuses himself of not having acted when it mattered, 'either morally or historically',[21] while at the same time recognising that both morality and history are concepts that crush the ordinary individual, 'this poor bundle of all too vulnerable flesh, indefinable emotions and impressions, this poor skin that wants only to protect itself against freezing cold and scorching heat. One can never be lenient enough', he writes, 'towards someone whose physically vulnerable existence grinds and devours him from within.'[22]

Améry cannot unsee the wretchedness of his historical condition, first in the camps in France, where he and Kurt Grelling had wrestled with the best means of conveying in clear, accessible language the rational, logical, empirical view of the world that both still believed in. If his memories had gone no further than these internment camps, perhaps he might more easily have borne them. But his fate would be so horrible – the experience of being tortured first physically and then mentally over time – that even thirty years later, and perhaps then more so than ever, he struggles to come to terms with both his helplessness in the face of murderous unreason and his selfish instinct to survive it. He is almost as contemptuous of his own impossible fate as all those citizens of Europe who had turned on, or turned their backs on, the Jews living amongst them, despising them for the same helplessness he is struggling to forgive. He concludes his essay with the following verdict on both the positivists who escaped to America and on himself:

> He did nothing. He didn't kill himself, which would have been a halfway manly act. His hand [...] was just strong enough to sweep the logicians' writings off the table. No pity is allowed for his poor skin, which he wanted to save and ultimately did save. Surviving was everything – and it was nothing. The logicians took up teaching positions elsewhere; he despised them, just as he despised himself. You had no right to survive without a fight. One can never have enough leniency [...] But only those who are prepared to judge themselves mercilessly can practise it. Counted, weighed. Found too light.[23]

It's an astonishingly harsh indictment of all survivors, however they survived, one that is haunted by memories of those who did not, and one man in particular. In the next essay, *Debakel*, or 'Debacle', Améry mulls over his period of internment in the South of France in conditions that were brutish but still far better than what awaited him in the east. At the heart of his reminiscence is his friendship with Kurt Grelling, a man he misnames, most likely through a failure of memory. It's an error, in the one book of note beyond those in his immediate field of activity in which Grelling is remembered, that can now be corrected.

Améry begins in the third person, but is so immersed in his memories that the first clause is in French.

> *Jamais il n'aurait pensé qu'il puisse faire tellement froid dans le Midi de la France* [Never would he have thought it could be so cold in the South of France], perhaps twelve degrees below zero, and the shattered wall of the Pyrenees was hidden in the fog. The barracks in the Camp de Gurs, where two men discussed philosophy, were unheated. The words, which were mere phonetic symbols without any living warmth, froze on their lips. Nevertheless, the discussion did not stop; it revolved around the joint writing of a work on neo-positivist philosophy. The professor had been appointed to a university in New York and wished to present a short, well-rounded, easy-to-understand book as an inaugural gift there. He had his material in his little finger, he lacked nothing, but he wrote, and knew it, in a tenacious style. So, he teamed up with his younger friend, to whom the sentence structures came more easily. Incidentally, there is no reason not to mention the professor's name: it was Georg Grelling, who belonged to the second to third line of neo-positivist philosophers and is rarely cited today. As they say, he didn't get a chance, but rather was driven onto a train that led him to Auschwitz. Laval had set the course.[24] The logician and mathematician was taught the logic of history, which he had previously wanted to know nothing about.[25]

The name slip is forgivable, seeing as Améry has taken the trouble to remember Grelling at all, though it is also certain that he could not forget him. But perhaps they had only ever addressed each other by their surnames, as is certainly the case in the numerous letters in which Grelling and his various correspondents write to one another about the people they know. Even among such good friends, each of them scrupulously maintains the formal *Sie* form of address rather than resorting to the familiar *Du*. It was a more formal time in every way, and perhaps in the camps more than anywhere a pressure was felt by many to uphold an idea of civilisation, a standard of conduct defying the barbarism that seemed always about to engulf them, both in the potential for violence from beyond the barbed wire and in the daily signs of squalor and degradation that were hard to ignore. Some were unable to resist; eyewitness reports from former internees at the mixed camp of Gurs lament the apparent promiscuity that took hold amid the filth,[26] though with the men kept apart from the women, such couplings, often husbands with wives, were grateful for the barracks that lay empty in different parts of the camp.²⁷ The uncivilised ones, the truly indecent, were those who held the blameless against their will.

Grelling's efforts to maintain good habits of personal and mental discipline, his consistent donning of shirt and tie, even when his clothing was threadbare, his exacting instruction in the rigours of positivism or mathematics or logic for anyone who would listen, were his own ways of keeping up an idea of civilisation for himself and those around him. But Améry sees in all the intellectual effort a futile denial of the reality in which they found themselves. The logic of history he speaks of is a notion that seems almost flippant, one he claims that Grelling did not understand when both the letters that Kurt exchanged with Neurath as well as his more formal writings, including *Anti-J'accuse*, suggest otherwise. There is a strong sense of hindsight at work in Améry's view of both Grelling and himself at the time; their recent biographies, first as refugees to Belgium, then as prisoners in the South of France, differ only in that, in the spring of 1941, Grelling had a realistic prospect of emigration whereas Améry did not. The cultural critic Walter Benjamin, a friend and colleague of Theodor Adorno and a Jewish contemporary of Grelling's from the same privileged Berlin background, saw history as an angel swept by the storm of progress helplessly into the future, but with its back turned, facing the past, watching the wreckage pile up in its wake. The image comes from Benjamin's late essay 'Theses on the Philosophy of History'. Written in the spring of 1940, it is fatalistic not only about the lives of men but also the spirit of history itself. When France was defeated, Benjamin had also been swept up in the debacle. In September 1940, when Grelling and Mayer still languished in the camp at Saint-Cyprien, he had passed nearby en route to the Spanish border. A supreme bibliophile, like his friend Hannah Arendt and many other German-Jewish intellectuals he had been an exile in Paris since 1933. Benjamin had come back to the city in March 1940, after a terrible period of six months' internment in a camp near Nevers, close to Bourges. In June, after the Nazi invasion, he'd been forced to leave behind his beloved personal library, fleeing the French capital for the South. Already suffering from a heart condition and also in a state of mind that was fragile at best, in September he set off from Marseille with a small group, bound for the Spanish border. But, even in 1940, there were many things that could go wrong. After the Spanish authorities refused them permission to enter, Benjamin and his party retired for the night to a hotel in the border town of Portbou, with the intention of trying again the following day. But Benjamin was fearful of being sent back to France, where the Vichy authorities and Gestapo agents already in the South were arresting and interning known anti-fascists and foreign Jews who were still at large, descriptors that both applied to him. The next morning one of his companions was summoned to his room to find life ebbing away from his body. Though some uncertainty persists, it is generally believed that the writer had opted to put an end to his suffering with an overdose of morphine rather than go on being crushed by a force whose baleful character he knew so well.[28]

Benjamin was one of thousands of mostly Jews but also others who chose their own manner of death over anything the Nazis might have planned for them or after what the Nazis had done to them. Among them all – exactly how many will never be known – were Moritz and Catherine Oppenheim, Guido and Irmingard Leser, Stefan Zweig and his wife Lotte, Walter Hasenclever, Clara Poll.

The angel of history in Benjamin's essay is helpless, powerless to stop the storm of destruction, despite wanting to restore what has been lost; the image is poetic, metaphysical, a woeful vision of a world in which the future may not be fixed but the tragic is preordained. Améry's logic of history is a more malevolent creature, too haunted by his own experiences to bear any resemblance to the rigorous logic of the positivists. Despite his commitment to the rational, he knows how fragile it can be, how quickly the forces of unreason can knock down the guardrails of civilised thought. His logic of history is something like the merciless logic of victory, a retrospective vindication of brutal events, the triumph of might in which history is written by the winners and those who lose are not just defeated but erased.

But in applying the logic of one who survived, perhaps Améry also risks adopting the same zero-sum view of the past as those who had tried to erase him: that those who perished, the 'submerged' described in *The Drowned and the Saved*, the last book by Primo Levi, were in some way responsible for their not having lived to tell the tale. In the unworldliness that settled upon Kurt Grelling during the years of enforced inactivity after the Nazis had seized power, as described by family and friends who knew him intimately, isn't there a danger, a subtle one to which none of us is immune, of seeing this as a critical element in the story of what later happened to him: that, according to one writer, 'When Oppenheim emigrated to the USA, Grelling did not join him despite Oppenheim's repeated urging';[29] or that, in the opinion of another, his 'reluctance to grasp what Hitler had in mind for Jews meant that he left the attempt to emigrate too late';[30] or even, in the view of one who adored him, that

Kurt had 'waited too long before realising the terrible logic of Hitler's Final Solution'?[31]

The dead have no voice beyond the words they may have left behind, so we'll never know how Grelling would have felt about this settled collective judgement on his fate. But as the detailed content of the letters has shown, and will go on showing, the reality is far less easy to explain, and was less within his power to control, than a mere lack of imagination on his part. But a failure of logic, the realm in which he excelled, is surely the claim that would have brought him up short. In any case, for Jean Améry, it is only in the context of the previous essay in *Unmeisterliche Wanderjahre* and in much of his other writing that the harshness of his sentence on the logic of history can be seen to reflect the far more pitiless excoriation to which we know he subjected himself. In parts of the rest of this essay, 'Debacle', it also becomes clear that his doctrine of survival brought with it a burden of guilt that was hard to live with over those who didn't make it, the millions of the murdered whose standard-bearer is his neo-positivist comrade from Gurs. Perhaps inflected by this feeling, the next sentence sees a switch in tone and personal pronoun to an intimacy that is almost shocking in its sudden access of warmth. 'A late greeting, then, over our misfortunes, friend Grelling! I liked you very much, and that's why I didn't tell you when we argued about whether the thing could be called a chain of events, or more pragmatically a purposeful constitution, that I was basically tired of the thing, that it didn't concern me any longer.'[32] Thirty years later, he is convinced that, in the harsh conditions of the camp, the 'logical game',[33] which had once enthralled him, now seemed 'empty and used up',[34] its abstract utility rendered meaningless by a visceral hardship.

Still, looking further back, Améry remembers with gratitude his first experience as an adult of the political system which, since the time of David Hume, with the importance it places on sceptical, autonomous thought – at least, in theory – had emerged as a natural corollary of early positivism and the scientific worldview. He is referring to the years in Belgium from his arrival in Antwerp in early 1938, where, as a Jew, like Kurt Grelling a few months later, he was given refuge by the Belgian government from the forces that wanted to destroy him. It was here that, for the first time, he found, 'Formal democracy, repressive tolerance, alienation, which masks itself behind law and the granting of rights, both of which need only to be examined more closely [...] in order to see that they contain injustice and the outweighing of all rights.'[35]

He is under no more illusions than the negativists, the critical theorists, about the shortcomings of 'bourgeois democracy', the sense that democracy was 'a larger-than-life farce and you shouldn't allow yourself to be duped by it',[36] as his Marxist friends dogmatically insisted. But he didn't believe them, because the 'pseudo-pluralism' of democracy, 'no matter how miserable, was still better than the open dictatorship, which no longer felt compelled to pretend';[37] and 'repressive tolerance was preferable under any circumstances to repressive intolerance'.[38]

His defence of democracy is all the more persuasive for its disenchanted clarity. Writing of the thrilling and direct experience he had had as an exile 'of very specific freedoms, which can only be defined by the unfreedoms that conflict with them',[39] Améry takes issue with the critics of democracy, and what he saw as their lazy depiction of an unavoidable complicity of democracy, both in principle and as practised, with the forces of intolerance that sought to dismantle it. So, despite what he calls 'the debacle of bourgeois democracy'[40] represented by the defeat of France, and despite its poor recent record, not only in Germany but also in the countries of western Europe whose timid leaders had simultaneously appeased both Hitler and their own electorates, who were tired of war; despite the long charge sheet of its failures, Améry is insistent that 'bourgeois democracy can lead both into fascism [...] as well as into a gentle, problematic but humane welfare state on the Scandinavian model. It can carry social oppression within itself, but also the coexistence of the have-a-lots and the have-littles, and can guarantee the have-littles that they will not become the have-nots.'[41]

At the end of his long, disillusioned defence of a failing ideal whose imperfect practical application he still favours over any possible alternative, Améry returns to his time in the camps and his friendship with the unheroic but principled bourgeois philosopher, the decent man of logic and staunch social democrat of whom he had grown so fond and who seems to have embodied the vulnerable idea he has been trying to defend.

> Now I thought about the hunger and the great cold in this valley, which resound[ed] with misery. And when he, the older friend, came and suggested that I write the short and easy-to-understand introduction to the neo-positivist world of ideas, I objected that I couldn't write with clammy fingers and the churning in my stomach. Whereupon the friend, who not only had letters from Einstein as recommendations for people who didn't even know anything about Einstein, but also small but regularly renewed sums of money that came to him from somewhere, suggested that he would guarantee me five francs per day in advance for the writing services. Beyond

friendship, it was a business like any other. We discussed things while the news became more and more sinister, because Yugoslavia also fell quickly into the hands of the aggressor, and there was hardly anything encouraging to be heard from any theatre of war – we discussed the concept of protocol sentences and their application, Wittgenstein's penchant for mysticism, Neurath's vigorous but also somewhat shallow empiricism, and recorded what was said in more or less pleasant, easily accessible sentences of Anglo-Saxon simplicity.[42]

The reference to letters from Einstein is intriguing given the great man's friendship with Oppenheim, though there is no record of any letter of Einstein's being sent in support of Grelling's application to the New School. But, given that he knew Grelling from the Berlin Group, and that Oppenheim would have told his lifelong friend of Grelling's predicament, it seems entirely plausible that he would have done whatever he could do to help. Whatever was the case, what comes next in Améry's recollection at the end of this essay is tragically confusing, even more so when set beside Grelling's own memories of why their collaboration came to an end. If we were to believe Améry's account, the younger man abandoned his older friend, seizing with a man of his own age a sudden opportunity to escape:

One day I treacherously broke the unwritten contract. I left the friend behind with his philosophy and his appointment to the New School for Social Research. Without warning, I set off one night with a random comrade: we broke out of camp and headed north, it turned into a long journey and, when I think about it, it hasn't ended to this day.
The breach of contract weighed heavily on me and weighed even more heavily on me when I found out much later that things had gone badly for my friend, that despite the Einstein correspondence and a proper appeal, he had lost the unequal battle and been handed over by the horse trader to the enemy's knife.[43]

In fact, though Améry is not wrong about his friend's ultimate fate, in other respects his memory is faulty. With an appointment to the New School confirmed, Grelling's emigration prospects had dramatically improved. On 12 March he was moved across the country to the Camp des Milles, close to Aix-en-Provence and a short train ride from the port city of Marseille. It was where anyone with a realistic chance of emigration was sent while they waited to receive the necessary paperwork – the various visas and other documents – and a place on a ship. In a letter to Oppenheim written on 28 March, Grelling describes life at the new camp, saying that it is *not very conducive to intellectual work. But even so I hope that my friend Hans Mayer will be able to come here as well, so then we can finish the well-advanced manuscript of our book. As far as our work together is concerned, it would be very nice if it could be printed soon, and if it's not possible in any other way, then in its current form. It would be very beneficial to me if this work could be printed by the time I arrive in the USA.*[44]

From the evidence of this letter, there is no indication that Mayer had left him behind, in fact quite the opposite, and this view is unwittingly confirmed in the continuation of the passage at the end of Améry's essay, in which he describes his escape:

> We wandered, the accidental friend and I, through France's blooming fields, which opened up so beautifully before us in the Basses-Pyrénées that I immediately took them, with a joyful heart, into the ideal-typical picture. There were good farmers, who offered hospitality with hay, bread, meat and wine, and there were bad ones, like the one who allowed us to dry ourselves from the rain by his fire while he sent for the gendarmes. Prison, release, train journeys without papers through the country ruled by the occupier, long searches for cigarette butts in Montmartre [...]. Field paths even higher to the north [...][45]

The hazards of their predicament, two undesirables on the run in ragged clothes, are clear from this passage. But Améry's memory of events is less reliable. If he had left Grelling and not the other way around, he would have to have done so in late winter or at the very latest with the first flickering of spring. But the reference to blooming fields opening up in the Basses-Pyrénées places his escape much later in the year, perhaps even early summer. As it turned out, in the year 2000, the date of the breakout was confirmed as 6 June 1941, when Améry's biographer, Irène Heidelberger-Leonard, spoke to Jacques Sonnenschein, the man (by then a very old man) with whom Mayer had made that perilous journey across the entire length of Occupied France and, in Mayer's case, back to his wife in Belgium. By the time they had seized their opportunity, it was almost three months since Kurt Grelling had been shipped to the Camp des Milles. So, why are Améry's memories of him so consumed with the sense that he had broken their contract and abandoned him to his fate? It's a question that, even then, no one alive could have answered who had not lived the experiences that Améry had had, and almost no one alive today.

Primo Levi, whom Améry had come to know when they were forcibly worked alongside each other in Monowitz-Auschwitz, is one who, many years later, was able to offer some kind of answer. In an essay in *The Drowned and the Saved* entitled 'Shame', written several years after Améry had taken his own life in 1978 and a matter of months before Levi's own untimely death,[46] he gives a sense of the weight of the burden that could be carried by one who had survived the unthinkable horror of the Nazi death camps, and Auschwitz above all, so consuming that it might have led him to distort his memories of the past so as to heap all blame upon himself. 'The "saved" of the Lager were not the best,'[47] he writes, 'those predestined to do good; the bearers of a message. What I had seen and lived through proved the exact contrary. […] I felt innocent, yes, but enrolled among the saved and therefore in permanent search of a justification in my own eyes and those of others. The worst survived – that is, the fittest; the best all died.'[48]

The final sentence in that passage, with its sense of a guilt that could never be fully assuaged, echoes Améry's recriminations in *Unmeisterliche Wanderjahre* about his own survival and that of others. But it's also a reminder that for every extraordinary story of survival that continues to be written, or could ever be written, there are two more of those who didn't make it. Most will never be told. These are the bare facts of the Holocaust, the numberless and thus, still, in some cases, nameless victims, some of whom Améry and Levi and the few who went through the hell of Auschwitz and survived it had seen with their own eyes and could not forget. With the Nazis persisting in deceiving them until the very end, most of those victims still hadn't realised what was happening even after they had disembarked from the trains. Because, even if their own murder was something they could bear to contemplate, given a method so original in its horror, what kind of logic could have led them to imagine *that*?[49]

A MAN IN
MY POSITION

In March 1941, with the coming of spring and his move from Gurs to the Camp des Milles, Kurt Grelling had made it to the waiting room, from where he should have left for America; it was logical to infer that he would. Why that didn't happen, and who was to blame for the failure, is the story that remains to be told.

Until economic circumstances forced its closure in 1937, the camp had been a tile and brick factory on the edge of the nondescript village of Les Milles, around 5 miles west of the centre of Aix-en-Provence. Requisitioned by the French government on 2 September 1939, the day before war was declared, the imposing, nineteenth-century, three-storey brick building was ideal for the intended purpose; if you didn't know what it was, you might have guessed it was a prison. Its first inmates were sent there in September and October, when 'undesirable' enemy aliens, German and Austrian nationals living in France, were summarily interned. Most of the men at Les Milles had been released by April 1940, when the camp was closed. But then a further round-up the following month, after the Nazi invasion, saw many of the same people, including the novelist Lion Feuchtwanger and the surrealist artist Max Ernst, returned to Les Milles. At this point, the camp housed as many as 3,500 internees, near double its intended capacity, crammed like tinned sardines into its two main, open floors. The vast majority were either Jewish or political refugees or both.

In their different ways, the French camps were experiments in environmental discomfort. Where at Saint-Cyprien, the so-called 'pesthole of France', sand got into every orifice, and Gurs was a muddy swamp, every surface of the former factory at Les Milles was covered with a thick layer of brick dust, which sometimes made it hard to breathe. In the open courtyard, the summer sun was so intense that most inmates couldn't stay out there for long; on the inside, the sunlight could hardly be felt: the

The main building at the Camp des Milles, near Aix-en-Provence, France. (© Julian Beecroft)

windows of the building had been blacked out to stop artificial light from offering a night-time target for enemy bombers, though the enemy at the time of the Debacle, in June 1940, was not the same one as a year later.

Kurt Grelling arrived there on 12 March 1941, after the refugee organisation the Centre Américain de Secours (CAS), based in Marseille, had taken up his case following his appointment to the New School for Social Research. By then the camp's population was less than half of what it had been the previous summer, the period that Feuchtwanger had spent in the camp, as depicted soon afterwards in his memoir *The Devil in France*. It seems likely that, as the French authorities had failed to lift a finger to make life better for the inmates, the deplorable, insanitary conditions he writes of in that book were much the same when Grelling got there, though as Feuchtwanger remarks, it was striking how even those who'd been accustomed to luxury in their former lives quickly adapted to the routine squalor of the camp. After ten months of wretchedness, Kurt had also become inured to the hardships of internment, above all the complete lack of privacy. In his letter of 28 March, he is even surprised by the improvement in living conditions, describing them as *slightly better than in Gurs*. The weather was also sunny and springlike and the food was *better for quality*,[1] though again it was never enough.

The main meal every day was served at eleven o'clock in the morning, with a further inadequate meal at 5 in the afternoon. In Feuchtwanger's time, the early lunch was normally a lentil or bean soup with a bit of meat, whose flavour was marred by the bromides added to suppress the sexual appetites of the men. By the time that Grelling arrived, with the diets of the general population increasingly restricted, there was little or no meat to be had for the men at Les Milles. Though there was a canteen at the camp, it quickly ran out of anything it was able to obtain. On the other hand, as Grelling reports in the same letter, *in Marseille, where you can go for a break every now and then, you can get all sorts of delicacies such as oysters and the like for a lot of money, though everything that has nutritional value is very tightly rationed. As you know, the French population is itself starving. I have lost about 25 pounds in the last 10 months and am trying my best not to lose any more weight. But I'm quite comfortable. There is no immediate danger to my health. All shipments of food, especially those with nutritional value (especially fat), are of course still welcome.*[2]

In fact, by the end of March, two or three parcels from the Hempels had reached him at the camp, along with another sent months earlier from Lisbon by Felix Oppenheim, Paul's son. The regime at Les Milles, under the jurisdiction of camp commandant Robert Maulavé and a detachment of Vichy's *gardes mobiles*,[3] was surprisingly relaxed. From November 1940, its status as an emigration camp meant that inmates could travel on day release or even longer to Aix and even to Marseille, where the US consulate and the CAS were based. Naturally, demand for visas and places on ships was high, and Kurt had already run into problems.

The CAS had been set up in August 1940 by the American journalist Varian Fry, who had been sent to France by the Emergency Rescue Committee in New York. His mission was to expedite the emigration of political and intellectual refugees from unoccupied France while there was still a good chance of saving them. But work that was expected to last mere weeks stretched out into more than a year before Fry was ordered to abandon the mission and return to America. The US State Department under Secretary of State Cordell Hull, and above all its visa division under Assistant Secretary Breckinridge Long, an antisemite and a private admirer of Hitler's *Mein Kampf*, had raised more and more barriers to Jewish immigration; by September 1941, when Fry himself was forced to escape through Spain and Portugal, the work of the CAS was completely at odds with US government policy as implemented by Long. But by then, instead of the couple of hundred that Fry had first been tasked with helping, with the assistance of the US vice-consuls in Marseille, this humanitarian hero had enabled as many as 4,000 Jewish refugees to obtain the US visas and other documents they needed to get out of Europe.

For more than a year, at great personal risk, Fry and his small staff worked every day from eight in the morning until midnight, dealing with the flood tide of petitioners. But, as with the number of applicants to the New School, there were always too many. The top priority were the famous cases, the storied list of names including Feuchtwanger, Ernst, Marc Chagall, Franz and Alma Werfel, Heinrich and Golo Mann, all of whom Fry was personally able to help; but for every one of these, there were dozens, less celebrated, who faced the same jeopardy. In his memoir of the work of the CAS, *Surrender on Demand*, Fry admits that one of the biggest problems was deciding who was in real danger and needed immediate help, and who was a lower priority. The sheer weight of these numbers would account for the frustrations that Kurt Grelling writes of over the lack of effort he thinks the CAS has made in his case.

He had already been to Marseille on more than one occasion by the time he wrote to Oppenheim on 28 March, setting out in detail how things stood. *During my first visit to M. (15/3) I contacted the CAS and found out that they had not done anything about my matter apart from intervening to transfer me to Les Milles. On my next holiday (18/3) I went to the consulate myself. There I discovered that my second letter (with the letters of recommendation) was not yet in my dossier. The classification of incoming letters at the local consulate generally takes a very long time, usually several weeks. The officer who processed me told me only that the New School was not recognised by the government and that an appointment there was therefore not considered a [qualifying] document for an nqv.*[4] *Since it was no longer possible to contact CAS again that day, I wrote a letter to them in M. and asked for an intervention from the consul. But that was completely unnecessary, because when I spoke to my head of department at CAS three days later, it turned out that he hadn't even read my letter. That was 21/3. I now received a promise from him that he would present the case to Mr. Fry, the chairman of the CAS. On 24th March, I finally received confirmation that Mr. F. would discuss the matter with the consul and, upon request, I was reimbursed for the cost of a cable to Johnson. Tomorrow (28/3) I will probably be able to go back to M., and perhaps then I will find out the consul's answer. I would then like to add a corresponding postscript to this letter. But you can already see from this description at what a snail's pace things are happening here.*[5]

As he had been since his deportation, Kurt was worried most of all about his family, which with the prospect of his own departure had become an acute concern. His children in Switzerland were now living on the kindness of strangers, and it was all he could do to trust that, whoever these people were, they would not abandon them. Greta's situation had not improved. Though she was somewhat circumspect in describing the hardships she faced, it didn't take much imagination to sense how desperate she felt. She wrote to Kurt that she lived very frugally and stayed up often late at night, knitting clothes to earn her keep. As Grelling reveals in the same letter, *She can't buy any clothes for herself, even though her own ones are barely wearable now. Most of her belongings in Berlin have been auctioned, which is connected with our emigration. Even though she suffers again from rheumatism, the lack of money means she can't look after herself. I'm desperate about her letters, and still she writes that first I should travel alone.*[6]

But Kurt was determined to take her with him on the ship once his own opportunity came up. As he would later spell out in writing to the US authorities, he was all too aware of the sacrifice she had made, as a non-Jew, simply to stand by him. But he also thinks that Greta would need to make a further, final sacrifice of the trappings of her former life. *I think that we might be able to cover the cost of my wife's passage by selling her jewellery when she comes here, assuming she can bring it with her. I don't yet know under what conditions she can get the visa, but I hope to find out soon.*[7]

He had also heard from his half-sister, Eva Oppenheim, and her second husband Felix. On 13 March, they had sailed from Lisbon to America with Eva's two children from her first marriage and were now living at the Barbizon Plaza Hotel on 6th Avenue in New York City. Soon after their arrival, for reasons that aren't clear but may well have been an attempt to disguise their Jewish origins, these Oppenheims would change their surname to Orey. Kurt had received money from Eva in January and February, but admits that this would soon be exhausted, *as in the coming weeks I'm facing large expenditures. I have to try to get a voucher to buy myself a suit. Neither the one from F. nor the one my wife sent me has arrived, and as you can imagine I'm looking very ragged. I may also have to undergo a hernia operation. Because of this I would like to ask you to send me a further 8,000 francs or even a bit more, because one doesn't know how long it will be possible to send things.*[8]

Despite these shortages, he was at least able to escape the camp on a regular basis, and, from his own letters to his sisters and brother-in-law – Else, Lotte and Hans Sachs – and to Oppenheim, it seems that, from the money he'd been sent, he'd allowed himself some of the ordinary comforts of life that could still be obtained in Marseille. *Can you imagine what it means, after 10 months, to be in a room by oneself and to sleep in a real bed and take a hot bath? Those and similar enjoyments have been granted to me in the past few days. It is something very beautiful that one can have that here, and one has to be grateful for it.*[9]

By now, some of his friends had managed to leave, successes that were hopeful signs for Kurt's own prospects. Pringsheim had finally arrived in New York, and Caro would soon depart for the same destination via the Caribbean island of Martinique, a colony of France and thus somewhere that didn't need a visa. He also asks about Felix, Oppenheim's son, in particular *about his destiny since May 1940*, though there is no evidence of any reply to this question. In fact, the detailed account of Felix's journey across France and the Iberian peninsula was not set down until Felix himself wrote it in retirement more than fifty years later. Briefly told, by the end of October he had made it to Bayonne on France's southern Atlantic coast. A Belgian company called Sofina, whose Jewish German-American CEO, Daniel Heinemann, was an important sponsor of Jewish refugees in Brussels, had organised a kind of 'underground railroad' to get people across this part of France's southern border. After problems he'd encountered with his Spanish transit visa, Felix succeeded at the third attempt, when the Spanish border guards had agreed to let him in. He took a night train to Madrid and was warned to keep a low profile by the Belgian consul in the city. The Spanish secret police, the Political–Social Brigade, had being trained by the Gestapo and were brutal in their repression of opponents of the Franco regime. Many young Belgians of military age who had fought in the recent civil war on the Republican side were now in the concentration camp of Miranda de Ebro, south of Bilbao. On the consul's advice, Felix spent every day in the Prado Museum, looking at paintings while hoping that no one was looking at him. Finally, after yet more problems with the Portuguese visa, he had made it to Lisbon at the second attempt and had soon found a place on a ship.

Felix was lucky, but the obstacles he had faced were common; as the war continued, decreasing numbers succeeded in escaping by that route. Having reached America at the start of January, he had already begun studying at Princeton to qualify as a US PhD by the time a Red Cross parcel he had sent from Lisbon reached Kurt at Les Milles on 5 April. The package, redirected from Gurs, contained the following contents: a shirt, a pair of socks, 2 bars of chocolate, a kilo of sugar, 2 packets of biscuits, half a kilo of coffee, a tin of jam, 3 Maggi stock cubes, 3 tins of sardines and a piece of soap. By the end of the month, two similar parcels from Felix had also arrived. Then another, containing a fountain pen and the suit he'd been promised, was followed by four suitcases of his clothes that Greta had sent from Brussels. This sudden affluence significantly improved Kurt's outlook, restoring some of the old pep from the earlier letters, even if he was only too aware of how precarious it was. *Those consignments and the small parcels my sister Eva still sends me mean that I have had relatively plentiful, tasty and nutritious food in the past few weeks. In the meantime, some private kitchens have appeared, and in Marseille, if one knows the area, one can eat very well. Nevertheless, my money is decreasing rapidly, even though under no circumstance do I allow myself any luxuries. (As per my letter of 28th March, I hope that you can help in this regard.) For two or three days a week I am in Marseille in a metropolitan civilisation, and so my outlook on life is very changed. The lack of freedom, the lack of hygiene and comfort, is not as bad as in Gurs. I don't really notice it that much anymore. It's a fact that sometimes I get the opportunity to converse with ladies. I can see that the final liberation comes closer. In short, I feel much better than at any time since 10th May* [1940].[10]

Kurt's situation had greatly improved, but he was keenly aware that there were more important concerns. The main subject of this letter to Oppenheim from 27 April is a detailed update on his US visa and the issue of finding passage on a ship. *Mr Fry discussed my case with Vice-Consul Standish on 1st April,*[11] *and Standish didn't even mention that they don't recognise the New School. On the negative side, he thought it impossible that I would get a non-quota visa, as I cannot fulfil the conditions, having not lectured in the past 24 months. Because of this, Standish has agreed to give me a common immigration visa, for which the work contract from the New School is seen as a substitute for an affidavit. Then I received a summons for a personal exam. It was only on 17th April that I managed to be received by another vice-consul.* <u>*This one gave me the general go-ahead for receiving the visa in May*</u>, *after I have secured a place on the ship and all the other formalities have been satisfied. This vice-consul didn't have the authority to give a positive answer as to whether my family can have a visa. I asked Mr Fry to discuss these points with Standish, with the result that on the 23rd I received a summons for my wife. I immediately sent her a certified copy of the paperwork. I hope that this will help her to get out of Belgium and into France. The question of the visas for my children is still open. I have again asked Mr Fry to intervene in the matter. I don't know the results. My wife had already asked for an exit permit on the 24th March, the date of her last letter. Up until the 15th, she was not allowed to leave Belgium, but now it's possible that she has already left Brussels. I hope that she will arrive here soon. I have written to her that I will wait for her here until the end of May, as I wouldn't be able to depart earlier anyway. As far as the children are concerned, for the time being we will leave them in their school in Switzerland. But I am determined when I arrive in the States to do everything I can to get them there as soon as possible.*[12]

His statement that *I wouldn't be able to depart earlier anyway* seems to indicate the difficulty at such short notice of finding a place on a ship; that's hardly surprising, given the level of demand. On this basis, it was both reasonable and unavoidable to wait until the end of May for Greta to arrive. He adds that he has made the decision to travel via Martinique with Greta, but they are still faced with the problem of finding money for the voyage. He lays out the sums needed for the passage to Martinique, the onward journey to New York and, before that, a stay of unknown duration on the Caribbean island. Oppenheim has already guaranteed a sum of $600 for Grelling's passage. Kurt asks his former employer whether he could lend them the money for Greta, if he feels unable to offer it as a gift, committing to *work to repay the loan if we get to America alive and healthy*. By now, there was no one else that Kurt could turn to. As anyone would in the same situation, he struggles to maintain his dignity. He insists that *all the money you have spent so wholeheartedly for me and my family since 10th May 1940 I would like to give back to you, if I'm in a position to do so. It's clear today that neither you nor I know if that will ever be the case. You are the best judge of the economic worth of a man in my position, for whom you have taken on the duty.* <u>*I have made the decision that I am not leaving here without taking my wife with me or at least having made the arrangements so that her own departure is secure in every respect.*</u> *I owe her this. Of course, it's possible given the current situation – or even highly probable – that the war will render all of these plans futile. But I don't see any way that I can plan for something like that, so I don't beat myself up about it (like your well-worn maxim).*[13]

With his family still so far away, and with a certain amount of freedom at the Camp des Milles, Kurt was more philosophical about his prospects than he might otherwise have been. But the letters and cables exchanged with Oppenheim over the next month convey a growing urgency based on a sense of foreboding that Oppenheim and the Hempels all seemed to feel. There was no new evidence to suggest that Grelling was in any kind of danger that hadn't been there before, but with the Nazis continuing to entrench their power through further conquests in distant parts of Europe – most recently in Greece – there was also a sense he wasn't safe.

On 30 April, Grelling cabled Oppenheim with the following message: *IF ALRIGHT TRANSFER MONEY HIAS TO AMERICAN LLOYD*[14] *NEW YORK FOR PASSAGE MARTINIQUE FAMILY VISAS AGREED*;[15] to which Oppenheim replies, an undated response that may well have been sent within hours and certainly within days: *LLOYD RESERVES PASSAGE ONLY PEOPLE PRESENT MARSEILLE PAY PASSAGE PREFERABLY USING GOLDSCHMIDT CREDIT*

FACILITY HOTEL ARTS RUE MAZAGAM MARSEILLE ADVISE LEAVE IMMEDIATELY MAYBE WITH GOLDSCHMIDT BEFORE FAMILY.[16] There was an Ernst Goldschmidt present in Brussels during their time there, someone who, as Grelling had written in early 1940, had just left for America with his family. But Oppenheim's friend went by the same name, so perhaps he was still in Europe after all, more than a year later. Either way, his pockets were deep enough that, even in time of war, a Marseille hotel was willing to extend him credit.

Then on 2 May, Oppenheim writes to Grelling of the lengthy correspondence he has had with Eva Hempel about approaching the people and institutions that needed to be contacted – including the New School, HIAS and American Lloyd, with the last of which HIAS has directed Grelling to deal exclusively. Oppenheim says Lloyd could be more practical and much cheaper in reserving passage for Greta, because the conditions were always changing. *I cabled Goldschmidt, whom you may know from Brussels, that he should transfer the 8,000 francs you have asked for. […] On the 28th, he cabled me the answer: 'Hope payments […] possible next week'.*[17] But Oppenheim impresses upon Grelling that none of his family members is currently in Marseille, so no one can come with him. *For that reason, it is the opinion of us all that you should be ruled by your head and not by your understandable feelings, and leave immediately, before your wife and/or children. If they arrive after you in Marseille, and their visa and exit only depends on getting a place on a ship, then this can still happen insofar as we've got the money together already. We've all said a lot about the principle of your family travelling, so I do not need to discuss it again today.*[18]

The cable that Grelling sent on 7 May almost certainly pre-dates the arrival of Oppenheim's letter, because otherwise it would seem he'd ignored his friend's advice. *OBLIGED WAIT FOR FAMILY END MAY GOLDSCHMIDT CREDIT FACILITY IMPOSSIBLE CABLE AMOUNT DOLLARS AVAILABLE TO ME, COST PASSAGE ONE PERSON VIA MARTINIQUE CIRCA 15,000.*[19]

Oppenheim cabled him back on the 9th: *FROM 500 DOLLARS AVAILABLE HOPE TO OBTAIN MINIMUM 50,000 INVESTIGATE YOUR CREDIT FACILITY AGAIN BETTER TRANSFER SON WILL BE HALF CABLE HOW MUCH NEEDED IMMEDIATELY TODAY.*[20]

In his next letter, dated 15 May, Grelling has a firmer idea of how much the trip via Martinique will cost: 4,300 francs per head, including Klaus, who will turn 11 years old on 2 June and, as a result, will have to pay full fare. There are also other expenses to be accounted for, including stays of unknown length for the family in Marseille while they waited to get places on a ship; the costs of luggage; further money for the stay in Martinique while they waited for a ship to New York; and a reserve fund in case anyone fell ill. Goldschmidt, who was leaving with his wife that day, had warned him not to underestimate the total cost. Grelling puts a figure of 35,000 francs on the amount they will need just to get them to Martinique. Jacques Weisslitz[21] at the CAS had told him that the journey from there to New York would be a further 5,500 francs each. It all seemed so complicated and expensive that it would hardly have been worth it had it not been for the crucial bit of news he had to tell: *Thanks to Mr Fry's active help, I was able to get visas for the whole family.*[22]

It was a result they would not have expected, given the demand for visas, but Fry had made it possible to think that they could all leave together at last. If Greta and the children had been in Marseille at that moment, such an outcome would certainly have seemed probable, even likely if the money could be found. But, as yet, he didn't have the visas in his hand, his children were in Switzerland, and Greta was in Brussels, unable to escape. *As you can imagine*, he continues, *I am waiting anxiously from day to day for news on this matter. Her last letter was dated 12th April. In the meantime, I have sent her the consul's summons, which she probably received at the beginning of May. I promised her that I would wait for her here until at least the end of this month, and that if she wasn't here by then, I would make everything ready to enable her to come with the children immediately. I continue to hope for their speedy arrival.*[23]

It was two weeks until the end of May. At this point, what could he have done when a mere fortnight was the window he'd allowed for himself and for Greta and, on the evidence of his letter of 27 April, the end of May was the earliest he could hope to have left? On top of that, he had managed to obtain the precious US visas. Perhaps if only his had been secured, he might have begged for a berth on any boat in the harbour, as Oppenheim had urged him to do in a letter that may not yet have arrived. But other families, like the Goldschmidts, had left together and were still leaving. With a wait until the end of May that was apparently unavoidable, and with the imminent prospect that the four of them might now leave together, even if his wife and children had yet to set off for Marseille, what should he have done? With so much uncertainty about the future, not only here in the South of France but across the continent of Europe, how would he have felt if he had left them behind and they had suffered for that decision, either badly or worse? How would he live with that?

To differing degrees, everyone involved could feel the jeopardy of the moment; that time was running out. But this foreboding was based on a future inferred less from facts or reason or even past experience than from a sense of how fragile the existing arrangements were, of the risk that even these would collapse. Set against this feeling of fragility was the prospect that his family would get there soon. Fear and hope were doing battle in Grelling's mind, and hope, for now, was winning. In any case, as he tells Oppenheim, his quality of life had greatly improved since arriving at the Camp des Milles. A better and more plentiful diet, largely down to the parcels he'd received, had seen him put on six pounds; he was able to come and go between the civilised haven of Marseille and his wretched billet at the camp; and the Nazis seemed to be content that the Unoccupied Zone should remain that way, a vassal state managed by the Vichy regime. All of these factors, he would have felt, led him not to a false sense of security but, through the exercise of dispassionate logic and bearing in mind the vagaries of induction, to keep its opposite at a distance where he could see it and assess it for what was true. He continues in the same letter of 15 May: *I don't know what is to become of us if, because of the war, we are unable to get away from here. But I have already written to you that I refuse to beat myself up about this at present. As luck would have it, such questions are not yet acute, and I don't see how I can plan for a case like that. If my wife should not be here a fortnight from now, and I don't know if she can come or when she will come, then I will hurry up with my departure.*[24]

At this juncture, the clause *I will hurry up with my departure* seems at odds with the statement in the letter of 27 April that it would not be possible to leave any earlier than the end of May. Perhaps at this point he might well have found a berth if he had put his mind to it, but feeling that *such questions are not yet acute*, he was dragging his feet for the sake of waiting for his family. So, maybe this was the chance he could have taken, the moment when the cold, self-interested logic of survival should have forced him to act. If that was the case, it was love, his concern for others, the best of any human being, that almost certainly stopped him from doing so.

Whatever was the case, by the time he received the next letter from Eva Hempel, dated 27 May, the question had become academic. She was writing to tell him that the $500 for the journey which they had so far secured had come from the following sources: $150 from Mr Forchheimer, who'd collected this from friends and acquaintances; $250 from the American Philosophical Society; and $100 from Grelling's half-brother-in-law Felix Oppenheim (Eva Oppenheim's husband, who would soon change his surname to Orey). All those sums, which Paul Oppenheim (no relation) and others had gathered through various efforts, were meant to pay for his journey. Oppenheim had had to guarantee $4,000 to the New School and his bank account was blocked, so this was an expense he didn't feel able to bear. And then the bombshell: that *there are rumors going around that a journey to Martinique is not possible anymore, and if this is true and all four of you have to go via Lisbon at $350 a head, then getting this amount together will be a big and probably insoluble problem.*[25]

Eva also asks if Kurt has shaved off the beard he had mentioned in his letters, echoing a point her husband had made in a letter of 18 March: that Gaby Oppenheim, Paul's wife, was *very keen that you should shave off your beard before arriving in New York, otherwise everyone will think you are a Polish rabbi (I say that without prejudice, but you are not one).*[26] This does seem a strange, even trivial thing to be worrying about. But clearly it reflects an anxiety that everyone was feeling, when every small advantage, every effort you could make to fit in, or to not stand out, seemed to weigh so much more, when so few were now being admitted. In America, attitudes had hardened and restrictions had grown tougher in response. Better to be culturally, even racially inconspicuous as well as intellectually uncontentious. Eva adds that she and Hempel were planning to go to the fishing village of Rockport for the holidays, like last year, where Peter would work on a manuscript on confirmation, another concern of early positivism and an area in which Hempel would soon leave a lasting mark. She adds that, *O. will also be coming to Rockport in August. And we still hope that you will join us.*[27]

Oppenheim's next letter, two days later, also warns of the rumour doing the rounds about the Martinique route. He urges Grelling to consider other options, in a way that he, Oppenheim, had done (and had clearly had the means to do) at those times when his own emigration, first from Germany and then from Belgium, had become an urgent need. *With all of these difficulties,* he writes, *I remind you of my other maxim, which helps me a lot: plan for every eventuality. If something goes wrong, and I find out that I didn't miss anything beforehand, then I have to resign myself that this was a higher power.*[28]

But the only alternative that Grelling could have planned for was to leave by himself, and, at least for now, he'd decided to wait for his family. Oppenheim's advice in the letter of 29 May was well meant but, in any case, arrived too late. On 3 June, it was Oppenheim who confirmed by cable that a voyage to Martinique was now impossible as the route had been withdrawn.

HOW NERVE-SHREDDING THIS CONSTANT WAITING IS

The loss of the Martinique route was a big blow. Grelling couldn't have known but may have feared that, with it, his best chance had gone; new obstacles, deliberately placed, would soon put the goal of emigration even further beyond his reach. On 12 June, he sent Oppenheim a cable that reflected the new reality: *RESERVE PASSAGE ME ALONE LISBON AFTER 14 AUGUST THROUGH HIAS NEED MONEY HERE GOLDSCHMIET* [sic] *FAILS CLIPPER WILL FOLLOW.*[1] The same day he also sent a long letter that set out the predicament he now faced. *The situation in the past few days has indeed fundamentally changed. Martinique is finished and for my wife to get here in the foreseeable future looks highly unlikely. Furthermore, the American consulate gave me 15th July as the date for issuing the visa, provided I have a place on board by then and that the other formalities have been completed.*

A legal departure from Brussels is impossible at present; the other kind doesn't seem to concern my wife, either because she doesn't dare or because she doesn't have the necessary funds. About a fortnight ago, there appeared to be a possibility to bring her out, but, unfortunately, we have not been able to make it happen.

Since I can no longer make my arrangements dependent on my wife's arrival, and since the change to the Lisbon route means that the fare issue has to be rearranged, I have decided to prepare everything now so that I can leave alone if necessary.[2]

The shipping lines were telling him that all places were sold out until the following March. But, apparently, HIAS had places in the summer. He again asked Oppenheim for money: his resources were nearly used up, and the money he had borrowed from friends now had to be paid back urgently. Acting on Oppenheim's and Hempel's advice, he had asked another organisation, known as HICEM,³ about the funds to pay passage for his family. Someone who worked there had told him that $300 per person would be enough. Grelling didn't know how that sum had been arrived at, but took it as the basis for his own calculations. He writes that if they could just get another $100, then with the help of HICEM the journey for both himself and his wife could be paid for. Then maybe another way could be found for the children. His plan was to leave Les Milles on 1 August, assuming that Oppenheim could get him a place on a ship from Lisbon in the last two weeks of that month. *I differentiate now between two eventualities: a) If my wife is not here and will not be for the foreseeable future, then I will depart; but I will still endeavour that everything will be arranged for when my wife and family comes here. b) My wife arrives before that or her arrival is anticipated soon. Assuming I have been able to get these 100 dollars, if the worst comes to the worst, if necessary, I will delay my departure and will try to exchange my place on the ship for one on a later ship, so that I can travel together with my wife. c) If it should have been possible by then to get the travel money together for my children, then of course I will take them with me. Otherwise, when I get to America, I will have to attempt to get the missing money as fast as possible.*⁴

He was planning for more than one outcome, as Oppenheim had urged him to do. The precious US visas he'd been given for the family had convinced him that, somehow, they might still leave together. But Greta, who wrote to Oppenheim from Brussels on the same day, 12 June, took a more pragmatic view. She sent greetings from various mutual friends – Maria, Eugen his former landlord,⁵ Frau Loewe and the Perels – among the many who had stayed there and had not, or not yet, been deported.⁶ *At the moment my mood is good because, in the past few days, I have received so many letters. For weeks I had hardly any news from Kurt and also from the little ones, and this got me down. About Kurt I wrote in great detail to the Hempels, but I would also like to ask you again to help him so that he can depart soon. As for my journey, I can't count on it happening, because I didn't get a pass. I still hope very much that Kurt will soon be able to start his work again. Our good angel will not abandon us. He will make sure that we'll be able to travel there soon.*⁷

From this evidence, it is clear that Greta had given her blessing to a plan that Kurt would leave on his own. If he could manage to get to Lisbon, then that might still be possible. She then directly addresses their benefactors. *How beautiful it is that the four of you can do your studies and your work there. I admire your wife. Heartfelt thanks for the money for the shoes. I haven't used it because at the moment, according to the calendar, it's summer and I am using my light shoes again. I think I will have to stay here a while longer and knit because I can't find a suitable job. The worst thing for me is that I haven't been with my loved ones for so long and am very lonely inside. I hope I can find the necessary strength until we can see each other again. You cannot imagine how often and how much we all think about you here. Should I say that we envy you? I often think about the beautiful days at the sea. How I would love to step on a jellyfish. When will I get Kurt's first letter from there? Oh, if only I had already received it.*[8]

The emotional strain that she hints at in her letter would not have been helped by the news that came from the USA later that month. The State Department had just issued a new 'relatives rule'; the poisoned brainchild of Breckinridge Long, it denied a visa to anyone with close family members still in territory occupied by the Nazis.[9] Among the first to be affected by it, even though Kurt was being held in supposedly unoccupied France, was his sister Else in Dublin. Her daughter Marion wrote to Oppenheim on 2 July. *I received your address today from my mother in Ireland, [who] told me in desperation that someone has taken the American visa away from her, which she has has had since last August, because of her brother in France. [...] My mother is of course very unhappy that she has not secured a passage for herself in time. Now everything looks quite hopeless.*[10]

Rather unreasonably, she asks Oppenheim what he or Kurt will do to address the problem, as if there was anything they could do to counter the cruelty of the US government, or the hostility of the majority of the US population who even after Kristallnacht, like that in Britain, did not want to admit more Jewish refugees.[11] Crucially, a letter to Eva Hempel from Elsa Staudinger of the New School, dated 21 May, some days before the closure of the Martinique route, had already informed her that US consulates had begun refusing to issue visas to people with close relatives in Germany or in countries occupied by the Nazis, in advance of the measure being adopted as official US policy. So, even the visa for himself that Kurt had been issued that month might not have worked if he had ever tried to use it.

Whatever the realistic chance had been, the 'relatives rule' was now a fact of life, and for Kurt it was a problem to be solved. As he put it to the Hempels in a letter at the end of June, he had written to Greta *that she will not get a visa under the new regulations while she is still in Belgium.*[12] But he also thought that there were reasons to be optimistic. For one thing, he was sure that Greta would try everything she could to get out of Belgium; for another, so many people were still trying to help them. One hundred dollars for the cost of Greta's journey had come from the Christian Ecumenical Refugee Council in Geneva, to be paid by the Rev. Leiper of the Federal Council of Churches, transferred by the lawyer and pastor Adolph Freudenberg,[13] as soon as Greta had reached the South of France.

For Karin and Klaus, as yet there was no money, but he had pressed a friend in Montreal who owed him some money, a man named Hermann Hamburger, to contribute, and had also asked the Quakers if they could bring the children to France. Nothing had so far transpired, but he remained convinced that he was going to get the money together, one way or another.

But it would all be in vain if they couldn't find a way around the main problem. *The biggest difficulty now is the new immigration rules,* he writes, *but at the moment I don't see any reason for pessimism, though in the past few days this has certainly taken hold in the camp. But, indeed, nothing will happen without an intervention from Washington. I think this request would best come from Johnson. I only just found out that Mr Fry is a friend of Johnson. Fry sent him a cable to ask him to intervene in my wife's case. In the event that Washington makes difficulties for her because her relatives are in Berlin, I am sending a memorandum about this point, which the person who intervenes can do with what they want. It is of course better if the fact that my brothers-in-law are in the party isn't mentioned. But it's possible that we can't get around that.* [...]

I was very surprised to hear from you that the $500 is not from Oppenheim but has been paid by other people and organisations; at the same time, it is understandably a relief. [...] *In this connection, I am very interested to find out whether my stepbrother Hans Grelling is in the group from whom Mr Forchheimer has collected the $150. I had already asked him (Hans G.) but I never got an answer.* [...]

You write that Oppenheim had to guarantee the $4,000 to the New School. What you and Oppenheim told me before about Rockefeller — my relatives in Ireland and England and Oppenheim should all share this sum. Therefore, there should not be more than $2,000 over two years falling onto Oppenheim, if you agree with this estimate.

As you can imagine, the stresses of the past few weeks, together with the heat, have reduced my ability to work. It's a shame that after my transfer to Les Milles, I have been separated from Hans Mayer, who stayed behind in Gurs. I had started to work on a collection of essays. It's a shame, but he has deeply disappointed me. He hasn't yet sent me those parts of the essays that were as good as finished.[14]

It is almost certain, given what Jean Améry later wrote about his flight from Gurs, that Grelling's manuscript was left behind when Mayer and Sonnenschein escaped. It seems that, from the evidence of this letter, while Kurt may not have expected that Mayer would follow him to the Camp des Milles, he did expect the younger man to at least send the manuscript he had paid him to work on. Perhaps Mayer had intended to do so but had never quite got around to it, or perhaps, being focused on getting out of Gurs, the manuscript had simply ceased to matter. In any case, by his own account, his escape plan was hatched on the spur of the moment, when a cumbersome sheaf of dog-eared papers would no doubt have been the last thing on his mind. Wherever he and Sonnenschein thought they were going, it was certainly northwards, away from the Unoccupied Zone, and nowhere near Provence. But perhaps, for a writer, this failure to send an important manuscript to the man who needed it was a part of what lay behind Améry's later sense that he'd abandoned his friend. After all, for Kurt, and possibly for Mayer too, the manuscript may well have been more than just a short introduction to neo-positivist philosophy or even a calling card for Grelling's future prospects in America; it was a testament to the survival of the mind in the worst of times, the love of thinking in which their friendship had been forged, even as Mayer was struck by its futility, as Améry would later claim.

But if that project had come to a premature end, there were other uses of Grelling's intellect that were just as pressing. Kurt encloses with the letter to the Hempels a copy of the memorandum he mentions about Greta's relationships with both her family and the Nazi regime. Not only was she trapped in Nazi-occupied Belgium, he seems to have felt that the loyalty of her brothers to the Nazis would be an automatic stumbling block for officials in the State Department with the power to issue or refuse them visas. This may have been a worry but, as the Smith Act[15] passed the previous year had spelled out and as may have been a factor in Kurt's own case, tighter US rules on immigrants with political backgrounds were almost entirely fixated on those with sympathies for the left.

The memorandum, dated 22 June 1941, in which he brings to bear all his powers of logical persuasion, is as follows:

About the relationship of my wife, Frau Margaretha, born Berger, with her family.

My wife comes from a Christian, Aryan, Berlin family. Her parents and her three brothers live in Berlin. The brothers are members of the NSDAP (Nazi Party).

I maintain that despite this, from the American government's point of view, there is no reason to deny her entry. In support of this assertion, I will prove two things:
1) My wife is a fierce opponent of the Nazi regime, and there is absolutely no reason to anticipate that her point of view will change through any other influences.
2) Any possible attempt from the Nazis to make my wife pliable by threatening reprisals on her parents, I can say categorically will not work.

Concerning 1) I emigrated in October 1938 from Germany to Brussels. For the time being my wife remained with our children in Berlin. Before I emigrated, I transferred my fortune of 125,000 Reichsmarks to my wife. Early in 1939, with my agreement, my wife brought our children to a school in Switzerland so that they would not fall under the influence of the Nazis. Soon afterwards, the Gestapo put pressure on my wife to divorce me. To give their intimidation more strength, they told her that an expatriation procedure had been issued against me and that a similar order would be made for her. But if she divorced me, she would not have to worry about this and could enjoy her (my) money. My wife categorically rejected all of their advice. In the meantime, I tried to get her a permit to come to Brussels. This was finally successful in December 1939. My wife came to Brussels on 1st February 1940, and she had to leave everything behind – the fortune and all our chattels.

On 10th May 1940, I was arrested in Brussels and two days later was transported to the South of France. My wife remained alone in Brussels. Soon after the occupation of Brussels by the Germans, new attempts were made to persuade my wife to return to Germany and divorce me. Now they brought up the argument that it would be impossible for us to be reunited. My father-in-law supported those attempts to persuade her. My wife was steadfast and waited for the possibility to get to me and to go with me and our children to the USA.

I believe that with this behaviour my wife has proved to me and to the world that she doesn't want to have anything to do with the Nazis, even though her situation is insecure and worrisome, and it is highly unlikely that she will ever see her elderly parents again.

For this reason, I think I have proved my statement (no.1).
Concerning 2) The second can be easily justified. First, I want to say that the relationship between my wife and her brothers since the Nazis took power has been downright hostile. It went so far that, when she still lived in Germany, two of her brothers denounced us on the grounds that we were trying to shift money out of the country.

I think it is highly unlikely that the German agents will attempt to blackmail her in the new country [by saying] that they would do something to her parents. But even if they do try it, without doubt my wife would reject those threats, and would say to the agents that her brothers are party members and are man enough to protect their parents. This is [sufficient] reason to think that threats like these would have no effect on my wife.[16]

On this evidence at least, Greta's brothers, like so many, had fallen under Hitler's spell. Given the hardship she had suffered, and the Gestapo's remorseless intimidation, the pressure she was under was immense, as is clear from all of her letters. One full of anguish from Greta to her parents, dated 21 March, the date on which she and Kurt had married in 1925, confirms the accurate portrait of his wife's integrity and the hardships she had faced that Grelling would draw so precisely in his profile written three months later. By the time she sent the letter, she had been in Brussels for more than a year; for most of that period, since 10 May 1940, she had also been alone. Clearly, her parents were now trying to help her and it seems that they had sent her a package of food to keep her going. She was grateful for the help but also clear about why she would not be coming back.

Sixteen years ago, I was married to a decent, good and noble man. Your loving letter and the small package came as a gift on this, my day of joy. [...] You, my beloved parents, know full well that I would love, dearly love, to be there with you. Unfortunately, I cannot go there because I have been done too much injustice and evil there. My long and hard year of suffering has been due solely to the false denunciation. Unfortunately, no one could be found to help me obtain justice. But the responsibility for my suffering rests neither with me nor with Kurt, but rather with the informers. I talk with many women here who are in a position like mine, but because they have not been denounced, they have been able to get their goods and possessions. [...] But I still believe so firmly in German justice that I continue to have hope.[17]

Greta still had faith that the principle of justice somehow survived in Germany, despite all that she and her family had suffered. But she is adamant that she won't take the children away from their father, knowing what that would do to them and also to her. *I didn't come here voluntarily,* she goes on, *but rather the same situation which has made my life so hard has required my emigration when I would not be divorced. [...] I'm in my unfortunate position, and there is nothing I can do about it. I only know that Kurt and I have never done anything wrong, that we must bear all this pain and sorrow even though we are innocent. [...] As long as I live, I will continue to fight to restore my honour. I will not allow anyone to besmirch or deny me my honour. Forgive me, please. I really intended to write you a loving and happy letter, but then I became bitter again. [...] But to whom should I speak of my unhappiness, if not to you, who surely have complete sympathy for the misfortune of your child. [...] I hope that I will not have to live such a lonely and abandoned life for very much longer. [...] It has become abundantly clear to me that I cannot live without Kurt and the children. [...]*[18]

The letter to her parents bears out everything Kurt writes about Greta in the profile of 22 June. But, even if their bond could not be broken by distance, he didn't want to leave her behind, when she had suffered so much on his behalf. In a letter dated 29 July, a month after writing that profile, he told Lotte, Hans and Else in Dublin that their emigration was being blocked by the new regulations, under which her presence in Nazi-occupied Brussels ruled out the issuing of US visas; he also adds the insoluble problem that the presence of Greta's family in Berlin might make it impossible that they would ever leave, even if she could join him in France. But, in other respects, he was doing well and had taken on a familiar role. *A lively intellectual life has developed here in the camp in the past few weeks. Lectures and concerts are organised, etc. I myself have started a working group on 'the new logic' with 12 participants and will start another one on the foundations of mathematics in the next few days. This is fun and takes my mind off my worries.*[19]

On this evidence, Grelling's thirst for disseminating knowledge was passing the stress test that life in the camps had posed. It might even have been strengthened by it, as is borne out by two testimonies, both sent to Karin, his daughter, after her father's death, written by men who had known him at Les Milles. Neither one is among the many that Grelling writes about in his extant letters from the camp, suggesting the depth and range of intellectual contacts he made there, too many for them all to be mentioned in the limited page space he had. The first was Hans Fraenkel, a German-Jewish journalist, a man of Grelling's generation who had also been baptised a Protestant as a child but had taken the doctrine far more deeply to heart. Fraenkel's description of Kurt tallies with so many others. *Day after day he studied his thick books*, Fraenkel writes, *and he was always willing to make himself available for lectures. One often saw him, armed with his folding chair and a book, aiming for the sunny side of the courtyard [...] or in summer a shady corner.*

At first, we didn't understand each other very well, because his philosophical and my theological interests were very much opposed to each other. I became very angry with him once when he destroyed a lecture I had given with the brief comment, 'I couldn't make any sense of a single thing you said.' Today I must admit he was right – the lecture was miserable [...].

Nevertheless, I treasured his intellectual honesty, and he valued me very highly, too. We developed feelings of mutual respect [...].

In May 1942, I was sent with others to a [forced] labour camp. The members of my Bible study group organised a farewell event which touched and honoured me, and it was really a great thing for me that your father attended, to show me his sympathy. It became clear to me what it was that drew us to each other, two such different people, namely, the mutual recognition that each was a man of character in his own way, who publicly acknowledged his beliefs – his philosophical and mine Christian.[20]

More testimony on Grelling's standing among the intellectuals at the camp comes from Wilhelm Traumann, a former judge deported from Heidelberg to Gurs on 22 October 1940, who, like Kurt, was later sent to the Camp des Milles. He survived the war and, in the summer of 1946, wrote two letters to Karin. Traumann is apparently the man lecturing in a photograph taken inside a building in the camp during 1941; Grelling sits at a table in the centre of the picture, listening with others to the speaker; he is sporting the neat beard he had first grown at Saint-Cyprien.

Kurt (with beard), sitting at a table in the Camp des Milles, listening to a lecture given by Wilhelm Traumann, autumn 1941. (© Kurt Grelling Archive)

Traumann writes that both he and Kurt were *very active in the well-developed 'lecture circuit' at Les Milles*. Grelling he describes as being *constantly busy, despite the unfavourable conditions in the camp. He would sit for hours at his place near the window, or working in the library at the University of Aix. In the camp, he gave lectures and taught a course in modern logic, the so-called 'new logic'. Because of the difficulty of the subject, naturally he didn't have many people in his audience. He also participated in our seminar, which examined the problems of the future peace.* […]

Above all, he tells the Grellings' 19-year-old daughter, *your father was a passionate democrat who loved to talk politics. That was surely a family tradition, since your grandfather wrote a political pamphlet,* J'accuse!, *which was very well known in its time.*[21]

Traumann doesn't seem to know of *Anti-J'accuse*, and Grelling wouldn't have mentioned it; given what he had suffered, he may have scarcely believed that he could ever have written such a book. But, in any case, the portrait of Grelling in these letters from Fraenkel and Traumann is very much the man of wide interests, both pure and applied, who emerges from the collective testimony of all those who had ever known him: the unworldly dreamer with concrete ideas for the improvement of society or the international situation. For everyone, such as Jean Améry or Felix Oppenheim, Paul's son, or Grelling's sister, Else Samter, who recalled him in an ivory tower, there were others, such as Gerhard Weisser or Arthur Rosenthal or Traumann, who remembered him down in the trenches.

Kurt's intellectual confidence was being sustained, in part, by continuing good news about the children. In the letter to Lotte, Hans and Else, dated 29 July 1941, he writes that the young ones *are healthy and learn well*, that Klaus continued to write poetry, which was published in the school magazine, and had also taken part *in a jousting competition*. Pastor Freudenberg, one of his teachers at the school, the same Adolph Freudenberg who would help with the transfer of money, regarded the boy as *'straightforward and happily unproblematic'*. Karin, on the other hand, sent letters that were *very sweet and thoughtful*, but in a recent one had written, very honestly, *'I don't actually know you anymore'!*[22]

Karin's frankness would have cut him to the quick. Already the sense of loss she would carry for the rest of her life had begun to plague her. Family bonds were now being painfully tested, and Karin in particular, then 14 years old, was suffering under the strain. But other kinds of separation would be meted out with a brutal finality, as Kurt makes clear. *I'm very interested in what Else writes about her expatriation*, he says. *Greta hinted at the same thing about us months ago; but so far, I have not been able to obtain any official confirmation, although in my opinion this could be of great value to me.*[23] In fact, no official confirmation had reached him because the expatriation didn't happen until 8 November, later that year.

On 29 July, the same day as Kurt's letter to his sisters and brother-in-law in Ireland, Eva Hempel wrote to Greta, whom she would have known from their time in Berlin, though maybe not that well. It must have been hard to strike the right tone with anyone in such a predicament, to be informal and open about the ordinary things, in the way that one would usually write to a good friend, when the writer lived in safety, even comfort, and the recipient lived in poverty and peril. Eva says that they were glad to hear from her in so much depth, that they think a lot about her and their other friends in Brussels – Maria and Eugen and Dr Hirsch. She says that they are also longing for the day when Kurt arrives in America and are doing everything in their power to speed things up. *But you also hear that things are getting more difficult*, she writes. *And after the new regulations one has to start again from the beginning. We are now trying to intervene in Washington* to his advantage. *And we received good documents from Kurt for this purpose. We do not give up hope, but one needs an awful lot more patience, and we know how nerve-shredding this constant waiting is.*[24]

Eva reveals that they have given up their New York apartment for a small summer house, which is *primitive but very peaceful, and Peter can work on the verandah. He has made a good convalescence and has already been working hard. This evening we're expecting the Carnaps here and on Sunday the Oppenheims, who will stay with us for a few weeks. We are directly on the ocean, so we don't have to suffer in the heat.*[25]

In a third letter from 29 July, Peter Hempel writes to Grelling at the camp, reassuring him that more money would reach him soon. He says that Johnson doesn't want to intervene in Washington himself, but that a private individual should do it, so they will do it. The money promised by Rev. Leiper and Pastor Freudenberg had not yet arrived, nor that sent by Hans Hamburger in Montreal. But, as Oppenheim now had to guarantee to the New School Grelling's entire salary of $4,000, he was trying to share the burden with others, including Kurt's relatives in England and Ireland, who were certainly willing to help. But all manner of problems had arisen over how to realise the various commitments, and Hempel didn't know at that moment how things stood.

For now, he had no way of checking. Oppenheim had gone away for several weeks on a tour of California with Felix and Gabrielle, leaving Stephan behind on a summer course at Harvard. The pressure to come good for Grelling and also for others was considerable, and Oppenheim would surely have needed the break. But all this talk of houses by the ocean and tours of California must have sounded strange to Kurt and Greta, like tales from another world. An unbridgeable chasm had opened up between the urgency and desperation they now felt and the more leisurely perspective of the friends who were trying to help them. But, as Oppenheim reiterates in a letter he wrote on his return, *no one can get a visa whose wife is in the occupied area. So, you can see how important it is, as you had planned, that you cable us immediately, as soon as your wife is with you. Then as soon as we get the news, we will immediately make the necessary arrangements. [...] In the meantime, we are in constant contact with the New School [...]. As the Hempels wrote to you, Johnson allegedly can't do anything officially. In the same post, I am also writing to the New School that they should inform me as soon as they have a way around those difficulties. [...] We understand your impatience, but we very much hope that your admirable intellectual and physical resilience will help you. As you know, your own resilience is the mainstay for your wife.*[26]

That resilience was being tested in so many ways, as new obstacles were placed in their path. Oppenheim says that he has also received a very nice letter from Mrs. H. Hamburger in Montreal, to the effect that Canadian regulations prohibited sending money to France. Hans Grelling hadn't contributed to the Forchheimer funds, and the help from Grelling's relatives in England and Ireland had failed because of the foreign exchange controls. He adds, *It would be of interest to you that Ernst Goldschmidt arrived here a week ago with his wife and child, but only after enduring a terrible odyssey, in the course of which he said he envied you. Here in Rockport, I'm enjoying the beautiful combination of a stay by the sea and scientific work. But this enjoyment is tempered by world events.*[27]

Goldschmidt may well have envied Grelling at the worst points on his own journey, but surely he would never have traded fates with anyone who was still in France.

A week later, on 28 August, in a letter of one single, characteristic paragraph, Greta wrote to Oppenheim in a state of acute distress. *In the past few days, I have received news from the school in Switzerland that destitute children will not be allowed to stay there any longer. The children will have to leave the school by the end of October at the latest because they can't afford to feed them anymore. They want to give the children to my parents, but for many reasons, this is a sheer impossibility. I have taken the necessary steps to get the little ones here if possible. As I am not able to solve this difficult problem by myself, I have asked Maria and Eugen for help. Eugen immediately started negotiations with the Belgian authorities and received the verbal go-ahead for them to come here. As soon as I have this authorisation in written form, then I must contact the relevant German authorities to ask permission. At the same time, I have asked again for my travel permit, stating truthfully that I and the children are totally destitute. My request was processed further, and now I have to wait for an answer. [...] Maria will try, in the event that the children can come here, to organise transport through the Red Cross. I don't know what Kurt's opinion is on the problem. I've had no news from him. Under the current circumstances, I think it's wrong if the children go to him. His present situation is very serious. He wrote to me that he has no money and because of that is unable to provide himself with even the most meagre diet. How would he be able to look after the children there? Kurt's physical and psychological state worries me immensely. Why am I so helpless and devoid of power? I do everything I can to get permission for my journey. If I don't receive the necessary papers, I will have to stay here, whether I want to or not. I am sure you can understand how unhappy I am. My landlords* are behaving honourably. *When I told them about my difficulties with the children, they immediately said I could have them with me in the house. What that means with the current food situation, you probably can't imagine. As you can see, I still experience real friendship, despite all my sorrows and worries. I still believe in the goodness of people, so I cannot totally lose my faith in humanity. My inner strength comes not least from this friendship, but I know that I live and act as a woman and a mother according to my conscience, even though I am often very desperate in my downright indescribable situation. But* [...] *everything I experience is so small if I think about Kurt. If only I could help him. I think about it day and night but find no possibility.* [...] *Healthwise, things are just about tolerable, but unfortunately the doctors can't help me. They say no stress, etc. Kurt has suggested I take a cure, but I can't do that. This seems to be very dangerous for me and has been forbidden in my case.* [...] *So, therefore, I have to live with my sufferings.*[28]

The following day, 29 August, Grelling also wrote to Oppenheim. A remittance of $50 sent recently through the Baden-Pfalz-Hilfe, a New York NGO, had made things easier for the moment. But he writes that his debts had grown *to such an extent that after paying back the most urgent of them, I only have enough left to live on for three or four weeks.* He says he has arranged for an agent to visit Greta, *to bring her here if it's possible; though I have hardly any hope that this will be accomplished. But should she be able to come, and I should then be obliged to pay the sum of 8,000 francs, for that, too, I will ask for your benevolent help.* [...] *I know that I get even deeper in your debt, but I don't know any way to help myself. I hope it's possible once I'm there to pay off the debt, in the worst-case scenario at the end of the war, which I hope is not too far away.* [...][29]

What his hopes for an end to the war were based on isn't clear. But the one way he could help himself was to do what he was good at. By the time he wrote at the end of October, he was nearing the end of his course on the new logic. *If there is enough interest,* he writes, *I anticipate reading up on 'logical syntax and semantics'.* [...] *The course on the foundations of mathematics continues. Some time ago, in the context of the evening lectures, I taught about races, people and languages and recently, in the scientific circle, about the basic ideas behind neo-positivism. On that subject, through your mediation, two years ago Horkheimer gave me the discussion of Mises's little reader. Is it still of use to him? I have got the book here and I could work on it now.*[30]

The reference to the old commission from Horkheimer came as Kurt was trying to find ways of contributing to the costs of his own departure. How he had got hold of the book by von Mises is not explained, though the most likely source would have been the library of the University of Aix-en-Provence. But, as Oppenheim would later write, the book review had long since been covered by someone else. The world moved on. But at least by then the money had been found to keep Karin and Klaus at the boarding school until the end of the year, after the good Pastor Freudenberg had agreed to pay it himself, or so it seemed. The most pressing issue was Greta's journey to the South of France. On 10 September, Grelling had written to Oppenheim that Greta had put in a request for a travel permit, and six weeks later he confirms that *now she wants to come here illegally if the request is refused. This gives me new hope that, one way or another, she will be here soon.*[31]

More and more wives of the men at the Camp des Milles were turning up in the South, in many cases with children in tow. Greta, as a non-Jew, would be allowed to remain in Aix, close by. But most of the women, Jewish like their husbands, were sent to live in the overcrowded, unsanitary conditions of the internment camps for women and children, established in cheap hotels in Marseille. And from that source, Kurt adds reasons why, even if her journey is successful, their troubles would be far from over. *I have just spoken to a lady who arrived from Brussels and who spoke to Greta 8 days ago. Greta fears that 1) we won't get over there even if she would be here in the camp; 2) that here she has no means of subsistence, whereas in Brussels she does have that. If, either directly or through me, you would be in a position to reassure her on those two points, a lot would have been gained. Then she would take on this risky endeavour.*[32]

By the end of October, Greta had confirmed to Kurt that, one way or another, she would arrive in Marseille on 18 November. So, she must have been preparing to leave by the time she wrote again to Oppenheim on the 11th of that month. *Unfortunately, I still don't know what is going to happen to me or the children. From the school I received the news that they can stay there until the end of December. My local friends […] advise me urgently against bringing the children here voluntarily. Probably they are right, because all of my attempts to improve mine and my family's situation have come to nothing. My one last hope is to get a travel permit for myself. But no human being can tell me if and when I will get it. I have been trying for months but until now without success.*

I haven't seen my children for two years now. That is a long time. But I don't want to give up hope, even with all those failures, that I can still get to be with my own. In recent weeks, I have been feeling very unwell. The many disappointments and stresses have hit me hard. The sparse nutrition and all my other problems and worries have almost silenced my humour. I believed strongly that I would see my family again in November, but unfortunately …[33]

There was so little to brighten her days that the arrival of a parcel from America was an event she looked forward to with gratitude. But she also asks for what she calls *a great request. If you could send me tea, that would be a great help for me. I only get something warm to drink in the morning, but then in the afternoon and evening I drink water because it's cheaper. But now in the winter it's often too cold. […] My landlords continue to be very good to me. But as I only pay a fifth of the money that the other guests pay, I don't receive the biggest and most beautiful plates of food. […] I regret that I can never write anything positive to you, but that's not because I'm a complainer, but because of the difficult circumstances in which we live. Here we already had snow in October and it stayed. I hope we don't have a hard winter, as our coal would not be sufficient to fight it off.*

I congratulate Stephan on the doctoral exam. How proud and happy you must be with your two sons. At present, Kurt's letters are fairly content. I hope he doesn't suffer too much from the disappointment. I cannot express how sorry I am for the children and the poor man. Whenever I think about them, I have to cry. Soon it will be Christmas. For us it's the third Christmas that we'll have been separated. I don't want to think about this. I hope I will soon be able to write you a more pleasant letter. I don't want to believe that our good angel has left. Therefore, I live in hope.[34]

From the content of the letter, with its request for tea and worries over insufficient fuel, it sounded as if Greta was preparing to bed down for another winter in Brussels. But this may also have been a sign that, whatever she wrote and no matter the journey that she would soon be making, living in hope, with its faith in the future, was almost more than she could bear.

ON LOVE ALONE

With the arrival of his wife, Kurt Grelling went silent for a few weeks. A letter he sent to the Hempels in December has not survived. Then, on New Year's Day 1942, he wrote to Oppenheim for the first time in more than two months, to thank him for a Christmas gift. *Yesterday, to my great delight, I received four parcels from Lisbon, as you requested. The parcels contained sardines, chocolate, Ovomaltine, coffee and biscuits, all things that are very welcome here, as you can imagine. If I think back to the last New Year, I have to think that my situation has significantly improved. The last winter was the lowest point of my suffering. The most beautiful thing is that my wife is near me, and I can see her almost daily. But apart from that, our current situation is wretched. In particular, my poor wife made a huge sacrifice coming here, because her living conditions have got a lot worse. She lives in a tiny room without any comfort, not even her own wash basin. The food is totally inadequate. What one gets on [ration] cards is not sufficient and the rest is so expensive that we can only very rarely afford it. At present my wife has only a provisional permit to stay, which further increases the difficulties. But we hope that she will soon get a full permit. Our children remain healthy, thank God, but it causes us great difficulties to get the means together for their keep. It goes without saying that they lack the right clothing for the season. Now two months have passed since you so kindly submitted the applications in Washington. It's a shame that we are still waiting in vain for the authorisation. As far as I can tell, they have put new difficulties in place for emigrants from the Axis countries. Do you know anything about this? As I wrote in a cable to Hempel, I haven't received your cable from the 29th October and I haven't received what you sent me in November. [...] I hope very much that soon something will arrive from you again. You can imagine that the two of us will use more than double what I used myself, [...] as all the prices have gone up rapidly in recent weeks. My wife couldn't bring any money from Belgium, because the last she had was spent on the very expensive journey, and she didn't want to add to the debts we already have with Eugen.*

I ask you again to do everything in your power so that I and my family can be freed from our dismal situation. From here, I have contacted all authorities whom I thought could help me in any way.[1]

The following day, Greta also wrote to Oppenheim from the home of someone called Meyer at 32 avenue Saint-Jerome, in the southern part of Aix-en-Provence. It is likely that the letters were sent in the same envelope. She sends greetings from Eugen. *Brussels I can tell you about up until 22nd November, only reporting the very best, as far as this is of interest to you and yours. Hopefully, I will soon be in a position to tell you everything in more depth in person. It will be of interest to you that a senior official of the university is now living in the house at 21 avenue Victoria. The house was furnished by Eugen, as you and I know. Tenants are liable for all damages, including the furniture; this is the responsibility of the city of Brussels, which asked Eugen to let them use the furnishings. The car is still there at the villa. As you see, I have a lot of interesting things to tell you, as I'm always attending to my post in a café. Today I received leave to remain. In the meantime, my few bits of clothing have arrived, but unfortunately a lot of it was stolen. Our situation is very difficult, but we are happy that we can see each other and talk to each other. The contents of your parcel are a ray of light in our cloudy days. I'm still hoping that we get out of here soon. We can't live on love alone.*[2]

This letter to Oppenheim, in marked contrast to the desperation of some of those she had sent from Brussels, is chatty and sociable, but also restrained and self-aware, even when discussing a material situation that was quite clearly far worse than what she had left behind. This is the woman depicted in the letters of Hans Fraenkel and Wilhelm Traumann to Karin Grelling, sent shortly after the war. Fraenkel credits Greta with greasing the wheels of his own friendship with Kurt, writing that *because I found [her] immediately approachable [...] through her I came closer to your father [...]*. But Fraenkel had also valued his friendship with Greta herself and was able to sketch out details of her activities in Aix, painting a selfless portrait of someone who for years had lived on half rations at best. *Through our constant association,* Fraenkel writes, *your mother and I developed a real fellowship. Her presence was of course a brave act of affirmation for her husband. As an 'Aryan' woman she could have remained in Aix, but she courageously supported her husband, who didn't have any hope left. In earlier days, she had brought food to people hiding in the forest. She held her head high. I came to understand that she was the one who carried your father, a man of the intellect, through life.*[3]

The identity of the forest or the people hiding there isn't known, but Fraenkel's sketch is corroborated by the picture that Traumann paints of Greta's strength and active concern for the welfare of others. *She lived in Aix in a very modest garret,* he writes, *where occasionally I visited her. In the camp* she cared for us men with great energy. I remember vividly how she cooked wonderful lentils for us. Her only weakness was her heavy smoking of cigarettes. She was clearly a very well-read woman who understood our need for mental exercise.[4]

The portrait, like Fraenkel's, is full of admiration and respect. But, as is clear from the tone of her letters, the *great energy* of her care that Traumann describes was almost down to its last reserves. Her conscience, which enabled Greta to hold her head up high, was almost the only part of her with any strength left.

A few weeks later, Oppenheim received a letter dated 20 January with news of Grelling from an unexpected quarter. Before the invasion of Belgium, Dr Friedrich Caro had spurned the opportunity to emigrate with his family and had then been deported and interned, leaving them behind in Brussels. He had made it to America some time ago, but had only recently found the energy to write.

I have been in the country for almost eight months. I feel guilty that I haven't contacted you in all that time. The reason for this is that, after being interned in France, I have been paralysed by passivity. Luckily, I have recovered slightly from this condition.

A discussion I had yesterday with the philosopher Paul Weiss [...] has now given me the reason to write to you quickly. Professor Weiss belongs to the committee whose work is to get philosophers from Europe to America. Now, it's a shame that I have lost connection with your friend Grelling – we were interned together – and I don't know where he is now. In the event that he is still in France, Professor Weiss would like to offer him help from the committee, and he believes he can help him. If you need help of this kind, it would be best for you, dear doctor, if you would write to Professor Weiss.

In my case, I would be grateful if you could let me know how he is and how his relatives are, and also what you know about your friend Grelling.

I am a member of the Cooperative College Workshop organised by the Quakers, and they are very good to me. It is awful that my wife and children can't get out of Belgium anymore. It was only possible to leave the country illegally and my wife can't risk it, and in most cases things don't end well. I have had no news from Belgium since November 41.[5]

It isn't clear what kind of help Professor Weiss had in mind for Grelling. But, in any case, Oppenheim and the Hempels were still trying everything they could think of. At the end of January, Eva Hempel wrote to Oppenheim in English (more and more of their correspondence is now in the new language) with news of her conversations with a Miss Blitz[6] about a possible Cuban visa for Kurt and his family; Cuba was one of a number of Latin American countries selling visas to Europe's Jews at vastly inflated prices. Eva asks Oppenheim directly whether, in order to obtain the visa, he was willing to put up the sum of $2,600 deposit for the whole family; she doesn't care to hide her frustration. *If you are not prepared to do this then I think we can forget about the whole thing; for I know that it will be impossible to find anyone else who would be willing to – certainly no committee, etc. And by now I am somewhat tired of doing lots of things all the time which don't lead to anything. I am so busy now and so tired when I come home that I just hate to do 'Leerlauf'' on top of it. And somehow I especially hate to phone Miss Blitz (though she is very nice to me); I think it would have been so much easier today if, instead of you phoning Peter, Peter phoning me, I phoning Miss Blitz and now writing you, you had phoned Miss Blitz yourself; don't you think so?*[8]

Since further restrictions had been introduced the previous July by Assistant Secretary Breckinridge Long, US visas for refugees from Europe were issued solely by the State Department in Washington and only after extensive vetting had been carried out. As intended, what already had slowed to a trickle of successful applicants was now reduced to a drip. Two days later, Peter Hempel wrote to Professor Weiss for help, telling him that Eva had made an application to the State Department at the end of October for visas for Grelling and his family, and they were now awaiting a decision. But he was not sure how the entry of the US into the war in December would affect its immigration policy.

By this point, the ability of the Grellings to survive as a couple on remittances meant for Grelling alone was being seriously tested. On 15 February, Greta wrote again to Oppenheim: *Please excuse me when today I write another begging letter to you. But, unfortunately, our need forces me to do that. I don't know any other people who can help us, so that's why I'm writing to you. I don't need to tell you how very grateful we are for all that you do for us, but the two of us can't live on this. We don't get any other financial help from anyone else. Kurt has written to his siblings about financial help, but without any success. Because of the situation here, two people can't live for more than a week on the 50 dollars you send us so generously. What shall we live on for the other three weeks of the month? If our need would not be profound, then I wouldn't be writing this letter. It's awful to have to ask you personally for help, but through no fault of our own we have become beggars. Isn't it possible to find kind institutions there who would provide for us? If we live very modestly, only to the extent that we don't feel hunger anymore, then we need at least 200 dollars a* month (based on current prices). You probably can't imagine our worries and hardship. But when I write to you that we are in desperate need, then you'll believe me. We are in dire need of immediate and generous help if we're not to go under. Please search for help for us, and don't hold this plea for help against me.[9]

On the same day, Grelling also wrote to Oppenheim, saying that Oppenheim's letter from 1 December had only arrived on 8 January, since when, apart from two cables, they had heard nothing from him. The American base at Pearl Harbor had been attacked on 7 December, and no post from America sent after that date had yet reached the camp.

I wrote on 10th December to the Hempels and on 2nd January to you. Who knows when that post will arrive in your hands? On 12th January I received 4,300 francs through the Quakers, and on 10th February 2,083 francs through the Baden-Pfalz-Hilfe. [...] Unfortunately, we can't live on 2,000 francs a month. Through the Quakers, I got in contact with the Sachses, and I hope that they will give me a top-up there. Unfortunately, they can only send £10 a month, and this is equivalent to 1,760 francs. I also wrote to my sister Eva on 19th January, only to send us a monthly top-up, but without much hope of success. My wife has already explained the situation to you, so I don't want to add anything more. But I don't want to omit to thank you again for all that you have done for us. Unfortunately, we will still be hungry and walk around in threadbare clothing if help doesn't come from somewhere.

My attempts to earn money here through work have so far been unsuccessful. I am giving a young woman 3 hours of mathematics lessons every week for 5 francs per lesson. Financially, if we want to use this high-falutin word, it's a drop of water onto a hot stone. But I do get some other advantages because of that. Also, the situation of the children is getting worse. Our Karin is now 14 years old, and she can't stay in the school any longer. She has to go at Easter as an apprentice to a household full of strangers. Klaus can stay in school. One is trying to get the means together for his continued stay through some charitable organisation. We very much wish that we could bring our children to us, as we have been separated for two and a half years. But we hardly know what we are going to live on ourselves, and at least the children have enough to eat and a roof over their heads, though I am sure that the situation with their clothing is probably a different one. It will interest you and particularly Hempel that a few weeks ago, I met Mr Lautman[10] in Aix. He is one of three Frenchmen who know me and my work. We have met up a few times and we had very interesting discussions on wholeness in mathematics. Lautman has also introduced me to a philosophical society in Marseille, where he gave a lecture about the idea of order in mathematics. The emigration unfortunately makes no progress. One says here that people who were born in Germany only have a chance if they have a special petition and are able to push that through in Washington. I plead with you again to try everything if in any way possible to free us from our miserable situation.[11]

Their predicament was indeed miserable, almost critical, though it is striking how contradictory it also was. Trapped by war and destitution, without the means even to feed themselves, while still free to think and discuss ideas with anyone they met, and even to attend lectures in Marseille. The mind he could feed.

With the coming of spring, Oppenheim and the Hempels were still awaiting news of the hearing they would have to attend when the State Department finally got around to assessing the merits of Grelling's case. They were liaising with the Oreys – Eva, Kurt's half-sister, and Felix, her husband – who had now been persuaded to send him some money after months when they seem to have been reluctant. But Eva Hempel had had a visit from Mr Goldschmidt, who had arrived from Marseille the previous year and whose credit facility Kurt had tried to use. Goldschmidt brought her the handy and very precise sum of $177.25, for the aid of either Grelling or a man named Rathenau, most likely another refugee they were trying to assist.

Then at the beginning of April a letter came with news of the hearing they needed to attend. For the sake of simplicity and therefore speed it was decided that Peter Hempel and Felix Orey would be the right combination to persuade the tribunal of Grelling's character and credentials. But there was still the issue of the travel costs for Grelling and his family. In a letter of 13 April, Hempel tells Oppenheim that he has been pressing Kurt's half-sister, Eva Orey, to offer a substantial contribution, emphasizing *very strongly to her that if we do not have the money or the guarantee together by the time we go to Washington for the hearing, then the whole thing will disappear down the plughole*.[12] Eva Orey had also told him that the $500 they had promised would need to be borrowed from friends, but if Grelling's relatives in England, his nephew Werner and niece Ilse, could commit to reimbursing her when the international situation allowed, she and her husband would be prepared to contribute more than double that sum. Hempel seems frustrated with the Oreys; it isn't clear exactly how deep their own pockets were, but it's not hard to see why they felt that other family members more closely related to Kurt should share the costs of his rescue. In any case, the lack of liquidity in the financial system in time of war made this kind of mutual lending and borrowing an unavoidable necessity.

In the end, with the addition of $400 from one of the many charity committees that Eva Hempel had approached, the Oreys were able to offer the necessary guarantees to secure the full amount needed, so that this condition of entry at least could be satisfied. But, as Hempel wrote to Oppenheim in a letter of 26 April, Eva Orey had expressed doubts as to whether it was possible for anyone to escape from Europe any longer. He says he told her of someone that he and his wife had met less than two weeks earlier, who had come on a French boat from Marseille to Casablanca, and from there on a Portuguese steamer via Cuba to the USA. People were still finding ways.

The Grellings also hadn't given up hope. Letters they seem to have sent in early spring may not have arrived. But, on 14 May, Greta wrote again to Oppenheim, with a keen awareness of how dependent on the help of others she'd become. *I still hope that I would not have to write you letters anymore, but could speak to you for hours – but, unfortunately, I must write. For 14 days Kurt was very unwell. He had a horrible stomach and diarrhoea, and that has taken it out of him. Now he is healthy again but is always hungry* [...]. *I can't remember today what I have told you about us, so please don't become impatient if you have to read everything twice. The house* [in Brussels] *is still empty. A city official asked Eugenie to give up her furniture to a Mr Hans D., who has a position at the university. For this she is paid a minimal rent. All rented-out items have been inventoried by an expert. The city will be responsible for any damage incurred.* [...] *I haven't seen or spoken to Eugenie for a long time, otherwise she would have told me things that would have been of interest to you. I don't know anything more from Maria and her mother. I don't hear from anybody now. We are so lonely here and cut off from the world. But Aix is like that. We live here as we lived 200 years ago. But Aix and the surrounding area are beautiful.*

As you can imagine, we are still hoping for a miracle, and it would be a miracle if we could come to the USA.[13]

A few days later, on 18 May, Grelling wrote to Oppenheim himself, giving Greta's new address, 32 rue Roux Alpherand, as his own correspondence address. *Since my last letter to the Hempels three weeks ago, so little has changed that I don't have a lot to report. Our hope of getting to America has almost vanished. In any case, we will try as best we can to wait until the end of the war in France. Various organisations are trying to get me out of the camp on the basis of 'forced residency'. But for this I need to have at least 12,000 francs available to me. Maybe it would be enough if you or someone else, or the Quakers, would consent to support me with 50 dollars a month. This is only a guarantee for my keep, as my wife is free anyway and for me 50 dollars would be sufficient. The French authorities will deem it sufficient. I'm also trying to get money through work again and in this regard have [...] been in touch with Prof. Dürr*[14] *to make contact with a Swiss publisher. Maybe you or the Hempels can help me with this, namely by identifying books in the English language that are suitable for translation. Has Russell published anything suitable? I would like to ask you to get in touch with the author and the publisher about the translation rights. I think we can arrange a project like that today, to plan for a time after the war. It would be of service to me if the publisher could pay me an advance on the fee in francs immediately after signing the contract.*

Enough about that. Healthwise I am reasonable despite constant malnourishment. Unfortunately, my wife has lost a lot of weight in the last 6 months and is understandably very nervous, even though she is very brave.[15]

In May 1942, waiting out the war in a camp in the South of France, planning for a time when it was over, did not seem a wholly implausible option; it was something they might have survived. At the same time, at that point any Allied victory was something of a pipedream, while victory for the Nazis was a prospect too appalling to contemplate. Aside from the few weeks during the previous May when he had waited for his family in vain, Kurt had tried everything he could think of to get away; he was still trying but had also accepted how powerless he was. His and Greta's main hope still lay with the hearing that was about to take place in Washington, and on that subject Eva Hempel wrote to Oppenheim in English on the 22nd with fresh insights into how it might go. *I have seen Miss Rasofsky and spoken to Mrs Staudinger over the phone. Both say that the committee is mainly interested in the political views and opinions of the witnesses and of the prospective immigrants. They grill you thoroughly on your ideas about politics, democracy, etc. in order to find whether you or the visa immigrant might not be a communist – which they are likely to suspect in the case of an intellectual. Mrs Staudinger said that they just won't believe that the writings of a philosopher can be quite unpolitic, and they want you to show that his writings are democratic. Miss Rasofsky said that she did not think that Mrs G.'s brothers were a serious obstacle, since she had been on bad terms with them for such a long time. By the way, Peter and I discussed possible questions yesterday, and there are several in which you might come in, after all, f. ex. Why, how and where did G. go to Belgium – or when Peter is asked if he sent money to G. and how much, he might have to mention you, because after all he would not* want to say any untruths, of course. And if they asked him about his income, it would be clear that he couldn't send $100 of his own in a month. Of course, P. will only speak about the things he is asked about, but he just wanted to mention these possibilities beforehand.

By the way, we sent G. a cable on May 16, after all; Peter was all for it, since we won't know about the outcome of the hearing before the end of June, probably. It read as follows: 'VLT Kurt Grelling Camp Les Milles. Thanks letter April 7. Sent 100 American Express. Washington hearing May 26. Chances favorable decision unknown. Warmest wishes Carl Hempel.'

I think that in Stephan's case the hearing won't be more than a mere formality, and that you won't have any difficulties. But we shall also [keep] our fingers crossed anyhow.[16]

Oppenheim sent Grelling a further remittance on 6 June, followed by a letter dated the following day, though this has not survived. A photograph taken in late March 1942 shows Kurt and Greta in a group shot

Kurt, Greta and four others in the courtyard at the Camp des Milles, 25 March 1942. (© Kurt Grelling Archive)

taken in the courtyard at the camp. Greta sits on one end of the front row next to a teenage boy, with what looks like his mother at the other end. In the back are three men, one of whom may well be the boy's father. Kurt, clean-shaven again at Greta's behest, stands right behind his wife, in jacket, waistcoat and tie in the bright sunshine of an early spring day. The people in the photo seem relaxed, even dignified in their proper attire. The increasing destitution described in the letters is far from evident in the image. But, then, keeping up appearances was key to keeping up morale; the camera can only record what it sees.

Peter Hempel wrote to Grelling on 1 August in English, the language in which he now thought. For Kurt, despite his long experience in translating from English, it may well have embodied the distance that now lay between them and the difference in fortunes that had kept on growing. Though it may be that the letter never reached him.

For many weeks all of us here have been expecting word from the State Department concerning your application for visas; but the procedure seems to be even slower now than it was before, and we have heard nothing; nor do we have any way of obtaining information as to the chances for your application to be granted. Mrs Staudinger, of the New School, with whom I telephoned about the matter, could assure me only that the cases of some of their prospective staff members, for whom visas have been requested, have been pending even longer than your case. Thus the only thing that is left to us to do is, unfortunately, just to wait and to hope for the best. We are very sorry not to be able to give you any more encouraging news than this. At any rate, I think that some hope might be seen in the fact that the State Dept. has not simply declined to grant the visas, and that the application therefore seems to be under serious consideration. And if you have heard about the various ways that spies have been trying to slip into this country, then you would understand that the State Dept. feels that it has to investigate each case with extreme care. But we are feeling very strongly that you of all people deserve the privilege to be granted admission to this country – and I emphasised that conviction also very strongly at the Washington hearing of your case –, and therefore we are really waiting with great impatience for word from Washington.

We wrote you last on June 10 from our short vacation at the sea. Now the summer term is more than half gone, and it has not been so bad, although we had a few days of sweltering heat, and although it often gets very humid – which does not increase the alertness of student or teacher. My teaching load is not heavy this term; I give only my elementary logic. Thus, I have some time left for reading and research, and I am back at the attempt to define the relation of confirmation between a general hypothesis and a class of basic sentences. It is a very tough problem, and I often despair of ever finding a reasonable solution. In addition, I do some reviewing, as before. I had to review Carnap's new monograph, Introduction to Semantics. It is a very technical book and less exciting intrinsically than the likewise technical Logical Syntax was. If I knew that the material really gets there, I would be glad to send you some books; I think Russell's Inquiry into Meaning and Truth would interest you more than the Semantics. What Oppenheim wrote Russell concerning the right of translation of the book, he has certainly written to you. I do not know whether he has heard from Russell yet. Oppenheim is at present in Rockport and continues his work on the 'Plane of Thought', now under the guidance of our friend Goodman,[17] who is staying at R., in his summer house, and who is an excellent applied and pure logician. The two seem to have revamped a good deal of the system, but I am not sure if it will ever lead to the results which O. has in mind – such as why the natural sciences have been able to discover more empirical laws than the social sciences, etc. Tarski seems to have got a position in the Mathematics Department of one of the great Universities in California; but I do not know the details. Zilsel[18] is in New York, writing and also teaching a little. I must say that I find him very clear and stimulating in discussions, and that his recent articles on problems of the sociology of science strike me as far above average. When I see him again, I shall ask him if he can give me some reprints for you. I shall also send you a reprint of one of my articles, of which I sent you a copy early in June. This may increase the probability that at least one of them will arrive. I shall enclose a reprint of an article by McKinsey[19] – a very able logician here – on the theory of relations. – Quine is in Rio de Janeiro as a guest professor for the summer; he lectures logic in Portuguese! He went there by plane, covering the enormous distance in four convenient, exciting day trips. Eva and I have been well; Eva is still the secretary of that nice psychoanalyst in Manhattan (a woman) and likes it.

Your last letter is dated April 30; we confirmed it in our previous letter to you and then sent it to the Oreys. They have been planning to help you, we hope you have since heard from them. Some time ago, Oppenheim sent us a letter from both of you which we read with great interest and deep sympathy. We are very anxious to hear from you again. In that latest letter to Oppenheim, you raised the question of your getting back to translating scientific books, and we hope very much that that plan will materialise. From here, of course, we are unable to judge just how great a market there would be for the translation, and whether some Swiss publisher might be interested in the idea. Yesterday we heard from friends in Zurich that Karin has left school and is doing household work. We are not sure just what kind of work that may be; perhaps your next letter will tell us about that? Several months ago, Oppenheim arranged for some food parcels to be sent to you; have any of them arrived yet? How is your and Greta's health? We so much wish we could send you both some clothing; but it would not get through.[20]

THE CHOICE

A month before the date of Hempel's letter, the Vichy government had agreed to round up all foreign Jews in both the Occupied and Unoccupied Zones of France, to deport them to an unknown destination in the east. Mass murders in Poland and the Baltic countries had been carried out since 1939 by mobile killing squads known as *Einsatzgruppen*; as the war went on, a growing cohort of willing executioners was drawn from local volunteers in these and other countries under German rule. By the summer of 1942, the unthinkable had become a mere logistical challenge for the Nazis, any moral objections a trivial concern when compared with the size of the task they had set themselves. The nature of that task had been spelled out on 20 January 1942, at a conference of Nazi officials at a house on the Wannsee, a lake to the west of Berlin, where a plan was agreed to exterminate all the Jews of Europe. They called it the Final Solution to the Jewish Question.

On 27 March, the first French trainload of 1,112 Jews – including many prosperous and influential French Jews from the Occupied Zone – was sent from a transit camp at Drancy in north-east Paris to the camp at Auschwitz in southern Poland. According to the paperwork, they were sent there for 'labour service', a typical Nazi euphemism. At a further meeting in Berlin on 11 June, Heinrich Himmler set quotas of Jews to be shipped from Belgium, the Netherlands and France. The numbers were arbitrary but, somehow, they would need to be met. France would supply 100,000 Jews across its Occupied and Unoccupied Zones. One of those at the meeting was SS *Hauptsturmführer* Theodor Dannecker, the head of the *Judenreferat* (the Jewish Office) in France. In July, he made a tour of the camps administered by the Vichy government – including, on the 15th, the Camp des Milles – to make a census of the numbers of Jews he found. He had decided to split the French quota down the middle, equally arbitrarily; the Vichy regime would need to find 50,000 Jews to deport. These would need to be foreign Jews, either interned or those still living in the community, if it was not to have to make up the numbers from the population of French Jews, a measure which in principle it opposed.

The first round-ups began in the Occupied Zone on 16–17 July, when 12,884 Jews in the Paris area were arrested and interned in the Vélodrome d'Hiver, a sports stadium without the facilities to host that number for more than a couple of hours; they were kept there for five days in conditions that soon became bestial. The stadium was in the Occupied Zone, but the Nazis did not have the manpower to carry out such a large-scale operation. The task was handed instead to the French police, the gendarmerie and the *gardes mobiles*. Many ordinary police officers, appalled at what they'd been tasked with, found ways to warn the Jewish population of the region; many Jews went into hiding before the round-up began, often with French non-Jews who risked their own safety to help them. In the end, those arrested were less than half the number selected for deportation. But still the number was huge.

Until June 1943, when the Nazis took over, the internment camp at Drancy was run by the French police. A modernist housing project begun, but left unfinished, before the war, its U-shaped series of three connected blocks, five storeys high, had been designed to accommodate some 700 people when completed. The thousands interned there were far more than it could ever have coped with, even if the facilities had been ready. To make matters worse, the neglect of even basic standards of food, sanitation and sleeping conditions that was typical of the camps in the South reached its nadir in Drancy. This indifference was worse than at any of the other camps for a simple, brutal reason: most who were sent to Drancy would not be there for long. Between March 1942, when the first train left, and August 1944, when the camp was liberated, some 67,400 Jews were deported to Auschwitz in sixty-four separate 'convoys'.

At some point during his time at the Camp des Milles, Kurt Grelling had been assigned to the spiritual care of the Protestant pastor Henri Manen, on account of his formal baptism as a child. Given the history of his thought, and the testimony of Hans Fraenkel, it seems unthinkable that he believed, or even pretended to, in the God of Jesus Christ any more than that of Moses. But, from a practical point of view, there were advantages to be had from being affiliated with a Christian sect. It is also true that Grelling's personal beliefs would not have mattered to Manen, one of the hundreds of French Christian clergy, both Catholic and Protestant, who risked their own safety to help or hide Jews.[1]

In the Unoccupied Zone, a few months earlier, the Vichy regime had put large numbers of Jews, including Fraenkel himself, into GTEs,[2] or foreign workers' groups, so as not to have to intern them; their wives and children were interned in hotels in Marseille – principally the Hotels Bompard, Terminus des Ports, Atlantique and du Levant – in conditions not dissimilar to those at Les Milles. On 3 August, two days after the date of Hempel's last long letter, they were all arrested and brought to the camp. Manen soon got wind of the planned deportations after a decision on 6 August by the Marseille Chief of Police, Maurice de Rodellec du Porzic, that the Jews interned at Les Milles would supply a good number of those who were needed to meet the quota. Selections for the first two consignments of Jews were made on 11 and 12 August. In these early deportations, children were separated from parents who'd been chosen for the trains. Manen's eyewitness testimony of what occurred on those days contains harrowing scenes informed by a deep Christian pity, as the enormity of what was happening overwhelmed the hundreds selected and the loved ones they had to leave behind.[3] There remains a question over what the nature of that enormity was in the minds of both the deported themselves and the policemen charged with carrying out the task. In many cases, according to Manen, the officers were hardly less affected than the people they were sending away. He praises them for their compassionate and humane demeanour toward the soon-to-be-deported: 'full of sweetness for all, sharing all their anguish, rejoicing in every deliverance, helping practically in any way they could', as Manen puts it.[4] But at no point in his record of events does any of the French officials choose to openly defy their orders, though several of the guards are known to have done so in secret.[5]

In *Au fond de l'abîme* (At the Bottom of the Abyss), the diary and memoir he made of the events of August and September 1942, Manen writes that on Saturday, 8 August, he insisted on an audience with Rodellec du Porzic. At the meeting he protested that he could 'not accept the idea of [the camp's internees] being sent to the ghetto';[6] by which he certainly means a form of segregation, completely abolished in the nineteenth century, now brought back by the Nazis in Poland. Rumours of what life was like for the Jews who were forced to live in the Polish ghettos would leak out slowly to countries in the west that were also under Nazi rule. But conditions in the new ghettos, though terrible, hardly differed from those at Les Milles. So, clearly, there was something worse about a transfer to the east – for 'labour service' – that Manen was determined to resist.

That evening the pastor returned to Aix. The following day, Sunday, the 9th, in an interview with the camp commandant he tried to find out whose names were on what he calls 'the fatal list'.⁷ Again, the diary suggests it was widely felt that the place to which the inmates would now be sent meant almost certain death. A report from the commandant of the Aix brigade of the gendarmerie nationale, dated 16 August 1942, spells out what they seem to have learned: that the fate reserved for them at this unknown location was 'mass execution'.⁸ So, by now, in the summer of 1942, the rumours were hardening into facts. Over the next few days and weeks, there were numerous attempts at suicide. Some were successful, like the young girl who, in front of her parents, threw herself from the upper floor of the tile factory to avoid being sent away. Several succeeded by this method, several more by other methods. But many of those who'd already been deported to France still clung to the hope that, even now, they might get to leave on a ship. As Manen puts it in his diary entry for Tuesday, 11 August, for some, when the time came to select those to be sent on the first train, to be forced to realise that the longed-for journey was not going to happen 'seemed to amount to something worse than a death sentence'.⁹

Interior, Camp des Milles.
(© Julian Beecroft)

The first train left for Drancy on the 11th, with 262 people on board; on the 14th, 236 of them were sent from Drancy to Auschwitz.

The second train arrived in Les Milles on the 12th. Kurt Grelling, for whom Manen had argued so vigorously, is one of those he writes about in his diary entry for this day.

> G. I got a promise on Monday that he wouldn't leave. Driven by a presentiment, his wife, who has just been operated on, presents herself to be interned and to leave with her husband. The Director, who has always been very humane, does not let her in and sends her away with the assurance that her husband will not leave. But on Wednesday at 4 p.m., a German general arrives. After his visit to the Chief of Police there is a real manhunt in the camp. A whole, large group of men who were not supposed to leave are brought together to be screened – that is, to have their situation examined again. G. is among their number. He is 58 years old.[10] Things are going very badly for him. Finally, it is only at 8.30 p.m. that this man will learn that he is not to leave. But the nervous shock was too strong for him, and he is destroyed.[11]

Grelling seems to have suffered a breakdown of some kind. The following day, he would still have been in shock when the second train left for Drancy, carrying 538 people, all apparently Jewish; all were sent on to Auschwitz.

It isn't clear what was wrong with Greta that warranted an operation. But without doubt things had turned out as badly for the two of them as she had feared. Kurt gives a strong sense of their physical and mental state in a letter he wrote to the Oppenheims – in French, for Gaby's benefit – dated 15 August, three days after his reprieve.

> *Many thanks for your letters of 7th June, which arrived here about 8 days ago. In the past few weeks we have gone through trials that I can barely describe. Fortunately, we are now out of danger, at least for the moment, because we never know what new trials are in store for us in the future. My wife especially has suffered a lot from this war of nerves, of which we were the object, and I fear that she is seriously ill. I hope*

that the cables I tried to send to the Hempels have reached them and that you are reassured about our fate.

I am very happy to learn that the hearing took place on 26th May. A letter from the Hs, arriving a few days after yours, gave us the details. Unfortunately, almost 3 months have passed since this date without authorisation having been received. Let's hope it doesn't take long to come. This is a vital question for the both of us, the importance of which seems to elude the State Department. As for our children, they are doing very well. We are very grateful for the interest that you, Madam, have been kind enough to take in our children. Fortunately, Pastor Freudenberg of Geneva, secretary of the ecumenical committee for refugees, takes care of them, and both are in favourable conditions.

Thank you again for your financial assistance. I suppose that I received all of your remittances through American Express, to which I always acknowledged receipt. Please send money in the future not to me but to my wife, whose address I have put at the head of this letter. In addition, I have received quite regularly – as far as I remember – 2 small parcels of sardines from Lisbon every month, for which I also say thank you.

Unfortunately, my wife's state of health does not allow her to write letters. She therefore asks you, dear friends, to be content with her warm greetings and thanks.

Please excuse my bad French! I too am in a state that doesn't allow me to pay much attention to it.[12]

On 13 August, the women and children living at the internment hotels in Marseille were moved to the Camp des Milles, to be ready for their own deportation. But even having arrived, sleeping again under the same roof as their partners, there was no guarantee that these women would be united with the men; Manen cites instances of wives and mothers who would not be parted from their husbands or sons and had to fight to share their fate. Of course, Greta wasn't Jewish, so to present herself voluntarily at the camp was indeed the brave act that Manen describes in his diary. But, even among the internees, there were other non-Jews, selected for the trains, reprieved at the last minute when the authorities were alerted to their clerical error; no one but the priests would point out the moral error. In one case, a non-Jewish member of the GTE was so shocked at what was happening to him that he lost the ability to speak. He was only pulled from the line-up after his Jewish comrades had spoken on his behalf to Manen, and Manen to the police; this man, at least, was saved. There was a quota to be filled but only by those who qualified for that dishonour by Nazi decree or, in one case, who may have chosen not to save herself when she could.

Pastor Freudenberg, Karin and Klaus's teacher, referred to again in this letter, was closer to events than Kurt may have realised. A week later, Freudenberg had received the manuscript of Manen's diary directly from Manen himself. Quickly printed and distributed, it was one of the first accounts to bear witness to events in the camps in the Unoccupied Zone. Freudenberg would have read the part concerning Kurt and Greta, but even if he'd been able to work out who they were, he may not have told the children. It is also likely to have been Freudenberg who received the small suitcase of Kurt's belongings that was handed to Karin at the end of the war.

The same day, 15 August, that Kurt wrote his letter to the Oppenheims, Bertrand Russell wrote to Oppenheim himself, from the address of Little Datchet Farm in rural Pennsylvania. Russell's fortunes were at something of a low ebb. His liberal attitudes to sex, as set out in various books he had written, had been exploited to have him removed from the post he had been due to take up at City College in New York, where Hempel would have been a colleague. The short note that Oppenheim received seems to have repeated a message that Russell had already sent regarding Kurt's comments about translating his work, which had failed to arrive in Princeton. *I have received your post card. I am afraid my answer to your letter must have gone astray. I am most willing to give any permission that will help Dr Grelling. He will, however, also need the consent of my English publishers, Allen & Unwin, 40 Museum Street, London W.C.1, who handle all translation rights for me. With kind regards, yours sincerely, Bertrand Russell.*[13]

It is likely that, on 12 August, having been turned away from the camp, Greta had returned to Aix. From the evidence of Kurt's letter of three days later, she would barely have had the strength to do so. But the correspondence address that Kurt shares with the Oppenheims is Greta's, the same one he had given in the letter of 18 May. Why he had made this change isn't clear. But, given how ill she now was, he was surely trying to stay with her in Aix, whenever he could next get away from the camp. This had been forbidden since 3 August, but after the second train had left, on the 12th, there was a lull. According to Manen, for a period of ten days, covering two weekends, the camp commandant permitted members of Christian congregations to attend services in Aix on the 16th and the 23rd, the two following Sundays in August.

A third train with 134 members of the GTE, who had been rounded up at the beginning of the month, left on the 23rd; this also went via Drancy to Auschwitz.

In the glossary of names at the end of Manen's published diary and memoir, where 'G' in the text is identified as Kurt Grelling, the reader is told that, having been saved in August, 'he was arrested a short time later, along with his wife'.[14] If Kurt had remained with Greta in her room in Aix, the police would have known where to find them. Neither was strong enough to have any hope of escape; without papers Kurt would soon have been arrested; without ration cards both would soon have starved. So, most likely they were rounded up in the night-time operations that took place across the whole of France over the following few days and, in the case of the Unoccupied Zone, from 26 to 28 August. The scenes at the Camp des Milles earlier in the month were now repeated across the country, as the French police swooped on their victims, shocking ordinary French citizens who witnessed these events. Many who had condoned earlier measures taken by the Vichy government against Jews both foreign and French, the laws and statutes passed specifically to exclude them from economic and cultural life, could now see the horror to which those measures had led.

The raids, while falling short of the quota that Pierre Laval, head of the Vichy government, had promised to the Nazi authorities of the Occupied Zone, gathered up a further 6,584 Jews. These men and women were distributed across the camps remaining open in the South. Camp des Milles, almost emptied out by the first three transports, received a further 1,200 Jews – from Germany, Austria, Poland and Russia. On 2 September, a fourth train left for Drancy with 574 people on board, of whom 558 were sent to Auschwitz.

Derelict concrete barracks at Rivesaltes, near Perpignan, France. (© Julian Beecroft)

By this time, it is likely that Kurt and Greta were both interned in the camp. Record cards in the departmental archives of the Bouches-du-Rhône list them as present there on 4 September; they had not been selected for the fourth transport.

The second part of Manen's testimony was written later, in tranquillity, as a memoir of what happened in the camp between 13 August and 10 September, the date of the fifth and final deportation train. According to Manen, the last transport contained all those who did not meet the conditions judged necessary for emigration, though given the closure of all the former routes to safety, it is hard to imagine anyone who would have by then. The 713 people carried by this, the largest transport, were sent to the camp of Rivesaltes, close to Perpignan. Rivesaltes was a sprawling campus of low concrete huts squatting on a treeless plain exposed to the piercing mistral wind. From here four trains in the previous month had also left for Drancy.

One of those sent to Rivesaltes on the train from Les Milles was Hans Fraenkel. He had lived in the camp with Grelling since March 1941. They were good friends by the time that Fraenkel was sent away with the GTE in May the following year, before being returned there in August, when the deportations began. His letter to Karin describes her parents' final days in the South of France.

We made the train trip to Rivesaltes together in the same cattle car, slept next to each other in the barracks, and had a lot of time to talk. Young Pastor Dumas[15] did everything for us; we were with him, he read the Bible with us, gave us a gift of date bread, and informed us the evening before the deportation that 8 of us had been removed [from the list of those to be deported]. So, we spent the morning of that terrible day in peace. At one o'clock it was finished. We were released to our new barracks, had our midday meal, bought some grapes, and enjoyed ourselves in the warm air in total comfort.

That evening at 8 o'clock came the sudden alarm. Once again, we were lined up alphabetically in the darkness. The commandant read names and more names from his list by flashlight. Three times he combed through the list. He came near to our names again. I was standing near your father and mother, who were chatting with someone. Then both names rang out. Your father stepped forward to explain that there must be some mistake. But the commandant is rude and doesn't let him say a word. Two policemen were sent with them to get their luggage. After a while I heard your mother call my name.

I answered, 'Here!' and she said, 'Tell Dumas!'

'Yes,' I said, 'as soon as I can, first thing in the morning.'

'Too late,' was the last thing I heard from her.

Your father remained silent. He carried a backpack and his suitcase, silently entering his fate.

Pastor Dumas had been at the train. The commanding officer assured him, in good faith, that his list of 8 names had been respected. In the darkness, he[16] did not see your parents. So, Dumas first learned about the misfortune the next morning, and he telegraphed as usual to Lyon, so that the error could be cleared up there and the people pulled from the train. But for the first time, the train was routed through Toulouse and, by the time Dumas telephoned, it had already crossed the demarcation line.[17]

A second letter written to Karin Grelling came from Wilhelm Traumann, the man who is lecturing in the photo including her father, taken at Camp des Milles in 1941. He was also among those deported to Rivesaltes on 10 September 1942.

There was another examination and selection of who was to go to Germany. For that purpose, we were pulled out of the barracks, which were in very bad shape because of unbelievable infestations of bugs. We had to carry our baggage outside, and spend hours standing in the hot courtyard of the camp. Once again, your parents were spared, were permitted to stay, and we believed that they had finally been saved. Then the following happened. Several of those who had been selected for transport thought to avoid deportation by getting across the barbed wire fence and fleeing. Now, there was a specific number of forced labourers that had been prescribed and the camp authorities were required to deliver, so they had to make up this deficit. So, they grabbed at random from those who had been protected until then, among them your father [...].

Your father yelled to me – we were unable to come closer – 'We're leaving.'

I yelled back, 'God protect you!'

That was it. Your mother went of her own free will.[18]

STOLPERSTEIN[1]

The train of 581 people left Rivesaltes on the evening of 14 September, arriving at Drancy the following day. Kurt and Greta Grelling were recorded as part of convoy 33, which left the station of Drancy-Le Bourget on 16 September at 8.55 in the morning.[2] Two days later, the train of 1,003 people arrived at the ramp in Auschwitz. In the case of both Kurt and Greta, given their age and physical condition, they were almost certainly among the 856 of those on board selected to be murdered by gas.[3]

AFTERLIFE

It took a while for news of the Grellings' deportation to reach America. In the meantime, some drew their own conclusions. On 17 September, Leo Forchheimer wrote to Oppenheim. *I have not been advised by you that Dr Grelling has arrived and therefore I must assume that your efforts to bring him here have been in vain.*

Under these circumstances, I feel obliged to return to Mr Max Schott the $100 and to Mr Hochschild the $50 which both gentlemen were kind enough to contribute towards the living expenses of Dr Grelling. Therefore, please be good enough to have the $150 refunded to me so that I can reimburse the above-mentioned gentlemen.[1]

Three weeks later, a letter dated 9 October arrived from the American Friends Service Committee, the Quakers, signed by Ruth J. Perry on behalf of Margaret E. Jones. *We have sent the following cable to our office in Marseille, for which there is a $3.00 cable and service fee.*

'PAUL OPPENHEIM-ERRERA FIFTY SIX PRINCETON AVENUE PRINCETON NEW JERSEY ASKS INFORM GRETE [sic] GRELLING THIRTY TWO RUE ROUX ALPHERAND AIX EN PROVENCE BOUCHES DU RHONE VISA DECISION EXPECTED SOON HERSELF AND HUSBAND'

It seems an awfully long time since the hearing was held – have you been in touch with one of the refugee committees, as to why there may be this long delay? We know it usually takes six to eight weeks but I cannot understand why no decision has reached you since last May.

Our office in Marseille has urged us to continue to cable them as often as possible any emigration data we may have for aliens trying to complete their emigration plans.[2]

Oppenheim wrote back in English by return of post. *In possession of your yesterday's letter I thank you very much for your interest in the above case. But unfortunately there is a great misunderstanding: In my letter of October 5 I only suggested keeping me, as far as possible, informed about the fate of Mr. and Mrs. Grelling and not to make any communications to them. Some, necessarily incomplete informations* [sic] *I added, as I emphasized, for you, had only the purpose to explain in quite a general way the situation. I did e.g. not mention their two children, for whom a visa had been applied for as well, and now the parents will be very upset that the childrens* [sic] *visa is not mentioned in your cable. Furthermore, in letters and cables everything was avoided to mention our, perhaps unfounded hopes regarding an early favorable visa decision in order to prevent disappointments; now they will not understand the contradiction between our news and your cable. Finally it is very disagreeable that my name appears in this connection, as the whole matter is handled by common friends, and the Grellings will not understand my suddenly appearing, which is a disadvantage for them because of my jewish* [sic] *name.*[3]

Oppenheim then asked Mrs Perry to send a second cable to try to intercept the first, though it was not until the 20th that Margaret E. Jones wrote back with the wording of the new cable. It seems that, by then, Oppenheim had got word of what had happened, and he wrote to tell them.

Then a short note from Hempel, dated the 27th, contained the following paragraph: *Orey called and asked us to tell you that Gr. has received Orey's 20,000 frs.; before being arrested by the Gestapo;*[4] *let us hope he was able to buy more clothes with the money! The news about the Gs is unspeakably shocking.*[5]

A letter to Oppenheim from Marion Samter, dated 14 November, confirms what Hempel's letter had strongly suggested. *Thank you very much for your letter with its sad news,* she writes, *which under the circumstances was not unexpected. Even so, one always had hope for a happy turn of fortune and even now I can hardly believe the news. Why, for example, should my aunt have been deported – she was 100 percent Aryan. After the events of the last few days, I have to give up all hope for the refugees who are still in France, and I have to find comfort that those will be saved who have only recently been sentenced to perish in building the Sahara railway.*[6]

Where are the children in Switzerland? I think Klaus must be in the same school, and Karin?

It's odd that you got a message about the hearing. I had a hearing for my mother on 1st May, and the outcome came back negative at the end of July. I can appeal against the decision in January, but I don't think it will be much use.[7]

There would soon be news of a terrible event that happened far closer to home. On 11 December, Oppenheim wrote a brief handwritten letter in German to the Hempels. It is almost indecipherable, but its opening passages seem to be: *Dear Friends, From the deepest sorrow, the deepest gratitude. You are the first to whom I write. No one was better able than you to find the right words in the face of the catastrophe [...]*[8]

It would have been tempting to overlook the letter altogether were it not for a postscript in French, in Gaby Oppenheim's own mellifluous (and legible) handwriting, in which the exact nature of the catastrophe her husband refers to starts to become clear. *My dear friends, your friendship does me good. Thanks. This wound can never heal; because life without Stéphane*[9] *is just a wound.*[10]

Initial research, later confirmed by Oppenheim's grandson Paul, as well as a letter that Oppenheim sent to Hans Sachs in July 1943, revealed that the Oppenheims had suffered a tragedy of exactly the kind that Oppenheim had feared in the letter he had written to the Hempels in late July 1939, a month before he and Gabrielle had followed their youngest son to America. On 28 November 1942, a fire had broken out at the Cocoanut Grove nightclub in Boston, spreading rapidly through the building. Exit doors had been locked and other fire regulations had also been ignored, in one case because the non-combustible gas that would normally have been pumped through the air-conditioning units could not be obtained in wartime; instead, a highly combustible substitute was used.[11] Of more than a thousand people present, twice the club's authorised capacity, 492 were killed, Stephan among them. It remains one of the worst such incidents in US history.

When the news became known, the first person to visit the Oppenheims to offer his support was Albert Einstein.

Felix, their remaining son, returned to Europe with the US Army after D-Day and later enjoyed a successful academic career. The Oppenheims' famous lunches continued at their Princeton home. Unsurprisingly, when Einstein and Bertrand Russell were finally brought together, as Kurt Grelling had insisted they should be, it was Oppenheim who set up the meeting.

Otto Neurath and Marie Reidemeister, his partner and scientific collaborator, spent three seasons as enemy aliens in separate internment camps on the Isle of Man, where conditions were at least far better than those in the South of France. But, with his customary energy, Neurath had soon managed to secure the affidavits he needed from eminent figures, a list that in their case did include Einstein. In February 1941, they were freed and soon were married. They settled in Oxford where, on the evening of 22 December 1945, Neurath died suddenly while sitting at his desk, quietly reading to his wife.

For a while after everyone else had assumed the Grellings were dead, the Hempels went on trying to find out exactly what had happened. In January 1943, they sent a cable to France via the Red Cross, but it came back with the message that the person concerned could not be reached. Then a year later, Peter suffered a tragedy of his own when Eva died soon after giving birth to their son. Within a few more years, he had married again and collaborated with Oppenheim on another, highly influential book. He became one of the leading lights in analytic philosophy in America in the post-war period. The pre-eminent school in the English-speaking world, its rise owed almost everything to the exodus of Europe's Jews.

Marion in the US reading a handwritten letter, 1941. (© Sheri Blaney, Samter Archive)

Else Samter had moved out of the Sachses' Dublin apartment in 1941, but it was not until the end of the war that she finally got to emigrate to America. Contrary to the impression she gives in her letters, Marion was far from happy at the news. According to her daughter Anita, during the war her mother had in fact been relieved that Else would not be coming to America. Despite the appearance of a close relationship in Marion's photos of the 1930s, in truth they didn't get along. As Anita describes it, *one of our family stories about how my parents happened to get married is that my mother got a letter from my grandmother, letting her know that she was coming to the US. My mother, in telling my father about it, started crying. He felt so bad for her that he put his arms around her and kissed her. Having kissed her, he felt that he must be in love with her and so he proposed.*[12]

Eventually, in the late summer of 1945, Else arrived. Soon afterwards, Marion and her Italian-American fiancé, Harvard graduate Ralph Savio, were married. Anita was born in 1949 and, for a long time, the family lived at the house in Arlington where, some three decades later on the pavement outside, Marion's negatives and notebooks would be found and then handed to Sheri.

Newlyweds Ralph and Marion Savio, October 1945. (Courtesy of Anita Savio)

Else chose not to set up home nearby but moved into an apartment in New York City, some distance from her daughter and grandchild, where she would live for the rest of her life. In time, she began making trips back to Europe with her sister Lotte, to reconnect with the world depicted in her daughter's photographs, in which she had seemed so at ease. But she may have noticed that the world she remembered had receded from view and may even have vanished from the places where she and Marion had been.

By the time that Else left Ireland, Hans Sachs had died. In steadily worsening health ever since his emigration, in March 1945 he suffered heart failure following a prostatectomy, a risky operation at the time. After the funeral, Lotte moved to England, to live with her children and their families. A consistent presence in the home in which John Cooke was raised, she made regular visits to those non-Jewish friends in Heidelberg who had stood by them in the Nazi years. As she always put it to her grandson, *I didn't leave Germany, Germany left me*.

Above all, she seems to have made it a personal mission to hold as many different parts of the family as she could in meaningful relation to each other, according to the motto she had impressed upon her grandson: *Man soll sich kümmern über die* Leute; you need to care about *people*.

Hans Grelling, Kurt's half-brother in Zurich, had kept in contact with the children during the war, sending them presents at Christmas and, by his own account, paying some of the costs of the boarding school in Gland. Though it was never enough to keep them there indefinitely, it seems to have been more than either Kurt or Greta disclosed in any of their letters that survive, and perhaps was more than they knew. They seem to have been equally unaware that Hans had also tried, and failed, to bring them to Switzerland on a similar arrangement to the one that failed in America. As Hans explained to Werner Sachs in a letter written in English, dated 24 April 1945, *When Kurt and Greta were brought to the concentration camp in Southern France, they got in touch with me and it was arranged that I paid a monthly amount to the college where the children were staying which, however, did not cover their whole expenses. Therefore – I believe in 1941 – the children had to leave the school and Klaus was taken by a Swiss family, Morgenthaler, […] whereas Karin after visiting a housekeeping school found a place as baby nurse at the Nil family in Aarau. Between Kurt and myself it was arranged that I would pay Klaus a monthly pocket money. Although at this time it was almost impossible to get a Swiss immigration visa for Kurt and Grete [sic], chaplain Freudenberg respectively the Christian Emigrant Council tried very hard whereby I guaranteed about half of their expenses, the other half being guaranteed by other institutions.*

Unfortunately, we did not succeed in time. So, Kurt and Greta were deported apparently to Germany and no news from them has come through since.

In March 1944 my wife and I met Klaus in Montreux and he stayed on Easter holidays 10 days with us, whereas Karin paid us only a two days [sic] visit on the same occasion.

In 1944 a section of the Red Cross approached me in connection with the two children when I gave them the address of Professor Sachs in Dublin as next relative. The Red Cross declared to me that according to the attitude of the Swiss authorities those children who have relatives abroad able to look after them would in due course be asked to join these relatives, but of course this should be done only when conditions are settled and there was the certainty that the children were well looked after.

As to Klaus I believe that there are no obstacles for him to finish the school here and to learn a job by which he can support himself afterwards either in this country or in view of the attitude mentioned above, also abroad. As to Karin I also believe that there should not be any too great difficulties for her training as a hospital nurse if the fees for such a course can be paid, and the Nil family gives her the necessary leave for attending the training.[13]

Claude Grelling, North Hall, Wartburg College, Iowa, 1948. (© Kurt Grelling Archive)

A second letter from Hans Grelling to Werner Sachs, dated just four days later, encloses a letter from Klaus, in German, in which he expresses his determination to become an engineer. In the end, in 1947, he emigrated to America under the auspices of Lutheran World Relief with the help of Eva and Felix Orey, who provided the assurances to the US government that any immigrant needed. He changed his name to Claude, became an American citizen, married, had three children and lived a long and happy life, as his temperament, if not his life experience, suggested that he would. In the end, he worked his whole career in the insurance business but kept up the lifelong passion for literature inculcated by his father. A tireless activist on behalf of others, described by his obituarist as 'no "bleeding heart" liberal' but 'simply a staunch advocate for the human race',[14] like many survivors, for a long time he never talked to his children about the past he had managed to escape. And he never went back to Germany, not even for the ceremony in 2008 to inaugurate the pair of brass *Stolpersteine* inlaid in the pavement outside Wilhelmstrasse (today Königsbergerstrasse) 13 in Lichterfelde-Ost. Perhaps if he had been younger, for that purpose he might have gone; he was certainly grateful for this small but permanent memorial to his parents' lives.

In an email from 1999 to Abraham and Edith Luchins, two researchers who wrote about Kurt Grelling a generation ago, Claude recalled the efforts of his parents to protect their children from the Nazis.

My sister and I were both baptised in a Swiss church, presumably at the request of our parents, while we attended the boarding school Les Rayons, probably in 1939. I have always assumed that our being baptised then was a kind of social insurance policy for us, rather than a religious affirmation by our parents. It certainly was not a religious affirmation by Karin or me – we had no idea what the ceremony meant, even though I was 9 and she was 12 at the time. So, did my father consider himself to be a Jew? I think he probably did, but only in the 'racial' and not the religious sense.[15]

Claude's view is certainly right in this regard; Kurt's letters support the idea that, throughout most of the 1930s, every Jew was obliged to consider themselves as such on the grounds of race, whether they wanted to or not. Beyond Germany, for the governments of Europe and America, that was first and foremost what he was. For this reason, above all others, Claude disagreed with the view of some that his parents' fate was one of bad luck.

I have long been uncomfortable with the idea that some may ascribe the negative events in my father's life, and ultimately my parents' death, to 'bad luck' or some 'twist of fate'. To my mind, there was nothing 'random' in these events. All can be ascribed to the virulent anti-Semitism which pervaded most of Europe (and much of America, too) before Hitler, and which that madman brought to a terrible apotheosis. Kurt and Greta Grelling were not unique, and their experiences were not unfortunate accidents. These events were shared by millions of other Jews and were the result of deliberate governmental policy under Hitler and less overt but nevertheless ugly discrimination before that. Bad luck had nothing to do with it.[16]

Karin remained in Switzerland, in Zurich, where she trained as a nurse. She later married a man named Hans Gimple and raised three sons. Lotte Sachs would make regular trips to see her, followed in later years by her grandson, John Cooke, who visited Karin on several occasions towards the end of her life. John's written memories of Karin also shed light on Lotte's great skill in practising what she preached. The following paragraphs are extracted from that memoir.

Karin Gimple at a care home in Switzerland in October 2021, shortly before her death. (© John Cooke)

It was always a source of grief and puzzlement to Karin that her mother had left her children to be with their father when she could (as an 'Aryan') have safely stayed in Germany. On the one hand, Karin understood the reasons. On the other, it was something to which she could never reconcile herself. She mentioned it every time we met, to the end of her life. I think that my grandmother would have had no hesitation in talking over Karin's feelings. She had a certain gift for this, and a very direct manner which enabled her to talk about difficult subjects. I remember how impressed I was as a teenager when someone telephoned her about a death. Others might have said just a few words of condolence. But she spent some time asking the grieving person for details of the death and events leading up to it – very therapeutic, I would think, as bereaved people need to talk many times about their loss. I feel that she would not have shied away from speaking with Karin about her parents' lives and deaths. [...]

Karin said that Klaus had put Germany and Europe behind him in a way that she had been unable to do. Perhaps it was because he was younger. Perhaps he simply cared less. She felt that she had always been the one with a duty to care. She was the elder of the two, and felt that she was expected to be good and to look after Klaus. She had gone on feeling this responsibility during the years that the two of them were in Switzerland without their parents. She had been very much alone in Switzerland: although she knew of Hans Grelling in Zurich, he had never wanted to do more than the minimum to help them (she felt that he wished to be uninvolved and to avoid any embarrassment of any kind). She remembered her Tante Lotte with great affection: when she had got married, with very little money, Tante Lotte had presented her with her wedding ring, with 'Hans' engraved inside it (her husband's name as well as Hans Sachs's). She remembered Lotte Sachs's visits to Switzerland (she remarked that, with three small children, she was completely worn out if Lotte Sachs came to stay, very fond of her though she was). Grete Grünfeld had also been very good and kind: although no relation, she had always made contact with her when staying at the Grand Hotel Dolder in Zurich (again, taking three small children to a formal tea, served at the Grand Hotel Dolder, could leave one worn out). There had also been some contact with her mother's side – the 'Aryan side' – but on the whole she had been pretty isolated. Klaus, she felt, had benefited more from the family in America: Eva Oppenheim (Orey) had sponsored him on his arrival, and Aunt Else and her daughter Marion had been present in New York. [...]

Karin wondered: had she had a good life? She thought on the whole she had. She wondered whether she had been 'damaged' ('beschädigt') by her parents' fate. Indeed, had the family as a whole been damaged, for reasons such as its high level of divorce? She felt that Aunt Else had not escaped unhappiness, partly for similar reasons and also through being widowed. I said that it seemed to me that 'damage' was hard to assess: down the generations it was perhaps given to some to put the past behind them and to others to find it more difficult to do so – a matter of temperament and inheritance. But in different ways the Holocaust must have affected the entire family and its sense of security and optimism. She noted that, at the end of the war, she and others had thought that the Holocaust was a once-for-all phenomenon, however inexplicable: but the world had now seen many other holocausts, even if small in scale, and they would no doubt continue.[17]

ACKNOWLEDGEMENTS

A large number of people have been indispensable in the making of this book. My wife Ulla Beecroft has given more of her time to the task of translating the letters at the heart of this story than I could ever hope to pay back; happily, she would never ask that I should. The intellectual scope of the letters presented one kind of challenge, their human warmth another; the long process of rendering them in accurate and empathetic English enriched us both.

Most important of all, of course, are the family whose story this is. I am profoundly grateful that the descendants of Kurt and Greta, Lotte, Hans and Else have entrusted first Sheri and then me with the memories, documents and photographs at the heart of the book. Anita Savio was the first to be approached and immediately supported the project, offering Sheri Marion's remarkable story, helping to make sense of the negatives and notebooks, then opening the door to the wider family. Also in America, Claude Grelling's children, Kevin, Karin and, above all, Dr Kent Grelling, have been diligent in their assistance throughout the process, searching their father's papers and providing numerous photographs to help unlock the emotional truth of what Claude, his sister and their parents were facing as the world closed in and, in the case of Kurt and Greta, shut them out. From America, the trail led Sheri to England, to the grandchildren of Hans and Lotte Sachs – Peter Sachs and his sisters Ursula Owen and Ruth Cecil and especially their cousin John Cooke. John shared Marion's photos during a visit in 2021 to Kurt and Greta's daughter, Karin Gimple-Grelling, who recognised herself and her brother Claude; Karin's son, Beat Gimple, was also instrumental in helping his mother in this process of remembering.

Karin passed away in 2022. Peter Sachs died in late 2023 but by then had offered numerous insights into the family history, beyond those in his self-published memoir. Nicoletta Gentile Pescarolo helped identify her mother, Annemarie Gentile, from the negatives, and also the Villa

Incontri. Above all, John Cooke has been tirelessly helpful, a generous source of letters, facts and insightful commentary into the family, their many friends and the world they all inhabited, the fruit of many years of his own research and both published and unpublished works about these remarkable people. I am grateful he has allowed me to use his own words in those places where nothing I could write would match them and also for the invaluable feedback he offered, having read an early draft.

The book has also been enriched by the stories of others whose lives intersected with the Grellings'. Paul Oppenheim's grandson and namesake has been a wonderful source of information, images and anecdotes in that regard. For access to the two archives of letters on which the story is largely based, I am also grateful to Laura Renee Brooks of the University of Pittsburgh Library; and Robert van Vuuren of the Noord-Hollands Archief in Haarlem, the Netherlands. Further documentary evidence came from Jakob Hübner at the Bundesarchiv in Berlin and Marie-Claire Pontier of the departmental archives of the Bouches-du-Rhône, and further assistance from Dr Laurence Ritter of the Camp des Milles memorial site.

I am profoundly grateful to Volker Peckhaus, professor emeritus at the University of Paderborn, who gave up so much of his time to review the manuscript; his indispensable commentary enhanced my understanding of Grelling's intellectual passions and the broader milieu in which he worked. I am also greatly indebted to Professor Frank Caestecker of the University of Ghent, for assistance on the situation of German and Austrian Jewish refugees in Belgium; to Dr Peter J.T. Morris, for biographical information on Victor Samter; to Catherine Uecker of the University of Chicago Library and Philippe Schulman at the Jewish Museum of Belgium; and to Mike Brown for a crucial conversation on the dispute of the critical theorists with members of the Vienna Circle.

Sheri would like to thank Jon Holmes for his invaluable feedback and encouragement with her manuscript, which inspired her to seek my help. She would also like to thank Kelly Horan, deputy editor-in-chief of the *Boston Globe*, for help in tracing Marion Samter's ancestry; Rosemarie Selm for deciphering Marion's German handwriting; and Lindsay Sprechman Murphy of The Wyner Family Jewish Heritage Center at the New England Historic Genealogical Society in Boston, for documents on Marion's US immigration. She is also grateful to James Lesnick, who rescued the notebooks and negatives from the sidewalk trash all those years ago; and to her husband Richard Share for reading her early manuscript.

Lastly, Sheri and I would like to thank Amy Rigg at The History Press for seeing the potential of the book and commissioning it, Rebecca Newton for guiding the project through the various stages of production, Jemma Cox for an elegant design, Paul Middleton for the copy edit and Laura Hayes for proofreading. Given so much expert help from so many quarters and the editorial oversight that followed, the text ought to be free of errors or glaring omissions; any that remain are entirely my responsibility.

TEXT CREDITS

Eva Ahrends-Hempel: Carl Gustav Hempel Papers, 1903–1997, ASP.1999.01, Archives of Scientific Philosophy, Archives & Special Collections, University of Pittsburgh Library System.
Jean Améry: Jean Améry. *Unmeisterliche Wanderjahre. Aufsätze.* © 1985 Klett-Cotta – J.G. Cotta'sche Buchhandlung Nachfolger GmbH, Stuttgart.
Friedrich Wilhelm Caro: Courtesy of Frances Colf, estate of Friedrich Wilhelm Caro; Carl Gustav Hempel Papers, 1903–1997, ASP.1999.01, Archives of Scientific Philosophy, Archives & Special Collections, University of Pittsburgh Library System.
John Cooke: Courtesy of John Cooke.
Leo Forchheimer: Archives & Special Collections, University of Pittsburgh Library System.
Hans Fraenkel: trans. Claude Grelling: Courtesy of Stephen Kuttner, descendant of Hans Fraenkel.
Karin Gimple-Grelling: courtesy of John Cooke.
Claude Grelling: courtesy of the Kurt Grelling family; Claude Grelling obituary: *Minneapolis Star Tribune*, 20 August, 2017.
Greta Grelling: Carl Gustav Hempel Papers, 1903–1997, ASP.1999.01, Archives of Scientific Philosophy, Archives & Special Collections, University of Pittsburgh Library System; courtesy of the Kurt Grelling family.
Hans Grelling: Courtesy of John Cooke and the Kurt Grelling family.
Kurt Grelling: Carl Gustav Hempel Papers, 1903–1997, ASP.1999.01, Archives of Scientific Philosophy, Archives & Special Collections, University of Pittsburgh Library System; Noord-Hollands Archief; John Cooke archive; courtesy of the family of Kurt Grelling.
Else Grelling Samter: Courtesy of Anita Savio and John Cooke.
Carl Gustav Hempel: Carl Gustav Hempel Papers, 1903–1997, ASP.1999.01, Archives of Scientific Philosophy, Archives & Special Collections, University of Pittsburgh Library System.
Max Horkheimer: © Max Horkheimer, 2002, 'The Latest Attack on Metaphysics' in *Critical Theory: Selected Essays*, translated by Matthew J. Connell, Continuum Publishing US, an imprint of Bloomsbury Publishing Inc.
Alvin Johnson: Carl Gustav Hempel Papers, 1903–1997, ASP.1999.01, Archives of Scientific Philosophy, Archives & Special Collections, University of Pittsburgh Library System.
Margaret E. Jones/Ruth J. Perry: Carl Gustav Hempel Papers, 1903–1997, ASP.1999.01, Archives of Scientific Philosophy, Archives & Special Collections, University of Pittsburgh Library System.

Primo Levi: Copyright © 1986 by Giulio Einaudi editore S.p.a., Torrino. English translation copyright © 1988 by Simon & Schuster, Inc. Reprinted with permission of Simon & Schuster, LLC. All Rights Reserved.
Henri Manen: *Au fond de l'abîme: Journal du Camp des Milles* (Éditions Ampelos, 2013).
Otto Neurath: Vienna Circle Archive, Noord-Hollands Archief.
Felix Oppenheim: Courtesy of Paul Oppenheim.
Paul Oppenheim: Carl Gustav Hempel Papers, 1903–1997, ASP.1999.01, Archives of Scientific Philosophy, Archives & Special Collections, University of Pittsburgh Library System; courtesy of Paul Oppenheim.
Stephan Oppenheim: Carl Gustav Hempel Papers, 1903–1997, ASP.1999.01, Archives of Scientific Philosophy, Archives & Special Collections, University of Pittsburgh Library System; courtesy of Paul Oppenheim.
Gabrielle Oppenheim Errera: Carl Gustav Hempel Papers, 1903–1997, ASP.1999.01, Archives of Scientific Philosophy, Archives & Special Collections, University of Pittsburgh Library System; courtesy of Paul Oppenheim.
Ursula Owen: *Single Journey Only: A Memoir* (Salt Publishing, 2019).
Nicholas Rescher: 'The Berlin School of Logical Empiricism and Its Legacy', *Erkenntnis* (1975–), Vol. 64, No. 4 (2006).
Bertrand Russell: Courtesy of the Bertrand Russell Peace Foundation Ltd; Carl Gustav Hempel Papers, 1903–1997, ASP.1999.01, Archives of Scientific Philosophy, Archives & Special Collections, University of Pittsburgh Library System.
Hans Sachs: Courtesy of John Cooke.
Peter Sachs: *Berlin Mitte: A Tale of Restitution,* © 2007. Courtesy of the descendants of Peter Sachs.
Marion Samter Savio: Courtesy of Anita Savio.
Anita Savio: Courtesy of Anita Savio.
R.T. Smallbones: Letter from Robert Townsend Smallbones, British Foreign Office (Consular Service.); courtesy of John Cooke.
Carl Wilhelm Traumann: trans. Claude Grelling: Courtesy of Katherine Sarver, the family of Carl W. Traumann.
Hans Wehberg: Obituary of Hans Wehberg.
Gerhard Weisser: Private recollections sent to Karin Grelling (later Gimple-Grelling) and Claude Grelling; courtesy of John Cooke.
Stefan Zweig: *The World of Yesterday*, 1942, trans. Anthea Bell (Pushkin Press, 2009).

Main archival sources

Letters of Kurt Grelling, Hans Sachs and Else Samter, personal archive of John Cooke (JCA).

Kurt Grelling correspondence with Otto Neurath No. 241, Vienna Circle Archive (VCA), Noord-Hollands Archief, Haarlem, the Netherlands.

Kurt Grelling and Greta Grelling correspondence with Paul Oppenheim, Carl Gustav Hempel, Eva Ahrends-Hempel et al., Series II, Subseries 2, Box 44, Folders 1–4, Carl Gustav Hempel Papers, 1903–1997 (ASP.1999.01), Archives of Scientific Philosophy, Archives & Special Collections, University of Pittsburgh Library System.

ENDNOTES

1: Discovery

1. Stefan Zweig, *The World of Yesterday: Memoirs of a European*, trans. Anthea Bell (London: Pushkin Press, 2009), p.351.
2. HIAS, or the Hebrew Sheltering and Immigrant Aid Society, was a global Jewish NGO that protected refugees during the Second World War.
3. Marion Samter, unpublished handwritten note courtesy of Anita Savio.

2: The Gypsy Life Isn't Beautiful

1. Entry for Else Samter, Volks-, Berufs- und Betriebszählung am 17. Mai 1938, held in the Bundesarchiv, Berlin.
2. John Cooke, email to Sheri Blaney and Anita Savio, 30.07.2021.
3. Peter Sachs, *Berlin Mitte: A Tale of Restitution* (self-published, 2007).
4. Weizmann lived in Germany from 1892, in Switzerland from 1899 and in England from 1904 until his emigration to Israel in the 1940s.
5. www.theatlantic.com/ideas/archive/2023/11/henry-ford-anti-semitism/675911; www.americanjewisharchives.org/snapshots/henry-ford-and-antisemitism-the-notorious-dearborn-independent
6. https://time.com/5684504/einstein-england
7. JCA/Hans Sachs to Else Samter/25.05.1939.
8. https://kitchenercamp.co.uk/research/bloomsbury-house
9. JCA/Else Samter to Hans Sachs/01.07.1939.
10. Ibid.
11. Ibid.
12. Ibid.
13. JCA/Else Samter to Hans Sachs/08.07.1939.
14. A port town near Cork in southern Ireland.
15. JCA/Else Samter to Hans Sachs/08.07.1939.
16. Ibid.
17. Ibid.
18. JCA/Else Samter to Hans Sachs/10.07.1939.
19. Hans and Lotte's daughter was getting married in Oxford that August to a man named Arthur Cooke.
20. JCA/Else Samter to Hans Sachs/12.07.1939.
21. Ibid.
22. Ibid.
23. JCA/Hans Sachs to Else Samter/18.07.1939.
24. JCA/Hans Sachs to Else Samter/16.07.1939.
25. JCA/Hans Sachs to Else Samter/18.07.1939.

3: An Irretrievable Separation

1. His official title was minister of economics.
2. Sachs, *Berlin Mitte*.
3. www.s197410804.online.de/Zeiten/1933.htm
4. Otto Westphal, '*den verdienstvollen Professor vor spontanen Angriffen zu schützen*', excerpt trans. Beecroft and Beecroft, 'Die nationalsozialistische Diktatur (1933–1945)' in Cser, Andreas, etc., *Geschichte der Juden in Heidelberg*, Guderjahn: Heidelberg, 1966, p.514, reproduced in the original German in Horst Dickel, 'Hans Sachs' in Gisela Holfter (ed.), *German-Speaking Exiles in Ireland* (Amsterdam/New York: Editions Rodopi B.V., 2006), p.197.
5. Charlotte Sachs, testimonial in support of Otto Westphal, 16.04.1946.
6. R.T. Smallbones, letter to Hans Sachs of 26.11.1938, reproduced in John Cooke, 'Hans and Charlotte Sachs', in Gisela Holfter (ed.), *German-speaking Exiles in Ireland*, p.224.
7. JCA/Hans Sachs to Gertrud Brenning/20.05.1939.
8. Ursula Owen, *Single Journey Only: A Memoir* (Cromer: Salt Publishing, 2019), p.59.
9. JCA/Hans Sachs to Else Samter/25.05.1939.
10. JCA/Hans Sachs to Else Samter/07.06.1939.

4: A Man of Letters

1. VCA/241/Kurt Grelling to Otto Neurath/18.11.1938.
2. VCA/241/Kurt Grelling to Otto Neurath/24.06.1939.
3. *The Analysis of Mind* (trans. *Die Analyse des Geistes*, publ. 1927); *ABC of Relativity* (trans. *Das ABC der Relativitätstheorie*, pub. 1928); *The Analysis of Matter* (trans. *Philosophie der Materie*, publ. 1929); *An Outline of Philosophy* (trans. *Mensch und Welt: Grundriß der Philosophie*, publ. 1930.
4. VCA/241/Kurt Grelling to Otto Neurath/18.11.1938.
5. John Cooke, unpublished memoir of Karin Gimple-Grelling.
6. VCA/241/Kurt Grelling to Otto Neurath/30.12.1935.
7. VCA/241/Otto Neurath to Kurt Grelling/18.07.1934.
8. The *Berliner Gesellschaft für wissenschaftliche Philosophie* was founded in 1927 by the philosopher Joseph Petzoldt (1862–1929) as the *Berliner Gesellschaft für empirische Philosophie*. The change of name came in 1931 under Reichenbach's leadership.
9. https://plato.stanford.edu/entries/reichenbach
10. VCA/241/Otto Neurath to Kurt Grelling/26.07.1934.
11. An academic journal for the Unity of Science movement, jointly published by the Vienna Circle and the Berlin Group.
12. VCA/241/Kurt Grelling to Otto Neurath/21.07.1934.
13. Ibid.
14. Arthur Rosenthal, letter to Grelling's friend and colleague Paul Oppenheim, dated November 1940. By then, Rosenthal was a lecturer at the University in Michigan, but had served with Grelling on the Western Front.

5: *J'accuse!*

1. Kurt Grelling, *Anti-J'accuse, eine deutsche Antwort*, excerpt trans. Beecroft and Beecroft (Zurich: Art Institut Orell Füssli, 1916), p.21.
2. Ibid., p.23.
3. Ibid., p.16.
4. Kurt Grelling, '*Philosophische Grundlagen der Politik*', excerpt trans. Beecroft and Beecroft (*Sozialistische Monatshefte*, October 1916), p.1047. Accessed at https://library.fes.de/cgi-bin/digisomo.pl?id=01956&dok=1916/1916_20&f=1916_1045&l=1916_1055&c=1916_1047
5. Ibid., p.1048.
6. Ibid.
7. Ibid., p.1046.

8   ASP.1999.01/II/2/44/3/undated (autumn/winter 1940).
9   Grelling, *Anti-J'accuse*, p.125.
10 He is referring to the nineteenth-century Manchester School of liberal politicians who advocated strongly in favour of free trade and against protectionism.
11 Grelling, *Anti-J'accuse*, p.125.
12 Hans Wehberg in Volker Peckhaus, 'Concerning the Political Views of Kurt Grelling', trans. Claude Grelling (original paper, '*Zur politischen Einstellung von Kurt Grelling*', dated 12.09.1985).
13 Richard Grelling, *The Crime* (Vol. I), trans. Alexander Gray (New York: George H. Doran Company, 1917), p.29.
14 Ibid.
15 He is referring to a major road near the old Reichstag in central Berlin, not the road on which Kurt would later buy a house.
16 Richard Grelling, *The Crime* (Vol. I), p.29.
17 Ibid.
18 Richard Grelling, *The Crime* (Vol. I), p.29.
19 Kurt Grelling, '*Sollte eigentlich Universitätslehrer werden*' (excerpt trans. Volker Peckhaus), in Volker Peckhaus, *Hilbertprogramm und Kritische Philosophie: Das Göttinger Modell interdisziplinärer Zusammenarbeit zwischen Mathematik und Philosophie* (Göttingen: Vandehoeck & Ruprecht, 1990), p.146, footnote 422.
20 Gerhard Weisser, unpublished private recollections sent to Karin and Claude Grelling.
21 Richard Grelling, *The Crime* (Vol. I) (1917), p.29.
22 VCA/241/Otto Neurath to Kurt Grelling/28.01.1935.
23 VCA/241/Kurt Grelling to Otto Neurath/18.02.1935.
24 VCA/241/Otto Neurath to Kurt Grelling/28.01.1935.
25 VCA/241/Kurt Grelling to Otto Neurath/18.02.1935.
26 VCA/241/Kurt Grelling to Otto Neurath/12.12.1934.
27 Kurt Grelling, '*aber können wir daraus, daß ein für die Wissenschaft unentbehrliches Prinzip weder logisch noch empirisch begründbar ist, nicht schließen, daß es eine Erkenntnis a priori darstellt*', excerpt trans. Beecroft and Beecroft, in Peckhaus, *Hilbertprogramm und Kritische Philosophie*, p.148, footnote 437.
28 Gerhard Weisser, unpublished memoir.
29 Else Samter, unpublished Leo Baeck Institute profile of Kurt Grelling, 1958.
30 Maynes and Gimbel, *Personal Memories of the Early Analytic Philosophers* (Cham: Springer Nature Switzerland AG, 2022), p.80.
31 Yiddish word meaning an incompetent person.
32 Maynes and Gimbel, *Personal Memories of the Early Analytic Philosophers*, p.80.
33 VCA/241/Otto Neurath to Kurt Grelling/28.11.1934.
34 Karl Popper (1902–94), Austrian philosopher of science.
35 VCA/241/Otto Neurath to Kurt Grelling/26.07.1934.
36 Kurt Grelling and Paul Oppenheim, 'The Concept of Gestalt in the Light of Modern Logic', in Barry Smith (ed.), *Foundations of Gestalt Theory* (Munich and Vienna: Philosophia Verlag, 1988), p.204.

6: The Invariant of Transpositions

1   Victor Klemperer, *I Shall Bear Witness: The Diaries of Victor Klemperer 1933–41*, trans. Martin Chalmers (London: Weidenfeld & Nicolson, 1998), p.290.
2   Felix Oppenheim, Recollections, unpublished memoir.
3   Ibid.
4   Max Horkheimer, 'The Latest Attack on Metaphysics' in *Critical Theory: Selected Essays*, trans. Matthew J. Connell (New York: Continuum, 2002), p.164.
5   Ibid., p.167.
6   Cf. Russell's *War: Offspring of Fear*, a pamphlet Kurt Grelling cites in support of his arguments in *Anti-J'accuse*.
7   VCA/241/Kurt Grelling to Otto Neurath/12.09.1937.
8   VCA/241/Otto Neurath to Kurt Grelling/22.11.1937.
9   Ibid.

10 VCA/241/Otto Neurath to Kurt Grelling/22.11.1937.
11 By September 1936, prospective emigrants were permitted to take out only 15,000 *Sperrmarks* for every 100,000 marks deposited with the treasury. Jews lost many millions in exchanging their capital for the *Sperrmarks*. *Jewish Telegraphic Agency* report, 28.09.1936. In addition, the Reichsmark had devalued considerably against international currencies over the previous few years.
12 VCA/241/Kurt Grelling to Otto Neurath/12.01.1938.
13 Ibid.
14 VCA/241/Otto Neurath to Kurt Grelling/14.01.1938.
15 https://mathshistory.st-andrews.ac.uk/Biographies/Scholz
16 VCA/241/Kurt Grelling to Otto Neurath/26.03.1938.
17 Grelling and Oppenheim, 'The Concept of Gestalt in the Light of Modern Logic' in Smith (ed.), *Foundations of Gestalt Theory*, p.204.
18 The concept of interdependence was further explored by the pair in a subsequent paper. Cf. Grelling and Oppenheim, 'Logical Analysis of "Gestalt" as a "Functional Whole"' in Smith (ed.), *Foundations of Gestalt Theory*.
19 VCA/241/Kurt Grelling to Otto Neurath/22.05.1938.
20 Ibid.
21 VCA/241/Kurt Grelling to Otto Neurath/undated (summer 1938).
22 Ibid.; Grelling uses the English phrase 'negro college' in this and subsequent letters.
23 Ibid.
24 Ibid.
25 www.digitalcommonwealth.org/search/commonwealth-oai:vm411754k
26 VCA/241/Kurt Grelling to Otto Neurath/28.01.1939.
27 Ibid.
28 Ibid.
29 VCA/241/Kurt Grelling to Otto Neurath/30.10.1938.
30 Ibid.

7: Everything Is a Risk

1 VCA/241/Kurt Grelling to Otto Neurath/19.07.1939.
2 VCA/241/Kurt Grelling to Otto Neurath/28.01.1939.
3 ASP.1999.01/II/2/44/1/Paul Oppenheim to Carl Gustav Hempel/25.05.1939.
4 This 'them' is assumed to mean the Australian embassy.
5 ASP.1999.01/II/2/44/1/Paul Oppenheim to Carl Gustav Hempel/25.05.1939.
6 Ibid.
7 VCA/241/Kurt Grelling to Otto Neurath/04.04.1939.
8 VCA/241/Otto Neurath to Kurt Grelling/05.04.1939.
9 Ibid.
10 Ibid.
11 Ibid.
12 VCA/241/Otto Neurath to Kurt Grelling/27.04.1939.
13 VCA/241/Otto Neurath to Kurt Grelling/27.04.1939.
14 VCA/241/Kurt Grelling to Otto Neurath/04.05.1939.
15 VCA/241/Otto Neurath to Kurt Grelling/15.06.1939.
16 ASP.1999.01/II/2/44/1/Paul Oppenheim to Carl Gustav Hempel/25.05.1939.
17 ASP.1999.01/II/2/44/1/Paul Oppenheim to Carl Gustav Hempel/03.07.1939.
18 Ibid.
19 Foreigners' visa.
20 The state security service.
21 VCA/241/Otto Neurath to Kurt Grelling/24.06.1939.
22 ASP.1999.01/II/2/44/1/Paul Oppenheim to Carl Gustav Hempel/20.06.1939.
23 Ibid.
24 VCA/241/Otto Neurath to Kurt Grelling/02.07.1939.
25 VCA/241/Kurt Grelling to Otto Neurath/09.07.1939.

26 ASP.1999.01/II/2/44/1/ Carl Gustav Hempel to Paul Oppenheim/29.07.1939.
27 Ibid.
28 The Red Star line.
29 ASP.1999.01/II/2/44/1/Paul Oppenheim to Carl Gustav Hempel/20.06.1939.
30 ASP.1999.01/II/2/44/1/ Stephan Oppenheim to Eva Ahrends-Hempel/04.08.1939.
31 ASP.1999.01/II/2/44/1/ Eva Ahrends-Hempel to Paul Oppenheim/20.06.1939.
32 VCA/241/Kurt Grelling to Otto Neurath/12.08.1939.

8: Letters from America

1 ASP.1999.01/II/2/44/2/Kurt Grelling to Paul Oppenheim/05.09.1939.
2 Ibid.
3 Felix Oppenheim, unpublished memoir.
4 ASP.1999.01/II/2/44/2/Kurt Grelling to Paul Oppenheim/15.09.1939.
5 Ibid.
6 He most likely means a Stuka dive bomber, an aircraft used by the Luftwaffe to attack shipping in the English Channel.
7 VCA/241/Otto Neurath to Kurt Grelling/23.10.1939.
8 Richard von Mises (1883–1953), Austrian mathematician and brother of the economist Ludwig von Mises (1881–1973).
9 Hans Kelsen (1881–1973), Austrian-Jewish legal philosopher.
10 Louis Rougier (1889–1982), French philosopher.
11 Aleksander Wundheiler (1902–57), Polish logician.
12 VCA/241/Otto Neurath to Kurt Grelling/23.10.1939.
13 Many other Polish-Jewish philosophers would be murdered by the Nazis.
14 With the help of Heinrich Scholz, Tarski's wife and children were able to obtain passports and leave Poland. Cf. Volker Peckhaus, 'Moral Integrity during a Difficult Period: Beth and Scholz', *Philosophia Scientiae* (Nancy) 3 (4) (1998/1999), 151–173. www.uni-paderborn.de/fileadmin-kw/fach-philosophie/peckhaus/downloads/beth.pdf
15 VCA/241/Kurt Grelling to Otto Neurath/25.10.1939.
16 ASP.1999.01/II/2/44/2/Paul Oppenheim to Kurt Grelling/06.11.1939.
17 Story from Paul Oppenheim by email, 05.02.2024.
18 ASP.1999.01/II/2/44/2/Paul Oppenheim to Kurt Grelling/06.11.1939.
19 ASP.1999.01/II/2/44/2/Paul Oppenheim to Kurt Grelling/12.12.1939.
20 Ibid.
21 ASP.1999.01/II/2/44/2/Kurt Grelling to Paul Oppenheim/14.12.1939.
22 Ibid.
23 ASP.1999.01/II/2/44/2/Kurt Grelling to Paul Oppenheim/11.11.1939.
24 He means Menière's Disease.
25 ASP.1999.01/II/2/44/2/Kurt Grelling to Paul Oppenheim/11.11.1939.
26 Ibid.
27 Ibid.
28 ASP.1999.01/II/2/44/2/Paul Oppenheim to Kurt Grelling/12.12.1939.
29 www.jewishvirtuallibrary.org/weidenreich-franz
30 ASP.1999.01/II/2/44/2/Paul Oppenheim to Kurt Grelling/12.12.1939.
31 ASP.1999.01/II/2/44/2/Kurt Grelling to Paul Oppenheim/01.01.1940.
32 VCA/241/Kurt Grelling to Otto Neurath/01.12.1939.

9: Many People Are Disappearing from Brussels

1 VCA/241/Otto Neurath to Kurt Grelling/12.12.1939.
2 VCA/241/Kurt Grelling to Otto Neurath/15.12.1939.
3 ASP.1999.01/II/2/44/2/Kurt Grelling to Paul Oppenheim/04.12.1939.
4 ASP.1999.01/II/2/44/2/ Kurt Grelling to Paul Oppenheim/14.12.1939.
5 ASP.1999.01/II/2/44/2/Kurt Grelling to Paul Oppenheim/01.01.1940.

6   Ibid.
7   Possibly the lawyer and socialist politician Piet (Pierre) Vermeylen (1904–91).
8   ASP.1999.01/II/2/44/2/Kurt Grelling to Paul Oppenheim/03.(01.)01.1940.
9   A temporary residency visa.
10 ASP.1999.01/II/2/44/2/Kurt Grelling to Paul Oppenheim/12.01.1940.
11 ASP.1999.01/II/2/44/2/Kurt Grelling to Paul Oppenheim/06.02.1940.
12 ASP.1999.01/II/2/44/2/Paul Oppenheim to Kurt Grelling/01.02.1940.
13 ASP.1999.01/II/2/44/2/Kurt Grelling to Paul Oppenheim/06.02.1940.
14 VCA/241/Otto Neurath to Kurt Grelling/20.02.1940.
15 Ibid.
16 ASP.1999.01/II/2/44/2/Kurt Grelling to Paul Oppenheim/06.02.1940.
17 ASP.1999.01/II/2/44/2/Kurt Grelling to Paul Oppenheim/02.03.1940.
18 Ibid.
19 ASP.1999.01/II/2/44/2/Paul Oppenheim to Kurt Grelling/13.03.1940.
20 Ibid.
21 ASP.1999.01/II/2/44/2/Paul Oppenheim to Kurt Grelling/12.(13.)03.1940.
22 This phrase is written in English.
23 This passage is written in English.
24 This sentence is written in English.
25 ASP.1999.01/II/2/44/2/Kurt Grelling to Paul Oppenheim/02.04.1940.
26 https://nws.dorsetcouncil.gov.uk/dorset-history-centre-blog/2021/05/03/ludwig-loewy-the-story-of-a-czech-jew-who-escaped-nazi-germany
27 ASP.1999.01/II/2/44/2/Kurt Grelling to Paul Oppenheim/02.04.1940.
28 Ibid.
29 Ibid.
30 ASP.1999.01/II/2/44/2/Kurt Grelling to Paul Oppenheim/16.04.1940.
31 VCA/241/Otto Neurath to Kurt Grelling/22.03.1940.
32 VCA/241/Otto Neurath to Kurt Grelling/20.04.1940.
33 Ibid.
34 Ibid.
35 Ibid.
36 aka the Caserne des Guides.

10: The Camp on the Beach

1   Marcel Bervoets, *La liste de Saint-Cyprien* (Brussels: Alice Editions, 2006), p.151.
2   JCA/Karin Grelling to Hans and Lotte Sachs/14.06.1940.
3   ASP.1999.01/II/2/44/2/Kurt Grelling to Paul Oppenheim/04.08.1940.
4   Ibid.
5   James N. Bade, 'From internment in Trial Bay to exile in Berkeley: the German physicist Peter Pringsheim and his connection with Australia', www.publish.csiro.au/HR/pdf/HR24006
6   Bervoets, *La liste de Saint-Cyprien* (2006), p.386.
7   https://scope.mannheim.de/detail.aspx?ID=1268507
8   Center for Jewish History: https://archives.cjh.org/repositories/5/resources/ 19206
9   www.geni.com/people/Friedrich-Caro-PhD/6000000031061497076
10 ASP.1999.01/II/2/44/2/Kurt Grelling to Paul Oppenheim/04.09.1940.
11 Ibid.
12 Ibid.
13 Kurt Riezler (1882–1955) was a German philosopher and diplomat.
14 ASP.1999.01/II/2/44/2/Carl Gustav Hempel to Kurt Grelling/28.09.1940.
15 Ibid.
16 ASP.1999.01/II/2/44/2/Kurt Grelling to Paul Oppenheim/22.10.1940.
17 Ibid.
18 Ibid.
19 Ibid.

11: The New School

1   There were sixty men in each barrack.
2   ASP.1999.01/II/2/44/2/Kurt Grelling to Paul Oppenheim/08.11.1940.
3   Ibid.
4   He means his half-sister Eva Oppenheim.

5 a.m.
6 JCA/Kurt Grelling to Hans and Lotte Sachs and Else Samter/08.12.1940.
7 Ibid; barrack 3, block C.
8 Bervoets, *La liste de Saint-Cyprien* (2006), p.405 and also https://gedenkbuch-wuppertal.de/de/person/spiro
9 Ibid.
10 ASP.1999.01/II/2/44/3/Alvin Johnson to Paul Oppenheim/15.11.1940.
11 ASP.1999.01/II/2/44/3/Alvin Johnson to Paul Oppenheim/12.12.1940.
12 ASP.1999.01/II/2/44/2/Carl Gustav Hempel to Kurt Grelling/14.12.1940.
13 ASP.1999.01/II/2/44/2/Paul Oppenheim to Kurt Grelling/28.12.1940.
14 Willard Van Orman Quine (1908–2000), American philosopher and logician.
15 Greta's and Kurt's landlady at 33 avenue Legrand, from early 1940.
16 ASP.1999.01/II/2/44/2/Greta Grelling to Paul Oppenheim/15.01.1941.
17 ASP.1999.01/II/2/44/3/Alvin Johnson to Paul Oppenheim/17.01.1941.
18 ASP.1999.01/II/2/44/2/ Carl Gustav Hempel to Kurt Grelling/28.01.1941.
19 ASP.1999.01/II/2/44/2/Kurt Grelling to Paul Oppenheim/08.02.1941.
20 Ibid.
21 JCA/Kurt Grelling to Hans and Lotte Sachs and Else Samter/15.02.1941.
22 ASP.1999.01/II/2/44/2/ Carl Gustav Hempel to Kurt Grelling/18.03.1941.

12: A Book of Essays

1 Grelling spells the first name 'Hans', the more common form.
2 Literally translated as 'years of wandering', the *Wanderjahre* are the journeyman years during which a newly qualified apprentice in a craft or trade in German-speaking countries works peripatetically in different places, before settling and establishing themselves in a particular location.
3 Améry was arrested in Brussels in July 1943, delivering leaflets for the Belgian Resistance. He was imprisoned in Fort Breendonk near the city of Mechelen, where he was tortured by the Gestapo before being deported to Auschwitz.
4 Monowitz was a sub-camp of Auschwitz, set up to supply slave labour for the firm of I.G. Farben, for whom Paul Oppenheim had worked until 1933.
5 Beyond Guilt and Atonement.
6 Johann Strauss II in fact had Jewish ancestry, a detail the Nazis overlooked in championing his music as a paragon of 'Greater German' culture. www.jta.org/archive/jewish-roots-of-the-waltz-king-emerge-amid-planned-celebrations-2
7 Jean Améry, *Unmeisterliche Wanderjahre*, excerpt trans. Beecroft and Beecroft (Stuttgart: Klett-Cotta, 1971), p.40.
8 Lion Feuchtwanger (1884–1958), German-Jewish novelist who escaped from the Camp des Milles in southern France to America in 1941.
9 Walter Hasenclever (1890–1940), German-Jewish poet and playwright who took his own life in June 1940 while interned in the Camp des Milles.
10 Hermann Kesten (1900–96), German-Jewish novelist and dramatist who emigrated to America in 1940.
11 Stefan Zweig (1881–1942), Austrian-Jewish writer who escaped to Brazil, where in February 1942 both he and his wife Lotte died by suicide.
12 Améry, *Unmeisterliche Wanderjahre*, p.38.
13 Ibid., p.34.
14 Ibid., p.44.
15 Ibid.
16 Ibid.
17 Ibid.
18 Ibid., p.45.
19 Ibid., p.52.
20 Ibid.
21 Ibid., pp.52–3.
22 Ibid., p.53.
23 Ibid., p.54.
24 Pierre Laval (1883–1945), head of the Vichy government from April 1942 to August 1944, executed for treason after the war.

25 Améry, *Unmeisterliche Wanderjahre*, p.55.
26 Cf. written testimony by former internees of Gurs held by the Wiener Holocaust Library in London.
27 Claude Laharie, *Le Camp de Gurs, 1939–1945: un aspect méconnu de l'histoire du Béarn* (Pau: Infocompo, 1985), p.203.
28 www.nationalww2museum.org/war/articles/walter-benjamin
29 Nicholas Rescher, 'The Berlin School of Logical Empiricism and Its Legacy', *Erkenntnis* (1975–), Vol. 64, No. 4 (Springer, 2006), p.285.
30 Owen, *Single Journey Only*, p.40.
31 Claude Grelling, undated email quoted in Abraham S. Luchins and Edith H. Luchins, 'Kurt Grelling: Steadfast Scholar in a Time of Madness' (2000), p.26. www.gestalttheory.net/uploads/pdf/GTH-Archive/2000LuchinsGrellingSteadfastScholar.pdf
32 Améry, *Unmeisterliche Wanderjahre*, pp.55–6.
33 Ibid., p.56.
34 Ibid., p.56.
35 Ibid., p.57.
36 Ibid., p.58.
37 Ibid.
38 Ibid.
39 Ibid., p.60.
40 Ibid., p.71.
41 Ibid., p.61.
42 Ibid., p.77.
43 Ibid., pp.77–8; the horse trader (*Roßtäuscher*) is taken to be Pierre Laval and the Vichy government.
44 ASP.1999.01/II/2/44/2/Kurt Grelling to Paul Oppenheim/28.03.1941.
45 Ibid., p.78.
46 Primo Levi died after falling from the third-floor landing of his apartment block in Turin in 1987. Officially recorded as suicide, this verdict has been disputed by many who knew him and by much of the evidence of what happened. https://www.bostonreview.net/articles/diego-gambetta-primo-levi-last-moments
47 Primo Levi, *The Drowned and the Saved*, trans. Raymond Rosenthal (London: Sphere Books, 1989), p.62.
48 Ibid., pp.62–3.
49 In 2013, Yad Vashem published a commemoration book with the names of 4.3 million Jewish men, women and children who had been murdered in the Holocaust and positively identified in the decades since the end of the Second World War. Its most recent edition, published in 2023, contains some 4.8 million names. Some 6 million Jews are known to have been murdered in the Holocaust. The book will be complete only when all the remaining number have been identified.

13: A Man in My Position

1 ASP.1999.01/II/2/44/2/Kurt Grelling to Paul Oppenheim/28.03.1941.
2 Ibid.
3 Holocaust Encyclopedia, https://encyclopedia.ushmm.org/content/en/article/les-milles-camp
4 A non-quota visa.
5 ASP.1999.01/II/2/44/2/Kurt Grelling to Paul Oppenheim/28.03.1941.
6 Ibid.
7 Ibid.
8 Ibid.
9 Ibid.
10 ASP.1999.01/II/2/44/2/Kurt Grelling to Paul Oppenheim/27.04.1941.
11 Vice Consuls Myles Standish and Hiram Bingham III at the US Consulate in Marseille were instrumental in helping hundreds if not thousands of Jews to escape, defying the obstructive policy of the State Department by issuing visas to those who needed them. https://statemag.state.gov/2022/05/0522feat03
12 Ibid.
13 Ibid.
14 US equivalent of Thomas Cook.
15 ASP.1999.01/II/2/44/2/Kurt Grelling to Paul Oppenheim/30.04.1941.
16 ASP.1999.01/II/2/44/2/Paul Oppenheim to Kurt Grelling/undated (May 1941).
17 ASP.1999.01/II/2/44/2/Paul Oppenheim to Kurt Grelling/02.05.1941.

18 Ibid.
19 ASP.1999.01/II/2/44/2/Kurt Grelling to Paul Oppenheim/07.05.1941.
20 ASP.1999.01/II/2/44/2/Paul Oppenheim to Kurt Grelling/09.05.1941.
21 Grelling in fact misspells this name as 'Weissnitz'. Jacques Weisslitz, who was Jewish himself, continued working to help refugees after Varian Fry had left. In 1942, Fry petitioned the State Department to issue him a visa, but this was refused. Weisslitz and his wife were later deported to Auschwitz, where, on 22 October 1943, they were murdered. https://museedelaresistanceenligne.org/media11542-Photo-de-membres-du-Comit-amricain-de-secours-la-gare-de-Cerbre-6-septembre-1941
22 ASP.1999.01/II/2/44/2/Kurt Grelling to Paul Oppenheim/15.05.1941.
23 Ibid.
24 Ibid.
25 ASP.1999.01/II/2/44/2/ Eva Ahrends-Hempel to Kurt Grelling/27.05.1941.
26 Ibid.
27 Ibid.
28 ASP.1999.01/II/2/44/2/Paul Oppenheim to Kurt Grelling/29.05.1941.

14: How Nerve-shredding this Constant Waiting Is

1 ASP.1999.01/II/2/44/2/Kurt Grelling to Paul Oppenheim/12.06.1941 (cable).
2 ASP.1999.01/II/2/44/2/Kurt Grelling to Paul Oppenheim/12.06.1941 (letter).
3 An umbrella organisation whose name is a combination of HIAS (see note 2, Chapter 1); the London-based Jewish Colonisation Association; and EmigDirect, based in Berlin.
4 ASP.1999.01/II/2/44/2/Kurt Grelling to Paul Oppenheim/12.06.1941 (letter).
5 Eugen seems to have been the owner of the house at 21 avenue Victoria, which the Oppenheims had rented from 1933 until January 1940, after their departure from Belgium in September 1939.
6 In the last few months of 1942, out of more than 66,000 living in Belgium (most of them refugees from Germany, Austria and Czechoslovakia), some 25,000 Jews in Antwerp and Brussels were rounded up and sent to the concentration camps of Dossin and Breendonk, near Mechelen. From there they were sent to Auschwitz where more than 23,000 were murdered either on arrival or by being worked to death.
7 ASP.1999.01/II/2/44/2/Greta Grelling to Paul Oppenheim/12.06.1941.
8 Ibid.
9 Holocaust Encyclopedia, https://encyclopedia.ushmm.org/content/en/article/immigration-to-the-united-states-1933-41
10 ASP.1999.01/II/4/44/2/Marion Samter to Paul Oppenheim/02.07.1941.
11 Holocaust Encyclopedia, https://encyclopedia.ushmm.org/content/en/article/immigration-to-the-united-states-1933-41
12 ASP.1999.01/II/2/44/2/Kurt Grelling to Paul Oppenheim/29.06.1941.
13 https://jewinthepew.org/2020/01/07/7-january-1977-passing-of-adolph-freudenberg-friend-of-bonhoeffer-lawyer-pastor-ecumenist-otdimjh/
14 Ibid.
15 Formally known as the Alien Registration Act 1940.
16 ASP.1999.01/II/2/44/2/Kurt Grelling/22.06.1941.
17 Grelling family archive/Greta Grelling letter to her parents/21.03.1941.
18 Ibid.
19 JCA/Kurt Grelling to Hans and Lotte Sachs and Else Samter/29.07.1941.
20 Hans Fraenkel, letter to Karin Grelling (trans. Claude Grelling), 20.09.1945, in Luchins, 'Kurt Grelling: Steadfast Scholar in a Time of Madness' (2000).
21 Wilhelm Traumann, letter to Karin Grelling (trans. Claude Grelling), 24.07.1946, in Luchins, 'Kurt Grelling: Steadfast Scholar in a Time of Madness'.

22 Ibid.
23 Ibid.
24 ASP.1999.01/II/2/44/2/ Eva Ahrends-Hempel to Kurt Grelling/29.07.1941.
25 Ibid.
26 ASP.1999.01/II/2/44/2/Paul Oppenheim to Kurt Grelling/20.08.1941.
27 Ibid.
28 ASP.1999.01/II/2/44/2/Greta Grelling to Paul Oppenheim/28.08.1941.
29 ASP.1999.01/II/2/44/2/Kurt Grelling to Paul Oppenheim/29.08.1941.
30 ASP.1999.01/II/2/44/2/Kurt Grelling to Paul Oppenheim/23.10.1941.
31 ASP.1999.01/II/2/44/2/Kurt Grelling to Paul Oppenheim/10.09.1941.
32 Ibid.
33 ASP.1999.01/II/2/44/2/Greta Grelling to Paul Oppenheim/11.11.1941.
34 Ibid.

15: On Love Alone

1 ASP.1999.01/II/2/44/2/Kurt Grelling to Paul Oppenheim/01.01.1942.
2 ASP.1999.01/II/2/44/2/Kurt Grelling to Paul Oppenheim/02.01.1942.
3 Fraenkel, letter, 20.09.1945, in Luchins, 'Kurt Grelling: Steadfast Scholar in a Time of Madness'.
4 Traumann, letter, 24.07.1946, in Luchins, 'Kurt Grelling: Steadfast Scholar in a Time of Madness'.
5 ASP.1999.01/II/2/44/4/Friedrich Caro to Paul Oppenheim/20.01.1942; Caro's wife and daughters survived the war and later emigrated to the USA.
6 Presumably not the same Ms Blitz who seems to have acted as Kurt's attorney in Brussels.
7 Literally 'freewheeling', i.e. pedalling without getting anywhere, she means an effort that yields no result.
8 ASP.1999.01/II/2/44/4/ Eva Ahrends-Hempel to Paul Oppenheim/26.01.1942.
9 ASP.1999.01/II/2/44/2/Greta Grelling to Paul Oppenheim/15.02.1942.
10 Albert Lautman (1908–44), French-Jewish professor of the philosophy of mathematics, later a member of the Resistance executed by the Nazis near Bordeaux in 1944. https://catalogue.bnf.fr/ark:/12148/cb12570113c
11 ASP.1999.01/II/2/44/2/Kurt Grelling to Paul Oppenheim/15.02.1942.
12 ASP.1999.01/II/2/44/4/Carl Gustav Hempel to Paul Oppenheim/13.04.1942.
13 ASP.1999.01/II/2/44/2/Greta Grelling to Paul Oppenheim/14.05.1942.
14 Professor Carl Dürr, a Swiss friend with whom Greta had stayed when taking the children to the school.
15 ASP.1999.01/II/2/44/2/Kurt Grelling to Paul Oppenheim/18.05.1942.
16 ASP.1999.01/II/2/44/4/ Eva Ahrends-Hempel to Paul Oppenheim/22.05.1942.
17 Nelson Goodman (1906–88), US logician and philosopher.
18 Edgar Zilsel (1891–1944), Austrian-Jewish philosopher and historian, moved to Mills College, California in 1943. He took his own life the following year.
19 J.C.C. McKinsey (1908–53), US mathematician.
20 ASP.1999.01/II/2/44/1/Carl Gustav Hempel to Kurt Grelling/01.08.1942.

16: The Choice

1 www.holocaustrescue.org/clergy-who-aided-jews-in-france
2 *Groupements de travailleurs étrangers*.
3 A similar, harrowing testimony appears in the diary of Raymond-Raoul Lambert (1894–1943). A French Jew, as president of the *Union générale des israélites de France*, Lambert was present at Les Milles during the first two deportations to plead with the authorities to have people removed from the list of deportees, with some success. Lambert was himself arrested in Marseille in August 1943, along with his wife and

four children. They were deported to Auschwitz and murdered there. Cf. Raymond-Raoul Lambert, *Diary of a Witness: 1940–1943*, trans. Isabel Best (Chicago: Ivan R. Dee, 2007).
4 Henri Manen, *Au fond de l'abîme: Journal du Camp des Milles*, excerpt trans. Beecroft (Editions Ampelos, 2013), p.35.
5 Of the four guards known to have helped Jews escape from Camp des Milles, one, Auguste César Boyer (1914–95), is recognised by Yad Vashem as 'righteous among the nations'. Boyer helped one Jewish family, a mother and three children, by hiding them in his home and went on to help many more Jews to escape. He was later arrested by the Gestapo and tortured on suspicion of having helped Jews, though he told them nothing. https://yadvashem-france.org/dossier/nom/2163/ Other guards who helped and, like Boyer, were also arrested and imprisoned were Aimé Bondi, Lucien Mercier and Jean-Louis Kissy. The camp commandant, Robert Maulavé, was arrested and imprisoned in September 1942 for refusing to hand over any more Jews. www.holocaustrescue.org/french-individuals-who-aided-jews-not-recognized
6 Ibid., p.16.
7 Ibid., p.18.
8 Report dated 16.08.42 by *Adjudant* Filip, commandant of the Aix brigade of the *gendarmerie nationale*, archives of the Camp des Milles. www.campdesmilles.org/histoire-archives.html#!prettyPhoto[galerie2]/0/
9 Manen, *Au fond de l'abîme*, p.19.
10 Kurt was actually 56 years old.
11 Manen, *Au fond de l'abîme*, p.23.
12 ASP.1999.01/II/2/44/4/Kurt Grelling to Paul and Gabrielle Oppenheim/15.08.1942.
13 ASP.1999.01/II/2/44/4/Bertrand Russell to Paul Oppenheim/15.08.1942.
14 Manen, *Au fond de l'abîme*, p.40.
15 Pastor André Dumas.
16 Dumas.
17 Fraenkel, letter, 20.09.1945, in Luchins, 'Kurt Grelling: Steadfast Scholar in a Time of Madness'.
18 Wilhelm Traumann, letter to Karin Grelling (trans. Claude Grelling), 18.06.1946, in Luchins, 'Kurt Grelling: Steadfast Scholar in a Time of Madness'.

17: Stolperstein

1 The programme of *Stolpersteine*, or stumbling stones, is an ever-expanding series of discreet commemorations installed in the pavements of towns and cities across Germany. The project was started by the German artist Gunter Demnig in 1992. The brass plaques fixed to the concrete 'stones', now numbering in excess of 100,000, record the details of victims of the Holocaust who lived at those locations. *Stolpersteine* can now be found in places outside Germany.
2 Serge Klarsfeld, *Vichy-Auschwitz: Le Rôle de Vichy dans la Solution Finale de la Question Juive en France, 1942* (Paris: Librairie Arthème Fayard, 1983), p.435.
3 Ibid., p.191.

18: Afterlife

1 ASP.1999.01/II/2/44/4/ Leo Forchheimer to Paul Oppenheim/17.09.1942.
2 ASP.1999.01/II/2/44/4/Ruth J. Perry for Margaret E. Jones to Paul Oppenheim/09.10.1942.
3 ASP.1999.01/II/2/44/4/Paul Oppenheim to American Friends Service Committee/10.10.1942.
4 It may have been one of the French police forces.
5 ASP.1999.01/II/2/44/4/ Carl Gustav Hempel to Paul Oppenheim/27.10.1942.
6 This is surely a reference to the first significant defeat on land that the Nazis had suffered – at El-Alamein on 11 November 1942.

7   ASP.1999.01/II/2/44/4/Marion Samter to Paul Oppenheim/14.11.1942.
8   ASP.1999.01/II/2/44/1/Paul and Gabrielle Oppenheim to Carl Gustav Hempel/11.12.1942.
9   Gabrielle has chosen the French spelling of her son's name.
10 ASP.1999.01/II/2/44/1/Paul and Gabrielle Oppenheim to Carl Gustav Hempel/11.12.1942.
11 www.firerescue1.com/mci-mass-casualty-incidents/articles/secrets-of-cocoanut-grove-fire-uncovered-ECzBiTBKQn24PwZx
12 Anita Savio, email to the authors, 29.09.2023.
13 JCA/Hans Grelling to Werner Sachs/24.04.1945.
14 Claude Grelling obituary, *Minneapolis Star Tribune*, 20.08.2017.
15 Claude Grelling, email to Abraham H. and Edith S. Luchins, 24.11.1999.
16 Claude Grelling, email to Abraham H. and Edith S. Luchins, 09.05.2000.
17 John Cooke, unpublished memoir of Karin Gimple-Grelling.

SELECT BIBLIOGRAPHY

Adorno, Theodor and Max Horkheimer, *Dialectic of Enlightenment*, trans. John Cumming (London/New York: Verso, 1997).
Aly, Götz, *Hitler's Beneficiaries: Plunder, Racial War, and the Nazi Welfare State*, trans. Jefferson Chase (New York: Metropolitan Books, 2006).
Améry, Jean, *At the Mind's Limits: Contemplations by a Survivor on Auschwitz and its Realities*, trans. Sidney Rosenfeld and Stella P. Rosenfeld (London: Granta Books, 1999).
——, *On Suicide: A Discourse on Voluntary Death*, trans. John D. Barlow (Bloomington/Indianapolis, IN: Indiana University Press, 1999).
——, *Unmeisterliche Wanderjahre: Aufsätze* (Stuttgart: Klett-Cotta, 1971).
Arendt, Hannah, 'We Are Refugees' (1943) in *Altogether Elsewhere: Writers on Exile*, Marc Robinson (ed.) (Boston, Mass./London: Faber & Faber, 1994).
Benjamin, Walter, 'Theses on the Philosophy of History' (1940) in *Illuminations*, trans. Harry Zorn (London: Bodley Head, 2013).
Bervoets, Marcel, *La liste de Saint-Cyprien* (Brussels: Alice Editions, 2006).
Braund, James and Douglas G. Sutton, 'The Case of Heinrich Wilhelm Poll (1877–1939): A German-Jewish Geneticist, Eugenicist, Twin Researcher, and Victim of the Nazis', *Journal of the History of Biology*, Vol. 41, No. 1 (Springer Nature, 2008), pp.1–35.
Brodersen, Momme, *Walter Benjamin: A Biography*, trans. Malcolm R. Green and Ingrida Ligers (ed. Martina Dervis) (London/New York: Verso Books, 1996).
Caestecker, Frank, 'Jewish Refugee Aid Organizations in Belgium and the Netherlands and the Flight from Nazi Germany, 1938–1940', in Heim, Susanne, Beate Meyer and Francis R. Nicosia (eds), *'Wer bleibt, opfert seine Jahre, vielleicht sein Leben', Deutsche Juden 1938–1941* (Göttingen: Wallstein, 2010), pp.45–65.
——, 'The flight from Austria between the Anschluss and the Second World War, March 1938–September 1939: a socio-political analysis of mass flight, the Belgian case', in Adunka, E., P. Driessen Gruber, F. Hausjell, I. Nawrocka and S. Usaty (eds), *Exilforschung: Österreich. Leistungen, Defizite & Perspektiven*, Vol. 4 (Wien: Mandelbaum, 2018), pp.72–89.
——, Frank and Bob Moore (eds), *Refugees from Nazi Germany and the Liberal European States* (New York: Berghahn Books, 2010).
Cartwright, Nancy, Jordi Cat, Lola Fleck and Thomas E. Uebel, *Otto Neurath: Philosophy between Science and Politics* (Cambridge: Cambridge University Press, 2008).
Churchill, Winston, *The Second World War: Volume I: The Gathering Storm* (London: Cassell & Co. Ltd, 1948).

Cooke, John, 'Hans and Lotte Sachs' in Holfter, Gisela (ed.), *German-Speaking Exiles in Ireland* (Amsterdam/New York: Editions Rodopi B.V., 2006), pp.215–48.
——, 'Karin Gimple-Grelling 30 August 1927–27 March 2022', unpublished memoir, 2023.
Davies, Norman, *Europe: A History* (London: Pimlico, 1997).
Dickel, Horst, 'Hans Sachs' in Holfter, Gisela (ed.), *German-Speaking Exiles in Ireland* (Amsterdam/New York: Editions Rodopi B.V., 2006), pp.183–213.
Duggan, Stephen and Betty Drury, *The Rescue of Science and Learning: The Story of the Emergency Committee in Aid of Displaced Foreign Scholars* (The Macmillan Company, 1948).
Edmonds, David, *The Murder of Professor Schlick: The Rise and Fall of the Vienna Circle* (Princeton, NJ: Princeton University Press, 2020).
Elon, Amos, *The Pity of It All: A Portrait of Jews in Germany, 1753–1933* (London: Penguin Books, 2004).
Ehrenfels, Christian von, 'On "Gestalt Qualities"' (1890) in Smith, Barry (ed.), *Foundations of Gestalt Theory* (Munich/Vienna: Philosophia Verlag, 1988), pp.82–117.
Feigl, Herbert, 'The Wiener Kreis in America' in Fleming, Donald and Bernard Bailyn, *The Intellectual Migration: Europe and America, 1930–1960* (Cambridge, Mass.: Harvard University Press, 1969), pp.630–73.
Feingold, Henry L., *The Politics of Rescue: The Roosevelt Administration and the Holocaust, 1938–1945* (New Brunswick, NJ: Rutgers University Press, 1970).
Fernau, Hermann, *Because I am a German* (London: Constable and Company, 1916).
Fetzer, James H., *Science, Explanation and Rationality: Aspects of the Philosophy of Carl Gustav Hempel* (Oxford: Oxford University Press, 2000).
Feuchtwanger, Lion, *The Devil in France: My Encounter with Him in the Summer of 1940*, trans. Elisabeth Abbott (Los Angeles, CA: USC Libraries, 2009).
Fry, Varian, *Surrender on Demand* (Boulder, CO: Johnson Books, 1997).
Goetschel, Christian, *Suicide in Nazi Germany* (Oxford: Oxford University Press, 2009).
Grandjonc, Jacques and Theresia Grundtner (eds), *Zone d'ombres 1933–1944: Exil et internement d'Allemands et d'Autrichiens dans le sud-est de la France* (Aix-en-Provence: Editions ALINEA et ERCA, 1990).
Grady, Tim, *A Deadly Legacy: German Jews and the Great War* (New Haven, CT: Yale University Press, 2017).
Grelling, Claude, 'A Long Time Ago in a Country Far, Far Away', chapter 1, unpublished memoir.
Grelling, Kurt, 'A Logical Theory of Dependence' in Smith (ed.), *Foundations of Gestalt Theory*, pp.217–26. https://philpapers.org/archive/SMIFOG.pdf
——, *Anti-J'accuse, eine deutsche Antwort* (Zurich: Art Institut Orell Füssli, 1916). https://archive.org/details/antijaccuseeined00grel/page/20/mode/2up
——, *Anti-J'accuse, une réponse allemande* (Zurich: Art Institut Orell Füssli, 1917).
——, 'Philosophische Grundlagen der Politik', *Sozialistische Monatshefte* (October 1916), pp.1045–55. https://library.fes.de/cgi-bin/digisomo.pl?id=SOHE191620&dok=1916/1916_20
Grelling, Kurt and Paul Oppenheim, 'Logical Analysis of Gestalt as a Functional Whole' in Smith (ed.), *Foundations of Gestalt Theory*, pp.210–16. https://philpapers.org/archive/SMIFOG.pdf
——, 'Supplementary Remarks on the Concept of Gestalt' in Smith (ed.), *Foundations of Gestalt Theory*, pp.206–09. https://philpapers.org/archive/SMIFOG.pdf
——, 'The Concept of Gestalt in the Light of Modern Logic' (1937) in Smith (ed.), *Foundations of Gestalt Theory*, pp.191–205, https://philpapers.org/archive/SMIFOG.pdf

Grelling, Richard (A German), *I Accuse! (J'accuse!)*, trans. Alexander Gray (New York: George H. Doran & Company, 1915). https://archive.org/details/iaccusejaccuse03grel/page/n7/mode/2up

———, *The Crime (Das Verbrechen)* (Vol. I), trans. Alexander Gray (New York: George H. Doran Company, 1917). https://archive.org/details/crimedasverbrech01grel/page/14/mode/2up

Handelman, Matthew, *The Mathematical Imagination: On the Origins and Promise of Critical Theory* (New York: Fordham University Press, 2019).

Heidelberger-Leonard, Irène, *The Philosopher of Auschwitz: Jean Améry and Living with the Holocaust*, trans. Anthea Bell (London: I.B. Tauris, 2010).

Horkheimer, Max, 'The Latest Attack on Metaphysics' in *Critical Theory: Selected Essays*, trans. Matthew J. Connell (New York: Continuum, 2002).

Hume, David, *A Treatise of Human Nature* (London: Penguin Classics, 1989).

Jackson, Julian, *France: The Dark Years, 1940–1944* (New York: Oxford University Press, 2001).

Johnson, Alvin, *Pioneer's Progress* (Lincoln, NE: Bison Books/University of Nebraska Press, 1960).

Kaplan, Marion A., *Between Dignity and Despair: Jewish Life in Nazi Germany* (New York: Oxford University Press, 1999).

Keynes, John Maynard, *The Economic Consequences of the Peace* (New York: Harcourt, Brace & Howe, 1920).

Klarsfeld, Serge, *Vichy-Auschwitz: Le rôle de Vichy dans la Solution Finale de la Question Juive en France. 1942* (Paris: Librairie Arthème Fayard, 1983).

Klemperer, Victor, *I Shall Bear Witness: The Diaries of Victor Klemperer 1933–41*, trans. Martin Chalmers (London: Weidenfeld & Nicolson, 1998).

Kolakowski, Leszek, *Positivist Philosophy: From Hume to the Vienna Circle*, trans. Norbert Guterman (London: Pelican Books, 1972).

Laharie, Claude, *Le Camp de Gurs, 1939–1945: un aspect méconnu de l'histoire du Béarn* (Pau: Infocompo, 1985).

———, *Petite histoire des Camps d'internement français (1939–1945)* (Morlaàs: Éditions Cairn, 2020).

Levi, Primo, *The Drowned and the Saved*, trans. Raymond Rosenthal (London: Sphere Books, 1989).

Liddell Hart, B.H., *A History of the Second World War* (London: Pan Books, 2014).

Lindqvist, Sven, *'Exterminate All the Brutes'*, trans. The New Press, in *Saharan Journey* (London: Granta Publications, 2012).

London, Louise, *Whitehall and the Jews, 1933–1948: British immigration policy, Jewish refugees and the Holocaust* (Cambridge/New York: Cambridge University Press, 2000).

Luchins, Abraham S., and Edith H. Luchins, 'Kurt Grelling: Steadfast Scholar in a Time of Madness' (2000), www.gestalttheory.net/uploads/pdf/GTH-Archive/2000LuchinsGrellingSteadfastScholar.pdf

Manen, Henri, *Au fond de l'abîme: Journal du Camp des Milles* (Paris: Éditions Ampelos, 2013).

Mann, Golo, *Reminiscences and Reflections* (London: Faber & Faber, 1990).

Marrus, Michael R. and Robert O. Paxton, *Vichy France and the Jews* (New York: Basic Books Inc. 1981).

Maynes, Jeffrey and Steven Gimbel, *Personal Memories of the Early Analytic Philosophers* (Cham: Springer Nature Switzerland AG, 2022).

Milkov, Nikolay, 'Kurt Grelling and the Idiosyncrasy of the Berlin Logical Empiricism' (2021), https://philpapers.org/archive/MILKGA.pdf

Neurath, Otto, *Empiricism and Sociology*, Neurath, Marie and Cohen, Robert S. (eds) (Dordrecht, Holland/Boston, Mass., USA: D. Reidel Publ. Co., 1973).

———, *Philosophical Papers, 1913–1946* Cohen, Robert S. and Neurath, Marie (trans and eds) (Dordrecht, Holland/Boston, Mass., USA/Lancaster, UK: D. Reidel Publ. Co., 1973).

Niewyk, Donald L., *The Jews in Weimar Germany* (New Brunswick, NJ: Transaction Publishers, 2001).
Oppenheim, Felix, 'Recollections', unpublished memoir, 1993.
Owen, Ursula, *Single Journey Only: A Memoir* (Cromer: Salt Publishing, 2019).
Pais, Abraham, *Einstein Lived Here* (Oxford: Oxford University Press, 1994).
Peckhaus, Volker, 'Concerning the Political Views of Kurt Grelling', trans. Claude Grelling (unpublished; original paper, '*Zur politischen Einstellung von Kurt Grelling*', 12.09.1985, shared by Professor Peckhaus with the author).
——, *Hilbertprogramm und Kritische Philosophie: Das Göttinger Modell interdisziplinärer Zusammenarbeit zwischen Mathematik und Philosophie* (Göttingen: Vandehoeck & Ruprecht, 1990), pp.142–49.
——, 'Moral Integrity during a Difficult Period: Beth and Scholz', *Philosophia Scientiae* (Nancy) 3 (4) (1998/1999), pp.151–173.
——, 'The Third Man: Kurt Grelling and the Berlin Group' in Milkov, Nikolay, and Volker Peckhaus (eds), *The Berlin Group and the Philosophy of Logical Empiricism* (Dordrecht: Springer Science + Business Media, 2013), pp.231–43.
——, 'Von Nelson zu Reichenbach. Kurt Grelling in Göttingen und Berlin' in Danneberg, Lutz, Andreas Kamlah and Lothar Schäfer (eds), *Hans Reichenbach und Die Berliner Gruppe* (Braunschweig/Wiesbaden: Friedr. Wieweg & Sohn, 1994), pp.53–73.
Rescher, Nicholas, 'The Berlin School of Logical Empiricism and Its Legacy', *Erkenntnis* (1975–), Vol. 64, No. 4 (Springer, 2006), pp.281–304.
Rees, Laurence, *The Holocaust: A New History* (London: Penguin Books, 2017).
Richie, Alexandra, *Faust's Metropolis: A History of Berlin* (London: HarperCollins Publishers, 1998).
Rietschel, Ernst Th., 'Otto H.E. Westphal (1913–2004)', *Journal of Endotoxin Research*, Vol. 11, No. 1 (2004), pp.63–4.
Robinson, Andrew, *Einstein on the Run: How Britain Saved the World's Greatest Scientist* (New Haven, CT/London: Yale University Press, 2019).
Russell, Bertrand, *The Autobiography of Bertrand Russell: Volume Two: 1914–1944* (London: Allen & Unwin, 1971).
——, 'The Philosophy of Logical Analysis', chapter XXXI in *A History of Western Philosophy* (London: George Allen and Unwin Ltd, 1947).
Ryan, Donna F., *The Holocaust and the Jews of Marseille: the enforcement of anti-Semitic policies in Vichy France* (Urbana, IL/Chicago: University of Illinois Press, 1996).
Sachs, Peter, *Berlin Mitte: A Tale of Restitution*, self-published memoir, 2007.
Sachs, Werner, extract from a history of the Grünfeld businesses, unpublished memoir.
Saini, Angela, *Superior: The Return of Race Science* (London: 4th Estate, 2019).
Sandner, G., 'Bringing Happiness: Otto Neurath and the Debates on War Economy, Socialization and Social Economy' in Stadler, F. (ed.) *Wittgenstein and the Vienna Circle. Vienna Circle Institute Yearbook*, Vol. 28 (Cham: Springer, 2023), pp.567–94. https://doi.org/10.1007/978-3-031-07789-0_18
Symons, John, Olga Pombo and Juan Manuel Torres (eds), *Otto Neurath and the Unity of Science* (Dordrecht/Heidelberg/London/New York: Springer Science and Business Media B.V., 2011).
Ziche, Paul, and Thomas Müller, 'Paul Oppenheim on Order – the Career of a Logico-Philosophical Concept' in Milkov and Peckhaus (eds), *The Berlin Group and the Philosophy of Logical Empiricism*, pp.265–90.
Zuccotti, Susan, *The Holocaust, the French and the Jews* (New York: Basic Books, 1993).
Zweig, Stefan, *The World of Yesterday: Memoirs of a European*, trans. Anthea Bell (London: Pushkin Press, 2009).

INDEX OF NAMES

Adorno, Theodor 97–100, 186, 189
Ahrends-Hempel, Eva 102, 114, 122, 123–24, 165, 204, 205, 207, 208, 211, 218–19, 220, 227, 230, 232–33, 235, 254
Améry, Jean 184, 185, 186, 187, 188, 190, 191, 192, 193, 194, 195, 212–13, 218
Arendt, Hannah 169, 189

Baekeland, Leo 35
Ballin, Albert 41
Benjamin, Walter 189–90
Bervoets, Marcel 160, 173
Blaney, Sheri 11, 12, 255
Brecht, Bertholt 185
Brenning, Gertrud 44, 45, 46, 60
Buber, Martin 174

Calderón de la Barca (Pedro) 149
Carnap, Rudolf 73, 93, 100, 107, 108, 114, 115, 165, 176, 185, 219, 235
Caro, Friedrich 148, 160, 161, 170, 202, 227
Cervantes (Miguel de) 149
Chagall, Marc 200
Chamberlain, Neville 56, 119
Cooke, Arthur 61
Cooke, John 40, 49, 71, 173, 180, 256
Courant, Richard 116–17
Curie, Marie 132

Daladier, Édouard 119
Dannecker, Theodor 237
Dante 144–45
Dollfuss, Engelbert 74
Dreyfus, Captain Alfred 82
Dubislav, Walter 78, 79, 100, 165
Du Bois, W.E.B. 110
Dumas, Pastor André 246
Dürr, Professor Carl 232

Ehrenfels, Christian von 105–07
Ehrlich, Paul 50
Einstein, Albert 36, 37, 38, 41, 52, 80, 90, 132–33, 192, 193, 253, 254
Eltzbacher, Arthur 160, 161
Eltzbacher, Hans 160, 161
Ernst, Max 197
Errera, Alfred 148–49
Errera, Jacqueline 132
Errera, Jacques 132–33, 162
Errera, Paul 132

Feigl, Herbert 100, 176
Feuchtwanger, Lion 185, 197, 198, 199
Forchheimer, Leo 176, 207, 212, 220, 251
Ford, Henry 41
Foy, Robert de 142
Franck, James 160
Franco (General Francisco) 202
Fraenkel/ Fränkel, Franz 160, 161
Fraenkel, Hans 216, 217, 226, 227, 238, 239, 246
Frank, Philipp 73, 100, 130
Freudenberg, Pastor Adolph 211, 218, 219, 222, 242, 243, 257
Fry, Varian 199, 200, 203, 206, 212

Gentz, Ismael 40
Gimple, Hans 259, 260
Göring, Hermann 55
Goldschmidt, Ernst 146, 148, 205, 206, 209, 220, 230
Goldschmidt, Richard 136
Goodman, Nelson 235
Grelling (later Gentile), Annemarie 75, 86, 179
Grelling, Greta (born Berger, Margaretha) Aix-en-Provence 226, 231, 243, 244, 251

111 (iii) avenue Bel-air, Brussels 159
emigration from Germany 141–43
political views 92, 213–15
relations with Berger family 141, 213–15
Grelling, Hans Richard 75, 86, 179, 212, 220, 256, 260
Grelling (later Gimple-Grelling), Karin 69, 70, 71, 75, 77, 159, 177, 212, 216, 218, 222, 229, 235, 243, 246, 247, 252, 256, 257, 258, 259–60
Grelling, Klaus (later Claude) 69, 70, 71, 72 75, 77, 92, 205, 212, 218, 222, 229, 243, 252, 256, 257, 258–59, 260
Grelling, Kurt
    Aix-en-Provence 197, 199, 229, 243
    Anti-J'accuse, eine deutsche Antwort 82, 83, 84, 85, 90, 93, 188, 217
    33 avenue Legrand, Brussels 130, 151
    economic views 89–90
    Erkenntnis 76, 108, 111, 116
    Eva Maria (adopted daughter) 91
    forced retirement in April 1933 38, 44
    German Peace Society 85
    Gestalt psychology 105
    Grelling Paradox 79–80
    lecture tour of Scandinavia 115
    Malvine (Haas, first wife) 91
    Menière's disease 134, 164
    protestant baptism 40
    race science 99, 110, 135
    Sozialistische Monatshefte 79, 81, 84, 85, 87
    Talladega College 110, 116
    Tatra Mountains 72
    teaching in the camps 164, 167, 216, 217, 221
    'The Concept of Gestalt in the Light of Modern Logic' 105
    'The Philosophical Basis of Politics' 84, 85
    translator of Bertrand Russell 11, 68, 80
    Walter-Rathenau-Oberrealschule 91
    Wilhelmstrasse 13, Lichterfelde-Ost, Berlin 28, 76, 129, 258
    work with Paul Oppenheim 100, 101
Grelling, Marta 86, 87
Grelling, Richard 33, 40, 75, 82, 84, 86, 87, 217
Grünfeld, Grete 54, 55, 59, 76, 173, 260
Grünfeld, Herbert 54, 55, 176
Grünfeld, Paul 54

Grynszpan, Herschel 67
Gumbel, Emil Julius 51

Hahn, Hans 73
Hamburger, Hermann 212, 219, 220
Hasenclever, Walter 185, 190
Hauptmann, Gerhard 86, 107
Heidelberger-Leonard, Irène 194
Helmer, Olaf 100, 108, 121
Hempel, Carl Gustav/Peter 88, 101–02, 104, 108, 113–14, 118, 120, 121, 122, 124, 129, 144, 145, 146, 164, 165, 173, 174, 175, 176, 178, 179, 181, 204, 208, 209, 210, 213, 219, 225, 228, 229, 230, 231, 232–33, 234–35, 237, 239, 242, 243, 252, 254
Heydrich, Reinhard 57
Himmler, Heinrich 39, 95, 237
Hitler, Adolf 24, 43, 51, 56, 96, 109, 119, 134, 147, 151, 155, 190, 191, 192, 199, 214, 259
Hook, Sidney 176
Horkheimer, Max 97–100, 131–32, 150, 186, 221
Hull, Cordell (US Secretary of State) 199
Hume, David 67, 191

Johnson, A.S./Alvin 164, 165, 166, 167, 173, 174, 176, 177, 178, 200, 212, 219
Jones, Margaret E. 251, 252

Kaila, Eino 138
Kaiser Wilhelm II 40, 41
Kaufmann, Felix 100, 164, 165, 176
Kelsen, Hans 130
Kesten, Hermann 185
Klemperer, Victor 29, 41
Köhler, Wolfgang 106
Kollwitz, Käthe 24, 27
Kranold, Hermann 110, 116

Landsberger, Richard 34, 38
Lautman, Albert 229
Laval, Pierre 188, 244
Leiper, Rev. 211, 219
Leopold III, King of the Belgians 95
Leser, Conrad 180
Leser, Guido 180, 190
Leser, Irmingard 180, 190
Leser, Walter 180
Levi, Adolf 160

Levi, Primo 190, 195
Loewy, Erwin 148
Loewy, Ludwig 148
Long, Breckinridge (Assistant US Secretary of State) 199, 211, 228
Lope de Vega (y Carpio, Félix) 149
Luchins, Abraham 258
Luchins, Edith 258
Łukasiewicz, Jan 103

Manen, Pastor Henri 238, 239, 240, 241, 242, 243, 245
Mann, Golo 51, 200
Mann, Heinrich 200
Mann, Katia 160
Mann, Thomas 160, 174
Maulavé, Robert 199
Mayer, Hanns (also Hans) 184, 185, 186, 194, 212–13
Mayer, Karl 160, 161
McKinsey. J.C.C. 235
Mises, Richard von 130, 149, 221
Mussafia, Maria 135, 140, 177

Nagel, Ernest 122, 176
Nansen, Fridtjof 71
Nelson, Leonard 79, 84, 88, 90, 91
Neurath, Otto
  Bavarian Republic 73
  death 254
  economy in kind 89
  moneyless economy 89
  Mundaneum Institute 100, 139
  Museum of Society and the Economy 73
  physicalism 115, 150
  pictorial statistics 73
  war economy 89
Neurath, Paul 67, 120
Nuttall, George 52

Oppenheim, Catherine 96–7, 190
Oppenheim Eva (born Landsberger, later Orey) 34, 39, 53, 171, 172, 173, 179, 201, 203, 207, 229, 230, 231, 258, 260
Oppenheim, Felix (later Orey) 54, 171, 201, 207, 230, 235, 252, 258
Oppenheim, Felix (son of Paul) 92, 96, 123, 128, 135, 140, 142, 150–51, 160, 171, 199, 202, 218, 219, 253

Oppenheim, Nathan Moritz 96–7, 190
Oppenheim, Paul
  21 avenue Victoria, Brussels 119, 150, 226
  art collection 96
  conversations with Einstein 133
  departure from Europe 124–25
  help for refugees in Belgium 118–19
  I.G. Farben 96
  Princeton 132, 251, 253
  work with Kurt Grelling 100–01
  work with Peter Hempel 101–02
Oppenheim, Paul (grandson of Paul) 97, 253
Oppenheim, Stephan (also Stéphane) 96, 122, 123, 124, 219, 223, 233, 253
Oppenheim-Errera, Gabrielle (also Gaby) 96, 123, 124, 128, 130, 132, 208, 219, 241
Owen, Ursula 56, 60, 263

Perry, Ruth J. 251, 252
Planck, Max 132
Plato 106
Poll, Clara 137–38, 190
Poll, Heinrich 135–36, 137–38
Popper, Karl 93
Pringsheim, Peter 160, 167, 170, 202

Quine, W.V.O. 176, 235

Rath, Ernst vom 68
Rathenau, Walther 41
Reichenbach, Hans 75, 78, 79, 80, 91, 100, 108, 165, 176
Reidemeister, Marie 165, 253
Riezler, Kurt 164
Rodellec du Porzic, Maurice de 239
Rosenthal, Arthur 78, 218
Rothstein, Luise 67, 68, 115, 120
Rougier, Louis 130
Russell, Bertrand 68, 79, 80, 99, 117, 120, 121, 132, 133, 147, 165, 166, 176, 232, 235, 243, 253
Rutherford, Ernest 132

Saarnio, Uuno 138
Sachs (born Grelling), Charlotte (also Lotte) 29, 36, 39, 42, 46, 47, 48, 49–50, 52, 53, 54, 55, 56, 57, 58, 59, 60, 61, 75, 86, 109, 111, 159, 165, 166, 172, 176, 179, 180, 201, 215, 218, 229, 255, 256, 259, 260

Sachs, Elias 49
Sachs, Emma 55
Sachs, Hans 39, 42, 43, 44, 46, 47, 48, 49–50, 51–3, 54, 55, 56, 57, 58, 59–61, 82, 109, 111, 137, 159, 165, 172, 176, 179, 180, 201, 215, 216, 218, 253, 255, 256, 257, 260
Sachs, Ilse (later Cooke) 45, 46, 51, 53, 58, 61, 75, 176, 230
Sachs, Peter 41, 54, 56
Sachs, Werner 38, 54, 55, 176, 230, 256, 258
Samter (born Grelling), Else 27–8, 30, 31, 32, 33–4, 35, 36, 38, 39–40, 42, 43, 44, 45–7, 48, 49, 60, 61, 65, 75, 76, 86, 92, 109, 138, 165, 172, 179, 201, 211, 215, 218, 255, 256, 260, 261
Samter (later Savio), Marion E. 24–6, 27–8, 29–32, 33, 35, 36, 37, 38, 45, 53, 55, 61, 75, 77, 109, 138, 180, 211, 252, 255, 256, 260
Samter, Victor 32, 34, 35, 41
Savio, Anita 26, 27, 28, 30, 32, 34, 35, 36, 39, 255
Savio, Ralph 255
Schacht, Hjalmar 54
Schlick, Moritz 73, 100, 164, 185
Schliemann, Heinrich 71
Schoenfeld, Frida 32
Scholz, Heinrich 103, 104
Schott, Max 251
Schrödinger, Erwin 60, 133
Schumann, Clara 96
Simon, (Henri) James 40
Simon, Ida 41
Simon, Isaak 40
Simon, Louis 40

Simon, Margarethe (later Grelling, later Landsberger) 33, 38, 86
Smallbones, R.T. 58
Sonnenschein, Jacques 194
Spinoza 133
Spiro, Ernst 173
Spiro, Friedrich 173, 180
Spiro, Herbert 173
Standish, Myles (US Vice-Consul) 203
Staudinger, Elsa 211, 232, 234
Strauss, Johann 106, 185
Strauss, Martin 117–18

Tarski, Alfred 103, 130, 165, 176, 235
Tillich, Paul 97
Traumann, Wilhelm 216–17, 218, 226–27, 237

Waldeck, Florian 160, 161, 170
Weidenreich, Franz 135
Weiss, Paul 227
Weisser, Gerhard 88–9, 90, 92, 93, 218
Weisslitz, Jacques 206
Weizmann, Chaim 41
Werfel, Alma 200
Werfel, Franz 200
Wertheimer, Max 97, 106, 164
Westphal, Otto 57, 58, 60
Whitehead, Alfred North 80
Wittgenstein, Ludwig 73, 193
Wundheiler, Aleksander 130

Zola, Émile 82
Zilsel, Edgar 235
Zweig, Lotte 190
Zweig, Stefan 20, 185, 190